KEYS TO THE DRAMA

Keys to the Drama
Nine Perspectives on Sonata Forms

Edited by

GORDON SLY
Michigan State University, USA

ASHGATE

Published by
Ashgate Publishing Limited
Wey Court East
Union Road
Farnham
Surrey, GU9 7PT
England

Ashgate Publishing Company
Suite 420
101 Cherry Street
Burlington
VT 05401-4405
USA

www.ashgate.com

British Library Cataloguing in Publication Data
Keys to the Drama: Nine Perspectives on Sonata Forms
   1. Sonata
   I. Sly, Gordon Cameron, 1958–
   784.1'83

Library of Congress Cataloging-in-Publication Data
Keys to the Drama: Nine Perspectives on Sonata Forms / [edited by] Gordon Sly.
     p.   cm.
   1. Sonata form. 2. Musical analysis. I. Sly, Gordon Cameron, 1958–
   MT62.K48 2009
   784.18'3–dc22   2008049687

Bach musicological font developed by © Yo Tomita.

ISBN   9780754656067 (hbk)
ISBN   9780754694601 (ebk)

Mixed Sources
Product group from well-managed
forests and other controlled sources
www.fsc.org Cert no. SA-COC-1565
© 1996 Forest Stewardship Council

Printed and bound in Great Britain by
MPG Books Ltd, Bodmin, Cornwall.

Contents

List of Figures

List of Music Examples

Contributors

Brian Alcgant is Professor of Music Theory at the Oberlin College Conservatory, and the past editor of *Music Theory Spectrum*. Current research projects include a book on the twelve-tone music of Luigi Dallapiccola, and the analysis and pedagogy of new music.

Alan Gosman is Assistant Professor of Music Theory at the University of Michigan, Ann Arbor. His research interests include counterpoint, music theory pedagogy, and Beethoven's sketchbooks.

Evan Jones is Associate Professor of Music Theory at the Florida State University College of Music. He holds the PhD in music theory and the DMA in cello performance and literature from the Eastman School of Music. He has presented extensively at national and regional conferences, and has articles published in *Perspectives of New Music*, *Computer Music Journal*, the *Journal of Schenkerian Studies*, and in several edited volumes of essays. He has performed in Merkin Hall and Weill Recital Hall, among other venues, and previously taught cello at Colgate University.

Edward Laufer is Professor Emeritus at the University of Toronto. He studied Schenker's approach with Ernst Oster. Over his forty-year career he has presented many papers and has published various articles on Schenkerian topics.

William Marvin is Associate Professor of Music Theory at the Eastman School of Music. His research engages Schenker's theory of tonality, form and tonality in eighteenth- and nineteenth-century opera, Broadway musical theater, and the pedagogy of aural skills and improvisation.

Neil Minturn is Associate Professor of Music Theory at the University of Missouri. He is the author of *The Last Waltz of The Band* (Pendragon Press, 2002) and *The Music of Sergei Prokofiev* (Yale University Press, 1997) and is currently working on a theoretical model of keyboard topography.

Frank Samarotto is Associate Professor of Music at Indiana University, Bloomington. He specializes in Schenkerian theory and analysis, especially in relation to rhythm and temporality, and has presented both lectures and workshops in these subjects internationally.

Matthew R. Shaftel is on the faculty at Florida State University and is the director of the Asolo Song Festival and Institute for Song Interpretation in Asolo, Italy. His research and many publications reflect an interest in opera, nineteenth- and twentieth-century art song, as well as early American and European popular music.

Gordon Sly is Associate Professor of Music Theory in the College of Music at Michigan State University. His research has focused on Schenkerian theory and analysis, nineteenth-century music, and on the pedagogy of analysis.

Preface

At the heart of sonata form's broad and longstanding appeal is surely the universality of its most basic trait: conflict or striving leading to final consummation—completion, achievement, resolution. Moreover, this fundamental quality appears almost infinitely malleable. It provides a robust vehicle for the "dramatic-dialectic" conception of Beethoven and the "lyric-epic" approach of Schubert,[1] for Haydn's frequent thematic uniformity and Mozart's invariable thematic contrast, for the norm-defining tonic-dominant orientation of the common practice to the tonal idiosyncrasies of Schubert and Brahms and the new tonal and stylistic worlds of Mahler and beyond.

It is precisely this universality that gives rise to the form's essential elusiveness. An immense and sundry repertory has attracted hermeneutic approaches that are both numerous and largely incompatible, often in complex and overlapping ways. Since the late 1960s, contributions by Edward Cone, Jan LaRue, Charles Rosen, Leonard Ratner, James Hepokoski, Warren Darcy, and William Caplin,[2] to name only the most widely read, have each illuminated the sonata's formal characteristics in important ways, but the fact of their disparate perspectives itself attests to this elusiveness, as does the weight of their cumulative conflicting structural terminology. Individual sympathies with respect to these varying perspectives notwithstanding—and sympathies for most are in evidence in the pages that follow—sonata forms are pervasively celebrated for their diversity, for the breadth in style, thematic design, harmonic language, and tonal architecture that they can support.

The underlying condition of the form—the sonata's "informing structure," as Northrop Frye would have it[3]—is fundamentally dramatic. This conception—that a sonata unfolds a dramatic architecture that engages the listener's imagination, creates and manipulates expectation through "the interplay of the anticipated and the actual,"[4] and ultimately finds the closure it requires—represents the common theme that runs through the essays in this collection.

Several of the papers focus centrally on specifically dramatic interpretations. Matthew Shaftel explores the first-act trio from the *Marriage of Figaro*, developing an interdisciplinary analytical model to address the work's complex interaction of musical and dramatic structures. Revealing how Mozart unfolds a dramatic

---

[1]   These characterizations are from Dahlhaus 1986, p. 1.

[2]   Cone 1968; LaRue 1970; Rosen 1972 [1997], 1980 [1988]; Ratner 1980; Caplin 1998; Hepokoski 2002a, 2002b; Hepokoski and Darcy 1997, 2006.

[3]   See Frye 1982, pp. 4–5.

[4]   This beautiful phrase is Edward Cone's. See Cone 1963, p. 25.

subtext through the use of an idiosyncratic sonata form, he illustrates how sonata-form principles underlie the work's musical and dramatic narrative. Shaftel's holistic approach to the work provides a compelling perspective on operatic formal structures. Frank Samarotto takes up the enigmatic opening movement of Beethoven's late quartet, op. 132. His study brings into focus the dramatic tensions that distinguish the work—in tonal, temporal, and formal domains. At the core of this extraordinary movement is an obsession with these inner dramatic sub-plots. Paradoxically, the movement's wholeness derives from this pervasive internal conflict. Neil Minturn offers a close reading of the opening movement of Mozart's D-Major piano Sonata, K. 311. He contends that the clearest and most meaningful image of the movement's thematic and formal irregularities is that which appears through the lens of its tonal drama. Brian Alegant's survey of development sections from eighteenth- and nineteenth-century sonata-form movements composed in A major reveals a number of prevailing tendencies that lead him to identify a small number of distinct tonal plans or strategies that recur across this literature. These strategies come to life when understood as dramatic plots, with their common tonal trajectories, prohibited tonal regions, and favored entry and exit patterns. Especially intriguing are Alegant's assertions that the broad tonal architectures that shape these development sections are signaled in their opening measures, and that these same events are often foreshadowed in the exposition. Alan Gosman delves into Beethoven's sketchbooks for two symphonic movements, arguing that the efforts and decisions involved in forging a main theme create a reservoir of dramatic tensions whose weight is felt at every turn in the finished movement.

Another area of focus in several of the essays is motivic organization. This plays the central role in Evan Jones's close reading of the opening movement of Schubert's "Arpeggione" Sonata, D. 821. Jones's stepping-off point is the considerable attention to "motive" that Schubert's music has attracted—by followers of Schenker and Schoenberg, certainly, but by others, as well, such as Edward Cone and David Lewin, who view the idea rather differently. While gratefully acknowledging all of these, Jones attaches himself to none. Rather, he fashions an approach to the motivic life of this work that is shaped by relationships that "participate in the dramatic momentum of the form itself." His contention, for example, that the opening melodic gesture defines an upper-neighbor motive *and* a 3rd-motive, even though these readings are in some senses mutually exclusive, attests to the sensitivity and breadth of his perspective.[5] Edward Laufer's study of Chopin's *Fourth Ballade* and my own investigation of Schubert's evolving sonata practice consider motive within the larger context of Schenkerian harmonic-contrapuntal structures. In both analyses, details in the motivic design influence

---

[5]   Jones's argument that the third note of the gesture, the eighth-note c, in addition to its interpretation as an escape tone that embellishes $\hat{2}$ over V harmony, be recognized as the upper 3rd of a larger unfolding of tonic harmony that subsumes that dominant finds support in Carl Schachter's remarks concerning the strikingly similar opening of Brahms's 2nd Symphony, 1st movement. See Schachter 1977, pp. 196–7.

ouı ıeading of the voice leading and help clarify questions that shape formal interpretation.

Finally, many of the essays focus on sonata forms that are tonally and/or formally anomalous—some strikingly so. Anomalies that characterize—perhaps define—the Beethoven quartet, as well as those required for the meaningful interaction of musical and dramatic structures in *Figaro*, have been alluded to. The Chopin *Ballade*, Laufer argues, may be read variously as a ternary, four-part, or sonata form; each interpretation illuminates aspects of the work's design, but each also demands substantial concessions. Laufer contends that the piece shares with classical sonata forms a number of qualities that define that tradition, and that viewing the *Ballade* in that light clarifies Chopin's poetic departures therefrom, which may in turn be understood to reflect the programmatic qualities of the music embodied in its title. William Marvin looks at the opening movement of Mahler's 3rd Symphony through the lens of James Hepokoski's and Warren Darcy's Sonata Theory. Paramount among the difficult interpretive problems here are those associated with a tonal work that begins in one key and ends in another. His argument that the movement is rhetorically and programmatically closed, but tonally open, with tonal closure now understood as a multi-movement process, might be viewed as a logical extension of cross-movement references in other domains that occur more and more frequently through the nineteenth century. Marvin closes with a discussion of how we might understand Mahler's tonal architecture in light of Schenker's tenet that the identity of opening and closing keys is a syntactic and formal necessity. Neil Minturn and I both deal with sonata forms that feature "off-tonic" as well as thematically reordered recapitulations. Minturn's view is that Mozart's modifications in K. 311 to the more usual tonal and formal procedures serve to point up specific relationships between its themes, part of his larger perspective on the movement as its composer's commentary on sonata form itself. I argue that such works within Schubert's output are part of an ongoing process that seeks to reconcile his penchant for various symmetries within his broad tonal designs with the tonal-structural norms of the classical sonata tradition.

This collection was spurred by numerous conversations about the interpretation of anomalous features in sonata movements that took place between and among its contributors over a number of years. The momentum of those conversations eventually prompted the idea for this volume, and, though our various schedules and commitments were not uniformly cooperative, we approached the project with uniform zeal—and that prevailed. To all, my heartfelt thanks for your diligence and fine contributions.

I wish also to thank James Forger, Dean of the College of Music at Michigan State University, for providing a generous grant to aid publication. His support, in that and other forms, is very much appreciated.

Finally, I owe an incalculable debt to Benjamin Ayotte, who, despite commitments to his dissertation and to a young family, found time to contribute to the preparation of musical examples, the editing, and the ironing-out of innumerable formatting wrinkles. That he invariably approached these tasks with verve, and reacted to each glitch with good humor, testifies mightily to his talent, character, and patience.

Gordon Sly
East Lansing, Michigan

Bibliography

Caplin, William E. 1998. *Classical Form: A Theory of Formal Functions for the Instrumental Music of Haydn, Mozart, and Beethoven.* New York and Oxford: Oxford University Press.

Cone, Edward T. 1963. "The Uses of Convention: Stravinsky and his Models." In Paul Henry Lang, ed., *Stravinsky: A New Appraisal of His Work.* New York: W. W. Norton.

———. 1968. *Musical Form and Musical Performance.* New York: Norton.

Dahlhaus, Carl. 1986. "Sonata Form in Schubert: The First Movement of the G-Major String Quartet, op. 161 (D. 887)," trans. Thilo Reinhard. In Walter Frisch, ed., *Schubert: Critical and Analytical Studies.* University of Nebraska Press.

Frye, Northrup. 1968, reprint ed., 1982. *A Study in English Romanticism.* New York: Random House; Chicago: University of Chicago Press.

Hepokoski, James. 2002a. "Beyond the Sonata Principle." *Journal of the American Musicological Society* 55/1: 91-154.

———. 2002b. "Back and Forth from Egmont: Beethoven, Mozart, and the Nonresolving Recapitulation." *19th-Century Music* 25/2-3: 127-154.

——— and Warren Darcy. 1997. "The Medial Caesura and Its Role in the Eighteenth-Century Sonata Exposition." *Music Theory Spectrum* 19/2: 115-54.

——— and Warren Darcy. 2006. *Elements of Sonata Theory: Norms, Types, and Deformations in the Late-Eighteenth-Century Sonata.* New York: Oxford University Press.

LaRue, Jan. 1970. *Guidelines for Style Analysis.* New York: Norton.

Ratner, Leonard. 1980. *Classic Music: Expression, Form, and Style.* New York: Schirmer Books.

Rosen, Charles. 1972, rev. ed., 1997. *The Classic Style: Haydn, Mozart, Beethoven.* New York: W.W. Norton.

———. 1980, rev. ed., 1988. *Sonata Forms.* New York: W.W. Norton.

Schachter, Carl. 1977. "More about Schubert's Op. 94 no. 1." In Maury Yeston, ed., *Readings in Schenker Analysis and Other Approaches.* New Haven and London: Yale University Press.

Chapter 1

The Divided Tonic in the First Movement of Beethoven's Op. 132

Frank Samarotto

The Problem

...quaquaquaqua...
—Lucky in *Waiting for Godot*[1]

The enigma in sound that is the first movement of Beethoven's String Quartet in A minor, Op. 132, is famously anomalous. One could speak of the paradox of its surface detail, an uneasy weld of contrapuntal rigor and chaotic discourse. Or one could address its notoriously idiosyncratic distortion of sonata form, especially the oddly configured development and recapitulation which restate the complete material of the exposition in the "wrong" key of E minor before restoring it to the conventional tonic key. This enigma has not escaped critical attention, but it is not clear that a perspective has emerged that gives the work's internal contradictions their fullest due.

A clearer sense of this work as an individual was once masked by sweeping up the movement in the celebrated (or supposed?) overarching motivic unity of the late quartets as a group. (Indeed, the first four notes of Op. 132 would often be adduced as the prime example of the source motive.[2]) This sort of unity is breathtakingly simplistic and, even at its best, speaks little of the extraordinary worlds these late works variously inhabit. This has more recently been replaced by a turn toward disunity and fragmentation, again applied to the late works as a whole. This new take also paints with a broad brush—are all these unhappy families unhappy in the same way?—and potentially trivializes the music in its degree of self-evidence. Oddly enough, whether unity or disunity is argued, the task of the interpreter is essentially the same: to give texture, depth, and breadth to every actualization of the unity/disunity tension, by its very nature a goal not

---

[1] All epigraphs are from the works of Samuel Beckett, published by Grove Press, copyright Grove/Atlantic, Inc.

[2] Ideas of overall unity in the late quartets have a venerable heritage but the *locus classicus* of this viewpoint is Cooke 1963.

meant to be realized but to be continually pursued as an ever deepening experience of this music.[3]

In the case of Op. 132, the complexity of this high-minded pursuit is obscured by a curious but little-noticed attribute of the work's musical language: its extraordinary simplicity. Not uncharacteristic of the later works but especially true of this opening movement is its unusually conservative tonal materials: there is scarcely a harmony, progression, or modulation that would be out of place fifty years earlier—indeed, C.P.E. Bach is routinely more adventurous. One is left with the inescapable conclusion that this work's enigma is the result of wresting anomaly from unremarkable premises. This movement is arguably Beethoven's most thoroughgoing essay in the art of problematizing the simplest of tonal relations and of discovering in them hitherto unexplored worlds.

Parallel to this and equally true is the quandary of its anomalous sonata form, which it clearly exemplifies, if anything too clearly, the individual components of exposition and recapitulation being almost trivially obvious to identify. It is only that it is snarled by the stubborn contradiction of a development too much like a premature recapitulation or the awkward redundancy of two recapitulations discrepant as to key that renders it seemingly impossible to resolve into a neatly conformant model. Given the work's dogged individuality, it would be as pointless to settle on a "correct" affixing of formal labels as it would be to declare the work unified or not. Either approach would sweep away the myriad details of its inner tensions, knotted together into a paradox of wholeness generated by internal conflict.

My attempt to recover this work's individuality will proceed from close examination of those most basic musical elements that Beethoven apparently renders so simply but whose hidden tensions permeate to the highest levels of form. My reading takes as its core the idea of a divided tonic, a tonic conflicted against itself, undermined by its equivocal presentation. A similar internal conflict is discussed in the motion of its phrase rhythm, and reveals itself as much in our perception of the movement's basic temporality. The conflict is brought full circle—but not resolved—in its contradictory realization of sonata form.

The Divided Tonic

> I can't go on, I'll go on.
> —*The Unnamable*

The opening tonic chord is the foundation on which a Classical piece stands; if it is not hammerstrokes that secure this base, then at least some clear enunciation is

---

    [3]   This movement has recently been discussed regarding the question of unity in analysis in general in Morgan 2003; among other analyses, Morgan critiques that of Op. 132 in Chua 1995; see also Chua's response in Chua 2004.

pro forma. It is clear that Beethoven assumes this eighteenth-century premise even into his late works, with exceptions clearly standing out as such (and in most the statement of tonic is not long in coming). The situation with Op. 132 is exquisitely subtle: there is no question of a tonic presence—indeed, the turn away from the tonic key at the very end of m. 29 is jarringly forceful—yet actual manifestations of an opening tonic are maddeningly elusive, compromised at every turn. To specify:

1. A lone tonic pitch does in fact appear in the very first bar, but it is, quite significantly, in a weak metric position, and, more important, caught up in the cello's four-note figure, a complex tonal configuration to be discussed presently. Moreover, the *Assai sostenuto* is presumably playing the role of slow introduction intended to prepare a more secure *Allegro*; as such, it is permeated with a sense of expectancy, one that favors the hearing of dominant tension over tonic stability.

2. That dominant tension also calls into question the first two full tonic chords; the first in m. 5—in six-four position, and not a viable candidate—and the second in m. 6, at last a full-voiced articulation of a tonic chord. But this latter tonic is also in a weak metric position, doubly so, in that it is the fourth half note within a two-bar unit; indeed, the *Assai sostenuto* so clearly falls into two-bar units that, even at the slow tempo, they group easily into an eight-bar group, placing the tonic chord of m. 6 into an even more subsidiary position. More subtly, the first violin's peak note C6 that caps off this tonic is immediately undermined by its repetition in m. 7 as the dissonant seventh of a diminished-seventh chord applied to the dominant; in effect, a possible arrival is retrospectively heard as an anticipation (and prepares an anticipation in m. 8, to be discussed later).

3. The next tonic harmony, in m. 10, is also weakly manifested, in first inversion and again in weak metric position. Less obviously, it is also an anticipation of a tonic harmony that is expected to appear in the next bar (its implication confirmed by voice-leading from the previous bass B) but which does not literally materialize. As if holding its breath, a repetition of tonic six-three is withheld and the cello instead strains to speak the first statement of the *Allegro*'s first theme. The curious vacuity of this moment confers a parenthesizing effect on mm. 11–12, and thus undermines the very moment when the *Allegro*'s tonic harmony and thematic material should be allied and confirmed.[4] The parallel statement in mm. 13–14 tumbles *ex medias res* from the first violin, and is in any case embedded in non-tonic harmony; its potential role as second stage of a *Satz* seems to materialize only gradually.

---

[4]   This reading of the phrase structure is supported by the brief analysis of the opening by Schmid 1994 p. 327.

4. These two-bar units, with their strong-weak accentuation, enforce the weak hypermetric placement of m. 16's root-position tonic, which is anyway swept up in the phrase's drive to the cadence (as is the six-three offshoot that follows). The drive culminates in:
5. the intensely focused six-four chord of m. 21, whose abrupt *Adagio* gives us a seeming infinity of time to be immersed in the sound of an A-minor triad, all the while acutely aware of its inexorable need to resolve to the dominant it represents.

This conspectus of tonic compromise is rounded off by the return of the first theme in m. 23, and even there a potential tonic is thwarted by the retention of F5, an implied suspension from the previous dominant ninth. (The apparent tonic in m. 24 sounds as a suspension to V, leaving only the thinly textured third in m. 26.) All this equivocation leaves one with a sort of cognitive dissonance: the stable ground of tonic is somehow there but at every turn eludes our grasp.

It may be useful to make a distinction between qualities which I will call *conceptuality* and *materiality*. It is so commonplace to refer to music being in a key that it is easy to forget how abstract this claim is. The sense that a tonic key or tonic prolongation pervades moments where no tonic is present is highly conceptual, a thing of the mind rather than of actual sound. This in no way negates the power of this idea; it simply points to a possible tension between the sonic experience and our comprehension of it (a tension that is inescapable, in tonal music at least). What mitigates that tension is the "tangible" reality of sounding pitches that anchor keys and prolonged harmonies as their literal representatives. (I speak here of the material and the tangible as metaphorical experiences of sound—more properly dead metaphors—much as we speak of musical space, distance, and so on.) Normally we expect a balance between our conceptual sense of key and its material representatives; exceptions—the lack of a tonic entirely, for instance—sound as such, and are typically used to create tension. It would be highly unusual in Schenkerian practice to speak of a prolonged harmony that is itself nowhere literally present, but it is not uncommon to identify a prolonged harmony that is not as prominent as subsidiary harmonies that surround it. The discrepancy becomes acute when the prolonged harmony that serves as the structural anchor of an entire movement must be assumed but its manifestations in sound are not nearly commensurate with its importance. In these situations we experience a tension between our conceptual sense of a tonic's structural superiority and the inability to latch onto a secure material presence.

An example of a character rather different from Op. 132 may serve to illustrate. The opening movement of Beethoven's Sonata in A major, Op. 101, is suffused with a Romantic longing, arguably unfulfilled until the final movement (where that opening is recalled!). Much of this affect derives from simultaneously implying and withholding the clear tonic from which this sonata form movement should proceed. To be sure, it begins with two bars of unequivocal dominant, followed by two bars in which tonic pitches are present. But the foundation of a root-position tonic remains out of reach, withheld, first in m. 3, by a plagal decoration and a late arrival of the bass, and then in m. 4, by a six-three position and an accented upper-voice neighbor note. (The six-four in the latter part of the bar represents dominant harmony, of course.) The deceptive cadence at m. 6 denies any hope of finding tonic footing anywhere nearby. There is a subtle separation of conceptuality and materiality that, I would suggest, is a structural realization of Beethoven's contradictory marking, "Somewhat lively and [but?] with the most inward feeling."[5]

An acute tension between conceptuality and materiality finds an even more exquisite expression in Op. 132's opening movement. Here the celebrated *Urmotiv* embodied in the first four notes must be considered beyond its face value as a pitch series performing some unifying function (and a vague and general one, at that). Quite the opposite: its tonal function is highly divisive, and carefully crafted as such.

The cello's G♯–A–F–E fragments the tonic chord into its component root and fifth, each placed in a weak metric position by the dissonant element that precedes and displaces it. I believe this is best interpreted through Schenker's technique of unfolding (*Ausfaltung*), in which intervals conceptually heard as sounding together are separated in time, unfolded, as it were, into a melodic sequence; in an abstract example, the melodic sequence E–C–B–F–E–C would stand for a major third, a diminished fifth, and the same third again. In this hypothetical, the effect could be quite serene: the dissonance is resolved, and the harmonic succession is clear (I–V⁷–I). However, unfolded intervals can be configured so as to maximize tension. An extreme case is Schubert's "Der Doppelgänger", whose ostinato, B—A♯—D—C♯, divides its I–V statements into two conflicting parts (a reading confirmed by the odd lack of thirds in two of the voicings, indicating a real separation of the harmonic components); this ostinato enacts an expression of the speaker's divided self.[6] Beethoven's use of unfolding is perhaps even more subtle, and is examined in detail in Example 1.1.

Example 1.1a shows my interpretation of the four-note motive: the G♯ and F belong together as a neighboring diminished seventh resolving into the A–E fifth. (The diagonal lines signify their conceptual realignment and the beamed eighth notes indicate not duration but connected units.) What deepens the division is that

---

[5]   The conflict is even more acute at the recapitulation, which arrives, of course, after an extended dominant prolongation, and where the tonic appearances are even more fleeting (until the closure at m. 77). It is plausible here that dominant continues in effect throughout the recapitulation, but I reject the possibility of similarly reading dominant harmony through the whole exposition as simply at variance with the music's effect and with a reasonable reading of its form. The complexity of deciding on tonic strength and the role of immediate experience in such decisions is particularly well discussed in Smith 1995. The contradictory performance directive is recently discussed in Sauer 2007.

[6]   I owe this example to Carl Schachter (personal communication). Also see Wagner 1995.

the fifth-that-would-be-tonic is broken apart, and forced into weak metric positions. Contrast this with the hypothetical arrangement in Example 1.1b, where the A–E at least acts as a boundary enclosing the neighboring dissonances and keeping them at bay. The tonic is further compromised by the harmonization of the E by the viola's G♯. In and of itself, this V could stand as prolongation of I; however, as Example 1.1c shows, the opening G♯ draws us toward hearing a prolonged dominant throughout this motive, raising the possibility of an entirely illusory tonic, one that slips from our grasp no sooner than we hear it. Nonetheless, and despite the tense affect of this introduction, I maintain that tonic is here somehow conceptually present, struggling to provide a base from which to proceed, but in divided form, unfolded into fragments we must mentally reassemble. Of course, since this motive reappears with notorious frequency throughout this movement, this specially contrived unfolding, with all the conflict it embodies, dominates the discourse, and undermines everything.

The struggle to achieve a tonic is palpable. The hypothetical in Example 1.1d shows that Beethoven could easily have supplied a tonic six-three by continuing the bass through B and C. However hypothetical, this actual line emerges in the first violin in m. 5, the first attempt at anything like a fluent melody, and an obvious adumbration of the main idea in mm. 11–12.[7] (And this line is further realized as the literal bass of mm. 15–17, which takes on the role of a sort of ostinato.) Indeed, much of the opening's melodic arch is focused around an ascent to the high C6 (in m. 6 and again in m. 21); Example 1.1e summarizes the conflicted harmonic underpinnings: Does one hear an overbearing V that resolves into a weak-beat tonic (in m. 6, only to collapse a moment later) or does one insist on tonic simply because one must, against all experience? Neither alternative fully captures this particular divided tonic.[8]

The uniqueness of this effect causes one to search for precedent. A hitherto unnoticed antecedent (if not a direct ancestor) for the special expressive *tinta* of this movement can be found in the peculiar canon *Languisco e moro*, reproduced with annotations in Example 1.2a.[9] An alternate version for single voice and piano confirms that A minor is the tonic, but this duet version is extraordinary in its quasi-Phrygian ending, and in its unstable opening, where tonic roots are approached and left as if dissonant appoggiaturas to V. (See also the annotations in Example 1.2a.) Beyond this curiously divided tonic, the motivic adumbrations of Op. 132 are even more specific: the melodic pairing E–F, G♯–A leads, in the third and fourth bars, to the same stepwise ascent to C observed in Op. 132. While

---

[7]   In a thoroughly trenchant review of the Chua 1995 cited in fn. 3, Nicholas Marston uniquely makes an insightful comment that, "one of the oddest ('illogical') details in the opening of Op. 132 [is] the suppression, in bars 5–6, of G♯"–a"–f"'– e"' in favour of G♯"–a"–b"– c"'." See Marston 1997, p. 283.

[8]   See also Kielian-Gilbert 2003.

[9]   Numbered as Hess 229 and first published in Beethoven 1971, pp. 145–6; this edition also includes the version with piano.

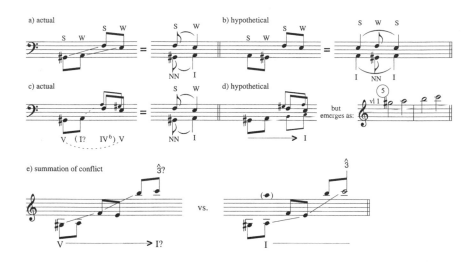

Example 1.1 Beethoven, String Quartet in A minor, Op. 132, the divided tonic

not chronologically close to the late quartet's composition, the canon is found in the Wielhorsky sketchbook of 1802–03 together with the sketches of the violin sonata Op. 47,[10] whose first theme features motivic content strikingly similar to both canon and quartet (see Example 1.2b); more subtly, the opening tonic of the sonata has a similarly unstable presentation.[11] And, to be sure, the use of a canon as inspirational source for a late quartet is familiar, most famously in Op. 135's final movement.[12] The canon's text, "I languish and I die, for you my dear whom I adore" need not be taken as a simplistic program for Op. 132, any more than the phrase "Es muß sein!" could be said to exhaust the content of Op. 135. Nonetheless, while the anonymous text of *Languisco e moro* is the epitome of stereotypical *Sehnsucht*, its musical setting is tonally extreme even for a canon (even allowing that strict imitation might require an exceptional ending). In Op. 132 the affect is taken past heartsickness to something maniacally obsessive, a malady perhaps more than physical.[13]

Perhaps more important, the canon points us to motivic material whose tonal content lies at the expressive core of the later work. The unfolded pairing E–F, G♯–A, a form of that heard in the quartet's opening motto, has already been

---

[10] Intervening are sketches for the oratorio *Christus am Ölberge*, Op. 85.

[11] The tentative status of the opening tonic is insightfully explored in Suurpää 2006. Lewis Lockwood also connects Op. 132 with Op. 47, but on the different grounds of its unusual (for Beethoven) key of A minor and its overall plan of movements; see Lockwood 2003, p. 453.

[12] See also Platen 1987.

[13] The connection of this whole quartet to illness is obviously suggested by the third movement and already invoked in Marx 1859.

mentioned. Even more pointedly, the melodic (and textual!) peak of the first phrase points us toward the same G#–A–B–C that struggles to emerge in Op. 132's *Assai sostenuto*. In both pieces, the filled-in diminished fourth presents us with the possibility of a tonic divided in its prolongational allegiance. Since it is not in and of itself a harmonic interval, this diminished fourth admits of at least two tonal interpretations: The G# can be a neighbor note to the tonic expression A–C, or C can be an auxiliary pitch to the dominant's G#–B. Neither canon nor quartet clearly shows either reading, and both do much to thwart certainty. Recall the effect already discussed of the precarious tonic arrival in the second half of the quartet's m. 6, and compare this to the fourth bar of the canon: The A and C on the downbeat would appear to assert tonic, except that the upper voice so strongly implies the half cadence on V that one easily expects at the fourth bar in. Returning to the quartet, we see inscribed in this diminished fourth the divided tonic engaged in an ongoing discourse of uneasy internal conflict:

- Example 1.2c shows the first appearance of the diminished fourth within the *Assai sostenuto*, febrile but tentative, its tonic harmonization weak and uncertain;
- Example 1.2d is a first strained attempt at a primary theme, parenthesized by its exceptional scoring and by a vacuity of harmonic support—an implied I^6; perhaps passing?;
- Example 1.2e supplies a stronger thematic statement, with more standard scoring, but caught within a cadential drive to V (see the augmented-sixth chord in m. 13) that denies it tonic status;
- Example 1.2f employs this idea as a bass, but, rather than provide clarification, its stepwise motion casts doubt on the stability of m. 16's tonic;
- Example 1.2g stumbles onto the diminished-fourth motive, and by mighty effort transfers it back to the highest register only to be undercut by a dominant bass;
- Example 1.2h's consequent statement is overridden by the first violin's F–E;
- Example 1.2i abruptly transposes this motive (interrupting the consequent phrase), and its expansion into a tritone (with its attendant key implications) provides a way out of miasma;
- Example 1.2j, the second theme that is the resolution of the tritone's dissonance, finally realizes this motive in a stable form, not only filling in a perfect fourth but clarifying that fourth as a third, F–A and a neighboring B♭. The ubiquitous conflict of the diminished fourth is here ameliorated, but only in a key removed from tonic stability.[14]

---

[14]   The progress of this motive loosely resembles the model of the tonal problem propounded by Schoenberg's followers, even incorporating a kind of developing variation; see Schoenberg 1994. A difference here is that this resolution of the diminished fourth's

Example 1.2 Beethoven, String Quartet in A minor, Op. 132, the *languisco* affect

This divided tonic is thus a complex entity bound up with several generating factors: the undercutting of clear tonic, forcing a conflict between its conceptual inference and its material presence; the unfolded presentation of the motto, exquisitely disposed as to create maximum tension; the diminished-fourth motive,

---

tonal problem occurs not toward the end of the piece, but within the second theme, and is temporary. Kofi Agawu sees a resolution of conflict in the movement's final moments; see Agawu 1987.

whose ambiguous tonal outlines evoke, both in specific pitches and in overall affect, the canon *Languisco e moro*. It is an equally complex task adequately to represent this tonic in a depiction of the voice-leading structure. Some special features of Example 1.3 (see pp. 12–13) seek to accomplish this.

Placed below the opening bar of Example 1.3a is a separate bass staff showing the conceptual tonic, existing outside the sounding reality of the piece, but more hidden in the cracks than filling the background. The surface is dominated by jagged unfoldings, pairings isolated from each other, out of which two continuities seek realization. The first is a rising stepwise bass, scarcely recognizable in its first pass, but crystallized into a whole by the explicit statement in mm. 15–21 (see the second system); the repetition here and in the following phrase earns this bass status as a quasi-ostinato, and it is so qualified in the analysis. (One should not fail to notice that this bass line frames tones not of tonic harmony but of dominant.[15]) The second continuity is the emerging diminished fourth in mm. 5–6, an almost-lyrical moment of tonic assertion that collapses before it can stabilize; for a moment, it is a brave attempt to attain the *Kopfton*, an attempt that fails.[16] The diminished fourth reappears in mm. 20–21 as a surface motive, but its initial G♯ is swallowed up in the passing bass; a separate strand of voice leading, a culmination of the upper-voice's reachings-over, re-attains C6, now on a downbeat, and marked by a *subito adagio*.[17] I take this attainment, the climax of the first theme, as the movement's most definitive statement of an initial *Kopfton*, a moment of clarity that immediately collapses.

This presentation as a voice-leading sketch sets in relief an extraordinary aspect of the opening page of Beethoven's quartet. The first two systems of Example 1.3 each show an attempt to reach $\hat{3}$ undergirded by similar stepwise basses, and they look very much like two versions of the same material. What is remarkable is that these two systems depict disparate passages that should function quite differently: the *Assai sostenuto*, presumably serving as a slow introduction, and the first sixteen

---

[15]   Thus the bass beaming of this ostinato is not to be understood as indicating a linear progression of a sixth, prolonging V. It is worth emphasizing that for this and other reasons it is far from implausible to read a dominant prolongation here and through much or all of this opening, which would certainly carry its own sort of harmonic tension. Leaving aside the difficulties this presents for the larger structure, it is precisely my aim to argue for a more special and particular treatment of the tonic, one which is inextricably bound up with this work's unique affect, and which would be lost in an unequivocal reading of dominant prolongation.

[16]   Structurally, this may be regarded as a large-scale anticipation (not to be confused with the local anticipation across mm. 6–7) of the more definitive arrival of $\hat{3}$ in m. 21; this latter is itself displaced from direct tonic support to arrive over dominant as a cadential six-four, altogether in keeping with this work's divided tonic.

[17]   The A–B–C third in mm. 20–21 obviously echoes the opening idea of the first theme, and similarly closes on a small-scale $\hat{3}$–$\hat{2}$ interruption.

bars of the *Allegro*, presumably acting as a thematic exposition.[18] Indeed, the bass-line of the introduction only completes itself six bars into the *Allegro*, coming to rest on a structural V. The formal divisions are as blurred as the formal functions are ambiguous. Under the domain of the divided tonic, the clarity that would set these apart is not possible; all is clouded by this *sub rosa* conflict.

The Divided Motion

> For to end yet again skull alone in a dark place...
> Long thus to begin till the place fades...
> *—Fizzle 8: For to end yet again*

The *Assai sostenuto*, with its insinuation of a slow tempo, is nominally an introduction. But it is full of endings. The opening bars clearly mimic the motet style more fully realized in the *Heiliger Dankgesang*'s evocation of *stile antico*. However, the intentionally weak attempts at overlapping entrances barely suffice to disguise how little this passage truly attains the contrapuntal fluidity of the strict style (a style in which Beethoven was otherwise quite fluent).[19] The eight-bar unit is solidly blocked into two-bar units by the rigid presentation of the motive. These blocks are torn by two opposing tendencies: on the one hand, they are sealed off from each other by apparent cadences every two bars; on the other hand, they tip unsteadily onto each other because of their harmonic instability. The relentless segmentation of this *Assai sostenuto* is clearly at odds with both the function of an introduction and the evocation of an older contrapuntal style. This is another enactment of internal conflict, and this time it is the sense of motion that is divided against itself.

These points require some explication. First, the cadence in m. 2 clearly evokes the traditional Phrygian half cadence (of Baroque heritage, and thus ending on V, but with an admixture of modal ambiguity in tow). The non-thematic filler begun by the second violin can do little to weaken this strong cadential effect. Subsequent to this, the cadences are progressively less stereotypical and therefore less well-defined; we might well choose not to call them cadences. Still, the reiteration of

---

[18]　Even given that voice-leading analysis tends to emphasize the general aspects of a piece, the resemblance is non-trivial, and includes significant salient features. To be sure, one finds pieces where elements of a slow introduction appear reworked in the body of the *Allegro*, but it is precisely the overall tonal structure that usually differentiates the functions of these sections (at least in the Classical tradition).

[19]　One may compare especially Bach's B♭-minor fugue, from Book I of the *Well-tempered Clavier*, which Beethoven copied out in parts, a *stile antico* fugue whose many overlapping (and irregular!) entrances remove any thought that Beethoven was consciously modeling this style at the opening of Op. 132.

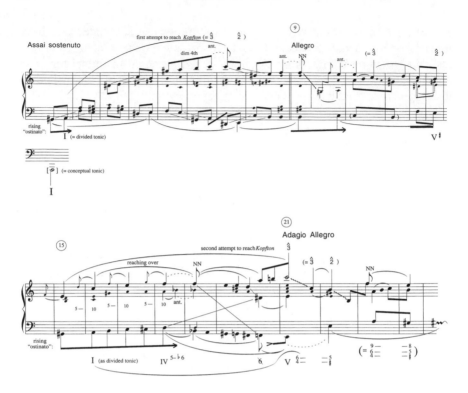

Example 1.3   Beethoven, String Quartet in A minor, Op. 132, voice-leading sketch
to entrance of second theme

the four-note motto carries with it the effect of momentary closure and confers that
closure on the V chord in m. 4, the I in m. 6, and, last and least successfully, the
dominant six-four in m. 8.[20]

Second, these cadential arrivals, enforced by their regularity, regularly arrive in
the weaker second half of the bar, in violation of eighteenth-century practice that
required metrically strong placement of the cadence (a convention that I believe
was still alive for Beethoven). Were this acting as a typical slow introduction, its
goal would be to drive toward a dominant chord, one given a relatively strong
metric position and a reinforcement sufficient to heighten its harmonic tension.
(Often, this reinforcement requires expansion of a basic duple phrase length, or at
the very least some emphatic reiteration of the final chord.) Our *Assai sostenuto*

---

[20]   The augmented-sixth chord on the downbeat is a traditional way to mark a dominant
arrival, but its effect is greatly undercut by the highly unusual "inverted" presentation. The
brief inflection to a diminished seventh is not uncommon, but again it is given here in an
odd voicing, to rather slack effect.

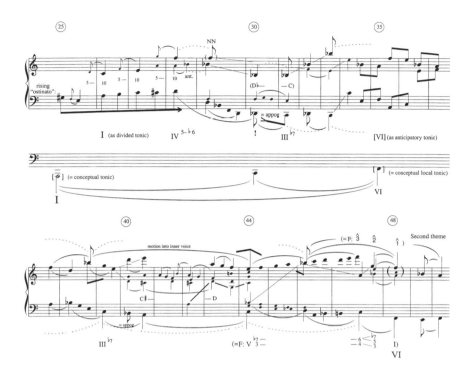

Example 1.3   Concluded

does the opposite. Example 1.4a underscores this discrepancy; to a simplified score it applies hypermetric groupings first to two-bar units and then to all eight (see the two sizes of numbering in between the staves).[21] The final dominant sonority in this putative introduction comes triply weakened, a six-four sonority on the last hyperbeat of a group of four. Example 1.4b shows a hypothetical continuation that would at least have pointed more effectively to the final dominant. (Again, if that had been the intention, then the final chords would likely have been durationally expanded beyond the basic model.) There is a sense that each closure of each two-bar unit is asserted but progressively degrades and becomes more porous. It is as if the music is torn between motivations.

To describe these motivations we may profitably turn toward A.B. Marx, whose organic model of form surely derives from Beethoven. For Marx, music took shape from within through two fundamental and opposed forces: *Gang*, a tendency

---

[21]   To be sure, the slow tempo does not allow for a strong metric effect, but I would assert that the severe regularity of the patterning makes the grouping as clear as it could be.

Example 1.4   Beethoven, String Quartet in A minor, Op. 132, rhythmic analysis of
             opening

to unimpeded flow, and *Satz*, a closing-off into segments.[22] The *Assai sostenuto*
is cast as a series of unrelenting *Sätze*, but the internal tensions of its unfolded
harmonies invest it with an intense *Gang*, a will for continuation which explodes
violently at the *Allegro* that ushers in the first theme. The container is burst, but

---

[22]   See *Marx* 1837–47. Given the unusual nature of the work under consideration, it is
worth remembering that Marx's model of organic growth from within asserted the essential
uniqueness of each musical form. The formal types were simplifications for beginners and
the characterization of Marx as schematizing forms is a corruption of his intent.

not entirely dissolved: the material of the first theme seems to be enclosed within the boundaries of the opening motive, now acting as a cantus firmus. Far from supplying mere motivic consistency, this cantus firmus is an element of conflict: It struggles to enforce the discipline of a *Satz* against the ongoing contra-pull of an unrestrained *Gang*. The precipitous gathering of energy toward the cadence of the first theme is abruptly brought up short by the *Adagio* of m. 21—indeed, it seems to require it, a moment to regain its balance after the vertiginous see-saws of *Satz* and *Gang*.

Elements of continuation accrue gradually: The anticipatory repetitions of C6 across mm. 6–7 and the awkward insertion of quarter-note motion in m. 8—the F♯ seems forced upward from the F♮—hint at the quarter-note anticipation of diminished-seventh harmony across mm. 8–9. Not gentle, but a shock, this anticipation opens up space into which sixteenths cascade. Example 1.4c characterizes this as a quasi-fermata, in which the meter seems suspended, or is at least not clearly articulated.[23] A corresponding anticipation on E (mm. 10–11) opens another space, in which the cello, as if from a distance, parenthetically anticipates the first theme. As shown in Example 1.4c, this represents a first, failed attempt at continuation, realizing the outer voices of the hypothetical continuation but stopping short of the cadence, having achieved neither a definite *Allegro* nor a stable theme. In mm. 13–14 the first violin falls into a parallel statement; this could be the beginning of a sentence but the apparent Phrygian half cadence seems to tell us that we are again in the segmented blocks of the *Assai sostenuto*.[24] It is neither symmetrical sentence nor isolated block but another attempt at continuation, one that succeeds in breaking through prior constraint by driving the bass upwards toward the dominant. (See again the "ostinato" in Example 1.3.) That it is to be taken as a whole phrase is confirmed by the repetition in mm. 23ff. (shown in Example 1.4d and aligned with the preceding phrase to show that relationship). But by no means does this phrase emerge without a struggle; to review:

- Mm. 9–10: pure *Gang*, a cadenza on a tense dissonance.
- Mm. 11–12: *Gang*, the "unmeasured" high E5 encloses *Satz*, the parenthetical statement.
- Mm. 13–14: *Satz*, the apparent half cadence, momentarily restrains *Gang*.
- Mm. 15–18: *Gang*, the mobile beginning on a V⁶, gradually renews itself.
- Mm. 19–20: *Gang* in control, pure forward motion.
- M. 21: a freeze on almost-closure (*Satz?*)…
- M. 22: …that collapses back into *Gang*.

---

[23]   The symbol of the quasi-fermata was introduced by Smith 1994.

[24]   The reader should not confuse my use of Marx's general sense of *Satz* with Schoenberg's specific term sentence (*Satz*) as the typical symmetrical Classical phrase formation (usually 2+2+4).

It is at the heart of this work's divided nature that all this conflict occurs in the only statement of the exposition's first theme that is wholly in the work's home key. Here also we may find it useful to invoke consideration of conceptuality and materiality. As a general concept, *Satz* seems to align itself with the quality of materiality, in that it requires the sounding realization of a cadential harmony for closure.[25] In this sense, *Gang* is more conceptual, a transitional movement towards something not literally present (and maybe not even defined). The contrast with conflicted first theme is nowhere more evident than in the second theme, shown in Example 1.4e. The preparatory bar on the tonic provides a solid material presence for the local tonic F major, easily subsuming the phrase's beginning on dominant-seventh harmony. The echo of the seventh bar and elision on the eighth does little to disturb the underlying symmetry of this *Vordersatz* and *Nachsatz* pairing. It is precisely the opening on V$_5^6$ and the faint echoes of the first theme's ostinato (see Example 1.3) that make clear that we are to hear it in comparison with m. 1, as a transformation of its tense conflict into flowing lyricism, a rehearing that goes far beyond the role of a *cantabile* contrasting theme.[26]

The path to that transformation is gradual. A look back at Example 1.3, beginning with the abrupt turn at m. 30, shows that a sense of F major is in the air almost immediately, but the lightness and delicacy of mm. 35ff. underplay that tonic's materiality, leaving us to reinforce its arrival conceptually. An aggressive drive toward a cadence is suddenly deflected to D minor, whose dominant brings in a punning play on the previously heard D♭–C, now reworked as C♯–D (as in Example 1.3, mm. 38–40). Floating (suspended?) above all this is B♭, the seventh awaiting resolution, the element of *Gang* that sustains this bridge's tension (even playing a dissonant role in the little fugato in D minor), until finding a home in the second theme.[27]

We may step back even further to assay the slow and quiet unsteady progress of increasing rhythmic motion from the *Assai sostenuto* to the second theme. Example 1.5 takes the descending step, first heard in m. 2, as a convenient measure of the movement's rhythmic evolution; the transparent motivic similarity, and the persistence of this motto into the *Allegro*, makes it easy to compare later instances

---

[25]   The symmetrical durational lengths of *Sätzen* can also be heard as material, if the temporal unit is thought of as tangibly appreciable. When the basic symmetrical unit is expanded (or, less often, contracted), an element of conceptuality is necessary to equate these phrase lengths. Even more in the temporal realm, no claim is made that conceptuality and materiality are mutually exclusive.

[26]   It should not be missed that the unfolded style of presentation characteristic of the opening bars is here regularized into simultaneous intervals (specifically a diminished fifth into a third), thus removing the tonal conflict described earlier.

[27]   The B♭ is articulated in three registers (see Example 1.3, mm. 30–33); the highest has particular significance because of the registral peaks in mm. 6 and 21. This upper B♭ makes an explicit resolution in this register when the closing material begins in m.57 (shown in Example 1.4e). Compare with the overview in Example 1.8.

Example 1.5   Beethoven, String Quartet in A minor, Op. 132, the descending step
as measure of rhythmic evolution

with the opening's steady half notes.[28] As already noted, the first note of this half-
note pair begins to take on the character of an anticipation in m. 6–7 (Example
1.5a). To the spasmodic elongations of the half-step shown in Example 1.5b is
added an appoggiatura decoration (see the harmony in the score).[29] Gradually,
the appoggiatura aspect becomes more forceful and foreshortened, accelerating
activity until the frenetic forward drive of mm. 44–47 (see Example 1.5i and the
score.) All the more striking that the energy invested in the initially enervated
step-motive is suddenly and comfortably absorbed into diminutions of the second
theme's accompaniment (Example 1.5j) and recreated as the opening's pacing[30]
(Example 1.5i). The accumulation of rhythmic energy is dissipated by coming full
circle, to a transformation of itself, languidness become lyricism, in a foreign key
that will not last.

---

[28]   As shown at Example 1.5c, the half notes of the *Assai sostenuto* must be taken as
more or less (but not necessarily precisely) equivalent in tempo to the whole notes of the
Allegro; this is usually how the piece is performed.

[29]   The C6 in m. 7 could already be heard as appoggiatura-like because of the
diminished-seventh harmonization.

[30]   Again, given the equivalence suggested above and in Example 1.5.

The Divided Temporality

> They make a noise like wings.
> Like leaves.
> Like sand.
> Like leaves.
> —Vladimir and Estragon in *Waiting for Godot*

The transformative pairing of the opening *Assai sostenuto* with the lyrical second theme is a curious linkage. This again involves the uncertain role of the opening slow music as an introduction; if that is what it is, then why this trajectory linking it to the second theme? Why not begin that trajectory with the first theme? One is tempted to say that, unlike a typical slow introduction, the *Assai sostenuto* is integral to the movement—except that "integral" is such an odd word to describe music that occasions such thorough conflict.

The uneasy relationship of introduction and *Allegro* begins with its performance rubric. The marking "Assai sostenuto" is ambiguous at best as a tempo indication, at once suggesting a slower performance, a legato style of playing, and perhaps even a certain indefinable character or mood.[31] All three of these seem to assert themselves by reaching outside of the space of the *Assai sostenuto*. Not only does the opening motto persist into the *Allegro* as an enclosing cantus firmus, it retains its sense of slow deliberate pacing, the whole notes of the *Allegro* in rough or even exact correspondence with the half notes of the *Assai sostenuto*. It is paradoxical, because one can hardly think of whole notes as conflicting with the *Allegro*'s metric hierarchy, but nonetheless tangible, because the *sostenuto* association with the ubiquitous motive is inescapable, and the *Allegro* provides no accompaniment active enough to persuade us that it is in fact a true *Allegro* that has cast off the thrall of the slow introduction.[32] The conflict previously discussed between two kinds of motion is paralleled by the simultaneous experience of two kinds of time, divided, as it were, between two tempi, that coexist uneasily through much of the movement. The effect is one of being mired and restless at once.

---

[31]   "Assai sostenuto" is not a very common marking in Beethoven's works; it is the opening marking of the *Missa Solemnis*, Op. 123, which carries the additional rubric *Mit Andacht*. Two examples of the use of "sostenuto" for a slow introduction are the Seventh Symphony, Op. 92 ("Poco sostenuto"), and the violin sonata Op. 47, ("Adagio sostenuto"), already mentioned in connection with Op. 132's tonal instability.

[32]   A comparison between the two works mentioned in the previous footnote is relevant: The *Vivace* of the Seventh Symphony is truly an active and fully realized fast movement; the violin sonata Op. 47, on the other hand, has passages of frenetic movement but is infected with a kind of stop-and-start, even simulating a slow tempo in its second theme by writing it in whole notes with no shorter values (see mm. 91ff.).

Example 1.5 has just taken us through the struggle the piece undertakes to arrive at the second theme – that is, to escape the mire of the *Assai sostenuto* and to recreate it as a genuine *Allegro*. (Especially given its cantabile character, it is significant that the accompanimental parts in m. 48 are marked *non ligato*, as if casting off the *sostenuto* associations.) The closing theme that begins in m. 57, though *dolce* in character, is truly an active fast tempo, realizing the full metric hierarchy of quarters against eighths-plus-sixteenths (and soon continuous sixteenths); there is a palpable sense of release from the divided tempo.

It does not last. The manically enthusiastic tonic arrival in m. 67 is immediately interrupted by *piano* half notes in the next bar; the dizzying contrast of rhythms is made even more acute by the juxtaposition of D♭–C (as dotted-eighth and sixteenth) with D–C (as even half notes).[33] A struggle of tempi ensues: the deliberate half notes stretch to three bars, *poco ritardando* (mm. 70–72). Faster chords follow *in tempo* but feel like throwaways; they fail to complete the cadence, hesitating on an offbeat tonic with added seventh. This ushers in the development; vague at first, but it is unmistakably the *Assai sostenuto* in both feigned slow tempo and four-note motto. This first theme creeps in and weaves its way through all parts; this much betokens a standard development, or at least a transition to development.[34] Indeed, the growing tonicization of C minor accumulates into a cadence in m. 91, one which resembles the build-up of *Gang* leading to a similar drive to a cadence. (Compare with m. 20.) That drive led to a subito *Adagio*—a confrontation of tempi; this one leads to silence, then the appoggiatura figures that populated Example 1.5 reappear, and haltingly reassemble the previous texture. One more attempt at a cadence (m. 102) is similarly confronted by an apparent slow tempo—this one the most vehement yet in the movement.

And it is a shockingly violent gesture for this work's relatively muted rhetoric. It is as if the persistence of the slow introduction into the *Allegro* suddenly takes on an aggressively active character, as if the languid *sostenuto* concealed a darker, more forceful side. Thus it is not enough to begin the development with a recreation of the opening material in its pianissimo and legato guise; this is soon dismissed. The hesitant continuations of mm. 74 and 92 are replaced by the opening motto stated as emphatically as possible: the whole quartet in triple octaves beginning *fortissimo*. What follows is famously called a restatement of the exposition transposed to E minor (with all the formal problems that entails), but it is not exactly that, and the differences are telling. Among them:

1. We have already seen in Examples 1.3 and 1.4 how the introduction and first theme share similar tonal and phrase structures, or rather attempts

---

[33]   This recalls the play on D♭ and C♯ in the bridge.

[34]   It is not uncommon for Beethoven to use a slow introduction within the development or as a transition to the development. The practice is found as early as the so-called *Kurfürsten* Sonata in F minor, WoO 47, #2, 1st mvt, see mm. 47ff. Unlike as in Op. 132, this usually occurs with a notated change of tempo.

at realizing them. The passage in mm. 103–118 recreates exactly the proportions of the *Assai sostenuto*; compare the hypermetric numbering of Examples 1.4a and 1.6a.[35] There are three differences: First, it lacks the harmonic alternation of tonic and dominant, remaining insistently in E minor. Second, the first theme's opening motive is interwoven into the motto, as if we are both continuing the development and also acknowledging that the interpenetration is complete. Lastly, the fourth hypermeasure, though it fills out the expected length as indicated in Example 1.6a, has more of the quality of a hypermetrical expansion, in that the top voice suspends its motion, the four-note motto (stated as simultaneous intervals!) dissolving into echoes in the accompanying parts. The anticipatory $\hat{6}$ (F5 in m. 8) is here expanded to five beats in order to rhyme with the pivotal cadential motions in mm. 91 and 102.

2. The divided tonic is here forcefully revived in the local tonic of E minor, especially in m. 103. The cadential drive in the previous bar prepares us for the tonic of E minor. We get the leading tone instead, materially a dominant, but the fortissimo dynamic stresses it as an appoggiatura, conceptually replacing the tonic. (I represent this in the overview in Example 1.8 in the same manner as the opening divided tonic.) The conflict inherent in this passage may explain why Beethoven does not alternate tonic and dominant of E minor and instead needs to insist on conceptually reinforcing this local tonic in the face of weak material representation.

3. A remarkable and far-reaching detail is found in mm. 107–108 and shown in Example 1.6a. Divided or not, the tonic here is clearly E minor, but Beethoven reworks the figuration to restate the diminished-fourth motive discussed earlier (see Example 1.2) on its original pitches (save the G♮ for the final G♯), in its original register, and *as if in its original key!* Besides the extraordinary reach of the opening into this distant area, the recall of a motive so exactly allows a long-range connection between the C6 of the *Kopfton* (first heard with this motive!) with the B6 that represents the motion to $\hat{2}$ and the interruption expected in sonata form. (Again, refer to the overview in Example 1.8.) This background upper voice motion is further clarified by the unambiguous top voice of mm. 114–121 and confirmed by the recomposition of the *Adagio* bar to include a high B as its peak. (Compare m. 21 where $\hat{3}$ is the high note with m. 130 where $\hat{2}$ is the peak.)

The *Assai sostenuto* is not done with imposing its dividing influence. As mentioned, the E minor passage just examined proceeds to a thorough transposition of the exposition leading to the same hesitating impasse at the end of the second theme,

---

[35]   Again, these equate the half notes of the *Assai sostenuto* with the whole notes of the Allegro without insisting on an exact tempo relationship in performance.

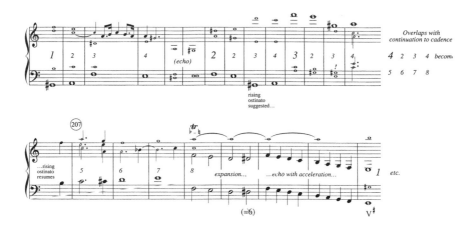

Example 1.6 Beethoven, String Quartet in A minor, Op. 132, rhythmic analyses of later passages

now extended for three more bars (see mm.189–192). This bit of searching leads to the same outcome, but the violent outburst of m. 103 is now transformed. Affectively its polar opposite, this recall of the *Assai sostenuto* is also in whole notes, but marked *piano*, and in four-part harmony. Example 1.6b shows that, like Example 1.6a, this passage is recreating the apparent hypermetric structure of the slow introduction (expanded by two bars of echo), again without its harmonic alternation. Its immediate referent is therefore that E minor passage and this time it seeks a way out. Unlike before, the fourth bar of the largest hypermetrical level is elided (in m. 207) to meld with the continuation to a cadence initially heard in the first theme (m. 17). This faster hypermeasure-in-progress is expanded to lead to an emphatic dominant that effectively eclipses any possibility of tonic prolongation. The turn away from exact repetition of the prior path together with the agitated expansion shown toward the end of Example 1.6b are a definitive sign: Control has been wrested from the *Assai sostenuto* and the suggestion of slow tempo does not return.

The Divided Form

> good good end at last of part three and last that's how it is
> —*How It Is*

It is late in the piece, not long to go, and the form has not been settled, not for the listener and not for the piece. The question is one of closure. It is not that we have not had enough of it (perhaps requiring an emphatic coda?)—we have not had any of it. (Even if we were to take mm. 194 or 202 as tonic returns, they are not closing tonics in any sense.) The piece is acting out a pantomime of sonata form, but its inner conflicts do not allow it to believe in its substance.

But perhaps not the second theme. We are accustomed to Beethoven casting the second theme as a moment of redemption or transcendence (especially in minor key works); this one comes as revelation. After a slight reworking of a part of the bridge passage (mm. 214–222, compare with mm. 40–47), a dominant is regained and we are prepared for the second theme. For a moment—as if holding its breath in disbelief—the bass is withheld and only enters a bar later via V–I. The major mode is expected but glares so brightly we want to shield our eyes. It is a passage of intense materiality, made more acute by the unique withholding of the bass note so clearly sounded before (especially its first statement, m. 48). The silent downbeat of m. 223 is a kind of ironic reversal of conceptuality and materiality: This is, I would argue, the most definite tonic presence in the piece thus far, and, for a moment at least, it takes the form of a rest.

It is this moment I take as a return to $\hat{3}$ (as $\sharp\hat{3}$) and to structural tonic. (See Example 1.8.) This is not a closing but the beginning of the end. Example 1.7 charts this closure. The A major statement of the second theme does not itself close and the echo in minor is a hint that it cannot. Where an eighth bar would complete the phrase, an elision intrudes, returning us to the first theme, in hopes of resolving its conflicts. (See Example 1.7a.) The divided tonic must be clarified, and the energy required to do so is considerable. The agitated rhythmic activity accruing in all parts finally realizes itself in m. 239, and again in 240. The hypermetric reinterpretation is crucial: m. 239 would have been a lower-level fourth bar (see Example 1.7a), but its *sforzando* emphasis and initiation of a cadential motion signals an elision into a new, higher-level, and greatly expanded hypermeasure. This has several phases, as shown in Example 1.7b:

1. The large bold hypermetrical numbers indicate the material need for cadential closure, whose tonic presumably would have come on the first strong beat of the next hypermeasure, with some closing extension (as is

typical). It is interrupted by

2. a parenthetical digression (a classic evaded cadence) that sets up another cadence,
3. the same parenthetical digression, the melody crazily extended through the first violin's registral sweep,
4. a last gasp of the cantus firmus enclosing the first theme (m. 247) (the suspension of bass register makes it clear that it is parenthetical),
5. a dissolution of both meter and hypermeter, from the shifting of chords to the offbeats mimicking prior rhythms (see the score m. 250; normalized in Example 1.7b),[36]
6. a complete suspension of metrical effect, *quasi ad libitum*; the tritone capped by a high D6 prepares for the descent of the *Urlinie* in its obligatory register,
7. which follows as emphatically as it can, and as normatively as it can, both tonally and hypermetrically.[37] (See m. 258ff. in Example 1.7b).

What finally are we to make of this as formal enigma? Example 1.8, already referred to, presents an overall picture of the tonal structure, and coordinates it with both a possible parsing of the form and, more important, the status of the conceptuality and materiality of the tonic. The movement does close with strongly material representatives of tonic and dominant, but with a conviction that seems to extend only to local events. The overall form is somehow represented, but the form as a whole is not satisfyingly consummated. This is because the stuff on which the form is grounded is itself conflicted to its core. It is not enough to say that the design simulates some possible sonata scheme. The material that informs it does not have the conviction to support that scheme.

This extraordinary movement, teetering at the edge of coherence, is obsessed with its inner tensions at all levels, forming a unity not of motives or formal schemes but of inner conflicts which it cannot resist—an uneasy unity of dividedness. All we can do is describe as accurately as possible and experience as fully as possible, but at last that's how it is.

---

[36]   The terminology here is that of Harald Krebs, from *Fantasy Pieces: Metrical Dissonance in the Music of Robert Schumann* (1999).

[37]   That $\hat{3}$ is in a metrically weak position allows us to hear the connection with the first theme, and thus makes this resolution even more palpable.

a) rhythmic analysis of second theme in recapitulation, mm. 223–39

b) rhythmic analysis of closing cadence, mm. 239–64

Example 1.7   Beethoven, String Quartet in A minor, Op. 132, rhythmic analyses
            of closing

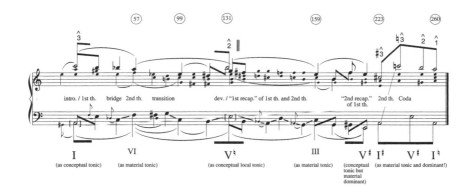

Example 1.8   Beethoven, String Quartet in A minor, Op. 132, voice-leading sketch
overview of entire movement

Bibliography

Agawu, Kofi. 1987. "The First Movement of Beethoven's Opus 132 and the Classical Style." *College Music Symposium* 27: 30–45.

Beethoven, Ludwig van. 1971. *Sämtliche Werke: Supplemente zur Gesamtausgabe*, XIV: *Volksliederbearbeitungen*. Ed. Willi Hess. Wiesbaden: Breitkopf & Härtel.

Chua, Daniel. 1995. *The Galitzin Quartets of Beethoven: Opp. 127, 132, 130*. Princeton: Princeton University Press.

———. 2004. "Rethinking Unity." *Music Analysis* 23/2–3: 353–9.

Cooke, Deryck. 1963. "The Unity of Beethoven's Late Quartets." *The Music Review* 24: 30–49.

Kielian-Gilbert, Marianne. 2003. "Interpreting Schenkerian Prolongation." *Music Analysis*, 22/1–2: 51–104.

Krebs, Harald. 1999. *Fantasy Pieces: Metrical Dissonance in the Music of Robert Schumann*. New York: Oxford University Press.

Lockwood, Lewis. 2003. *Beethoven: The Music and the Life*. New York: W.W. Norton & Co.

Marston, Nicholas. 1997. Review of Daniel Chua, *The Galitzin Quartets of Beethoven: Opp. 127, 132, 130*. *Music and Letters* 78/2: 281–3.

Marx, A.B. 1837–47. *Die Lehre von der musikalischen Komposition, praktisch-theoretisch*. Leipzig: Breitkopf & Härtel.

———. 1859. *Ludwig van Beethoven: Leben und Schaffen*. Berlin: Otto Janke.

Morgan, Robert. 2003. "The Concept of Unity and Musical Analysis." *Music Analysis* 22/1–2: 7–50.

Platen, Emil. 1987. "Über Bach, Kuhlau und die thematisch-motivische Einheit der letzten Quartette Beethoven." *Beiträge zu Beethovens Kammermusik*. München: Henle Verlag, 152–64.

Sauer, Amanda Stringer. 2007. "Cognitive Dissonance and the Performer's Inner Conflict: A New Perspective on the First Movement of Beethoven's Op. 101." *Music Theory Online* 13/2.

Schmid, Manfred Hermann. 1994. "Streichquartett a-Moll, op. 132." In *Beethoven: Interpretation seiner Werke*. Ed. Alexander L. Ringer, Albrecht Riethmuller and Carl Dahlhaus. Laaber: Laaber Verlag. Vol. ii, 326–37.

Schoenberg, Arnold. 1994. *The Musical Idea and the Logic, Technique, and Art of its Presentation*. Ed. Patricia Carpenter and Severine Neff. New York: Columbia University Press.

Smith, Peter H. 1994. "Liquidation, Augmentation and Brahms's Recapitulatory Overlaps." *19th-Century Music*, 17/3: 237–61.

——. 1995. "Structural Tonic or Apparent Tonic?: Parametric Conflict, Temporal Perspective, and a Continuum of Articulative Possibilities." *Journal of Music Theory* 39/2: 245–83.

Suurpää, Lauri. 2006. "Non-Tonic Openings in Three Beethoven Introductions." *Essays from the Third International Schenker Symposium*. Ed. Allen Cadwallader with Jan Miyake. Hildesheim, Zürich, New York: Georg Olms Verlag, 51–66.

Wagner, Naphtali. 1995. "No Crossing Branches? The Overlapping Technique in Schenkerian Analysis." *Theory and Practice* 20: 149–76.

Chapter 2

Types, Tokens, and *Figaro*: Musical Structure and Dramatic Narrative in the Act I Trio from Mozart's *Marriage of Figaro*

Matthew Shaftel

Scholars and musicians generally agree that sonata form presents a fundamentally dramatic process. Whether one focuses on thematic juxtaposition or harmonic structure, the essential dichotomy of the exposition and its (typical) resolution in the recapitulation displays the primary characteristics of an archetypal plot structure, what M.H. Abrams refers to as the tripartite *romance narrative*: "unity, unity lost, and unity-to-be-regained."[1] Most scholars acknowledge that a dramatic narrative underlies sonata forms; Charles Rosen sees this as the very *raison d'être* of the sonata:

> The advantages of the sonata forms over earlier musical forms might be termed a dramatized clarity: sonata forms open with a clearly defined opposition (the definition is the essence of the form) which is intensified and then symmetrically resolved. Because of the clarity of definition and the symmetry, the individual form was easily grasped in public performance; because of the techniques of intensification and dramatization, it was able to hold the interest of a large audience.[2]

Surprisingly, given its ultimately dramatic understructure, the translation of sonata narratives from music into other forms of language typically results in the production of strict structural outlines, wherein musical details (such as motives

---

[1]   In the *Marriage of Figaro* trio, the tripartite model can be represented as follows: presentation of characters—conflict—resolution. Most operatic sonata forms follow some adaptation of this fundamental narrative (although typically the characters are more individualized in terms of keys). Note that Abrams argues that this model stems from the Christian view of the "lost and future paradise." For more on the romance narrative, see Abrams 1971, 181. See also Korsyn 1994, 124–33. The merits of a harmonic, rather than a thematic, conception of sonata form (or, according to Edward T. Cone, "sonata principle") have been debated for decades, perhaps starting with Tovey 1927, 131–55. An elegant commentary on this debate can be found in Hepokoski 2002, 97–104.

[2]   Rosen 1980, rev. ed. 1988, 12.

and keys) are filled into blanks that are elastic, but relatively fixed in place.[3] The dramatic ramifications (as opposed to the music-structural ramifications) are, in fact, largely ignored in the musicological literature.[4]

On the flip side of the coin, research on the nature of meaning and its connection to musical events only infrequently explores what would seem to be an obvious connection between drama and formal structure. Robert Hatten's book *Musical Meaning in Beethoven: Markedness, Correlation, and Interpretation* is a noteworthy exception. Although it does not take formal structure as its focus, sonata form principles and the possibility of thematic *markedness*, the foregrounding of an event or idea against an *unmarked* background, provide an essential framework for his elucidation of meanings within several sonata-form movements (I will return to this later).[5] Nowhere might the drama-structure connection be more evident, however, than in opera, where the formal units must somehow interact with dramatic considerations, both on a local, or inter-scene, level and on the opus-wide level. The numbers operas of the eighteenth century provide ample opportunities for exploring how sonata narrative can influence or be influenced by an extra-musical plot. Although some authors have begun to explore this relationship (cited in note 9 below), they rarely push beyond a one-to-one correspondence of structural outline to localized plot elements, what Carolyn Abbate calls the technique of *mimesis*.[6] What is needed, then, is a model for music-drama interaction that includes form, but also incorporates other modes of analysis.

---

[3]   Ethan Haimo's work on Haydn provides one of many such examples: "[The Sonata principle] … is a remarkably suggestive idea, describing a basic principle of Haydn's approach to form: highly etched statements outside the tonic, toward the beginning of a movement, create a formal imbalance that needs to be corrected by the restatement of that material in the tonic toward the end of the movement." Note that the *romance narrative* described above is clearly in play, but it has been translated through singularly formalist rhetoric. Haimo 1995, 4.

[4]   Rosen 1972, rev. ed., 1997 is another case in point. Despite his claim about the dramatic advantages of sonata form, there is virtually no acknowledgement of narrative process in his entire work. Even Chapter 3, "Aria," which argues for the origination of sonata form in vocal music, never engages the possibility that the dramatic needs of aria and opera may have indeed given rise to the eighteenth-century sonata. This may have been a deliberate omission on Rosen's part, given the restrictions of space and scope. Note, for example, a passage from his book: "To say that sonata style provided an ideal framework for the rendering of what was most dynamic on stage is to oversimplify only insofar as it does not take account of the important role that opera itself played in the development of the sonata style" (296). Nonetheless, a complete absence of the role of dramatic narrative here and in many other discussions of sonata form is noteworthy.

[5]   Hatten 1994.

[6]   Abbate 1991, ix–xii. Abbate probably takes the meaning for *mimesis* from Jean-Jacques Rousseau, who conflated it with the rhetorical trope of *imitatio* in his eighteenth-century *Dictionnaire de Musique* (1768).

This essay explores the interaction between formal structure and drama in opera, presenting an interdisciplinary model of investigation and closing with a discussion of the first-act trio from Mozart's *Le Nozze di Figaro*. The trio's adaptation of sonata-form principles provides an ideal case study of the interconnectivity of intramusical and extramusical dramatic narrative. The methodological model integrates current music theoretical approaches to form and critical mechanisms from the fields of semiology, pragmatics, cognitive linguistics, and iconology. The focus of the methodology is the analysis of signs in the "language" of musical structure, but it allows a parallel track for the interpretation of operatic drama, culminating in a final, integrated level of exegesis. Ultimately, this critical examination of sonata form in conjunction with its intra-opus and extra-opus context leads to a rich understanding of dramatic narrative, expanding the exiguous scope of many music theoretical considerations of opera.

Types, Tokens, and Opera

The field of music theory takes the understanding of musical structure as one of its primary goals. Several recent volumes attempt to classify and catalog formal archetypes in music, focusing on particular instrumental repertoires or examining a single instrumental genre.[7] None of these volumes, however, explores vocal forms in any depth, undoubtedly due to the great challenges presented by their constant divergence from the instrumentally derived archetypes. In semiotic terms (Figure 2.1), vocal genres seem to exaggerate the differences between *type* (the culturally defined formal model) and *token* (the musical manifestation of a formal strategy in a particular work).[8] Indeed, careful text setting may have required composers to reexamine their formal strategies, leading them regularly to defy the culturally defined expectations of particular formal *types*.[9]

---

[7]   Particularly well received is Caplin 1998. See also Darcy and Hepokoski 2006, and Mathes 2006. Only Mathes discusses vocal forms in any detail.

[8]   Deborah Burton 2004 argues for a similar understanding of the ways in which broken "rules" create meaning: "... those who argue heatedly over whether or not musical coherence can exist in opera my also be somewhat disarmed: if an analysis can ferret out which musical 'rules' (to which Mozart referred) have not been broken, there is no logical reason why those rules cannot comprise a coherent—or even unified—organization." The difference between "type" and "token" is discussed further in the methodology section below.

[9]   Webster 1990 argues for a similar view of the role of structure in opera: "It cannot be accidental that, from *Idomeneo* on, Mozart always ended his operas in the key of the overture, always articulated the central finale in a different key, and always ended a finale in the key in which it began" (216).

> Vocal genres exaggerate the differences between type and token.
>
> Type: the culturally defined formal model.
>
> Token: the musical manifestation of a formal
>
> strategy in a particular work.

Figure 2.1   Essential dichotomy between type and token

With a few notable exceptions, scholars of musical form have especially avoided the operatic genre, perhaps because of the need to consider both immediate and long-term dramatic narrative.[10] Indeed, the untangling of the mutual interplay between musical substance and non-musical events presents significant challenges to any formal typology. Music theorists have likewise been reticent to explore the possibilities of extra-musical meanings in their relationship to formal structures, while still calling for this very type of study. Witness the comments of well-respected scholars who have identified a need for closer investigation of formal *tokens*, while themselves placing structural analysis outside the primary focuses of their work. The implicit call of Lehrdahl and Jackendoff in their statement, "to approach any of the subtleties of musical affect, we assume, requires a better understanding of musical structure"[11] has been echoed by many. Edward T. Cone's well-known article, "Schubert's Promissory Note," states: "If verbalization of true content—the specific expression uniquely embodied in a work—is possible at all, it must depend on close structural analysis."[12] Even Kofi Agawu, whose borrowings from semiology provide some of the foundation for my own study, does not go beyond the identification of basic syntax within formal structures (he identifies

---

[10]   Given the breadth of interest in and literature about opera, the scarcity of research on this topic is surprising. Some noteworthy exceptions: Levarie 1952 presents one of the first attempts at connecting operatic forms with dramatic considerations, but it presents an awkwardly outdated (and often times inaccurate) music theoretical perspective. Abbate 1989 (92–124) warns about the dangers of viewing operatic forms as having an existence outside of their dramatic contexts. Cherlin's 1983 study of *Moses und Aron* approaches the opera from a formal perspective, but recently discovered biographical information provides a new historical context for this opera's interpretation, as discussed in Shaftel 2003 (311–31). John Platoff (1984) has published several short articles on the formal procedures in opera, all stemming from an intriguing dissertation. Deborah Burton's 2004 article in *Studi Musicali* addresses many of the issues that plague opera analysis. Carter 1990 goes so far as to suggest that "the sonata principle governs nearly all Classical instrumental and vocal forms" (90).

[11]   Lehrdahl and Jackendoff 1983, 8.

[12]   Cone 1982, 233.

musical paradigms that signal beginning, middle, and end) while claiming that the goal of a successful semiotic analysis is to describe a work in a manner that integrates the "domains of expression ... with those of structure."[13] In response to this call, the model presented here seeks to combine the domains of expression and structure for a study of operatic works.

Methodology

From iconology, the study of meaning in works of art, I have adopted a three-tiered hierarchy of critical investigation and adapted it for the interpretation of operatic works.[14] In his seminal book *Studies in Iconology*, the art historian Erwin Panofsky proposed three levels of study for the examination of art works, moving from intra-opus relations on the first level (the structural elements contained exclusively within the art work) to extra-opus relations on the third (the interpretation of connections with historical and cultural context).[15] Panofsky's method is summarized in the chart in Figure 2.2.

While three levels may suffice for the visual medium, it is necessary to include a fourth level of inquiry for the study of opera. The additional level allows for the integration of the separate domains of music and dramatic action.[16] The first three levels maintain a separation between these domains; this is not to say that aspects of the drama do not inform the music at the earlier levels, but rather that it is more convenient to keep them separate as long as possible for the purposes of analysis.[17] On the fourth level of investigation, however, drama and music are interpreted as the integrated whole that defines opera as a genre.[18]

---

[13]   Agawu 1991, 24.

[14]   Burton 2004 cites the work of art as a useful analogy for operatic music: "... the same artistic medium—paint—serves in a variety of capacities to express both representational content and the artist's choices in how to convey that content."

[15]   It was Erwin Panofsky who first made the distinction between the terms *iconography*, as a term for the description and classification of artworks, and *iconology*, which refers to the interpretation of meaning in images: Panofsky 1939 and 1955, 40–41. For other discussions of iconological systems, see Warburg 1999; Gombrich 1960.

[16]   Other scholars have adapted Panofsky's hierarchy to their own studies of signs in literature and art: See Wittkower 1977, 174–87, and Mitchell 1986.

[17]   One could imagine, for example, that a moment that might initially seem to suggest closure in a musical phrase will instead be perceived as continuing to move forward if the text that it is setting is in the middle of a clause.

[18]   It is important to note that the separation of levels is only intended as an explanation of an integrated process. The earlier levels allow at least some mitigation of personal bias, although Panofsky himself recognized the difficulties of analytical agency, ascribing much of the interpretation to "synthetic intuition" which will necessarily be conditioned by the analyst's "Weltanshauung." See chart in Figure 2.2 and Panofsky 1939, 38.

OBJECT OF INTERPRETATION	ACT OF INTERPRETATION	EQUIPMENT FOR INTERPRETATION	CORRECTIVE PRINCIPLE OF INTERPRETATION (History of Tradition)
I Primary or Natural subject matter: (A) factual, (B) expressional— constituting the world of artistic motifs.	Pre-iconological description (and pseudo-formal analysis).	Practical experience (familiarity with objects and events).	History of style (insight into the manner in which, under varying historical conditions, objects and events were expressed by forms).
II Secondary or conventional subject matter, constituting the world of images, stories and allegories.	Iconographical analysis.	Knowledge of literary sources (familiarity with specific themes and concepts).	History of types (insight into the manner in which, under varying historical conditions, specific themes or concepts were expressed by objects and events).
III Intrinsic meaning or content constituting the world of "sym-bolical" values.	Iconological interpretation.	Synthetic intuition (familiarity with the essential tendencies of the human mind), conditioned by personal psychology and "Weltanschauung".	History of cultural symptoms or "symbols" in general (insight into the manner in which, under varying historical conditions, essential tendencies of the human mind were expressed by specific themes and concepts).

Figure 2.2   Synoptical table of iconological model; from Panofsky, *Meaning in the Visual Arts* (1955). Originally published in *Studies in Iconology* (1939).

Level	Music	Drama
1	The primary level of investigation explores the intra-musical aspects of the work, what Edward T. Cone calls "the musical persona."* The result is the identification of purely structural features of the music.†	The exploration of the drama at this level focuses on structural aspects of the drama (plot/character synopsis).
2	The secondary level, what Panofsky called the "conventional level," focuses on four elements of music that have *denotative* meaning:‡ 1) Formal structure as a semiotic *type* (as opposed to a *token*, discussed in level three). 2) *Topics* are direct musical references to extra-opus musical styles or genres. The relationship between a style and its appearance in the operatic work is one of *iconicity*, wherein specific musical similarities relate the signifier, the section or aspect of the aria, to a generic perception (a *token*) of the signified style. 3) Musical gestures as icons, but rather than referring by similarity to other music, they relate to physical motion by way of *metaphor*. Thus an "ascending" musical line can be interpreted in terms of a MUSIC AS MOTION metaphor, wherein the perception of gradually higher frequencies over time is mapped onto a physical ascent.§ 4) *Leitmotifs* are musical themes or motives that are associated by proximity to a specific person or idea.** The relationship between signifier and signified here is essentially arbitrary (although sometimes topics and gesture can play a role in the defining of a leitmotif). Obviously, Leitmotifs cannot be established without a connection to the text, but they don't have any *connotational* meaning until they begin to interact with the larger context of drama, formal structures, and other leitmotifs.††	The *denotative* meanings of the drama are examined at this level, essentially drawing associations between the libretto and the familiar aspects of the specific culture that is represented within the plot (but not its *connotations* for the historical period in which the work was written or in which the audience members are living). Also, this level requires an examination of the relationships between characters, especially as they take part in various dramatic events. Finally, the identification of the *type* of drama (comedy, tragedy) at this level, will lead to certain expectations that may or may not be met in the investigation of the *token* in level three.
3	Level three focuses on the *connotational* meanings of the elements of music suggested above. This is essentially a *pragmatic* undertaking—, that is, it examines the relationship between musical signs and their contexts. The meanings that will have a significant bearing on interpretation at this level are derived from *marked* musical events or interactions. 1) Formal structure: this level seeks to interpret the dissonances between the expectations created by *type* and the physical manifestation of the formal structure in a particular operatic example, the *token*. 2) Topic: this level explores the meanings connoted by the particular style or genre that is evoked by the topic. 3) A connotative understanding of gesture occurs when the denotated metaphor (MUSIC IS MOTION) is then interpreted through an additional metaphor (CHANGING EMOTIONAL STATE IS MOTION).‡‡ 4) Leitmotifs create connotative meanings when they interact with plot elements or each other. This essentially falls under the purview of the fourth level.	The *connotational* dimension of the drama relates it to the broader context, not simply relating meanings to the society within the drama, but acting as a possible commentary on "those underlying principles which reveal the basic attitude of a nation, a period, a class, a religious or philosophical persuasion."§§
4	It is at the fourth level that the drama and music are integrated with four possible outcomes. The music can: 1) *Paraphrase* or correspond with the meaning of the drama 2) *Polarize* (define) an ambiguous dramatic content. 3) *Contradict* or *ignore* the drama. 4) *Supplement* the drama, frequently in the form of a subnarrative or subtext.	

---

* In his book *The Composer's Voice* (1979), Edward Cone explores song as an interaction between the vocal and musical personae, the latter of which, in his view, acts as a direct representative of the composer's own voice.

† These are the aspects of music that fall into Eero Tarasti's category of "isotopies." See Tarasti, 1994.

‡ *Denotative* meanings are the most obvious and direct meanings for their signs. *Connotative* meanings are removed by some intermediate semiotic relationship from their signs (this is discussed in further detail below).

§ This understanding of *metaphor* comes from the work of George Lakoff and Mark Johnson in the field of cognitive linguistics. Although Peirce also identified a sub-category of *icon* as metaphor, the universality of Lakoff and Johnson's approach has essentially redefined work in the field of linguistics since the late 1980s. Only now, however, are music scholars beginning to explore this model of how humans understand and experience "one kind of thing in terms of another." See Lakoff and Johnson, 5. Note that the capital letters are used to identify larger categories of conceptual metaphors that govern groups of individual metaphors.

** This is what Peirce identified as an *indexical* relationship.

†† For example, the "sword" motive is played during the original conception of Wotan's sword in the beginning of Wagner's *Das Rheingold*. When it returns in *Die Walküre*, it denotes sword, but it connotes other aspects of the first opera's drama, including Wotan's grand plan.

‡‡ For example, this might allow one to interpret a rising musical line in terms of the growing anger of a specific character.

§§ Panofsky (1939), 30.

Figure 2.3   Synoptical table of the operatic model

Figure 2.3 shows a summary of the elements found at each level of investigation. Rather than describing the general approach to all four levels and *then* demonstrating their manifestation in *Figaro*, I will discuss each level in turn, citing relevant features and interpretations of the third-act trio of Mozart's *Le Nozze di Figaro*. Note that the current essay focuses primarily on the manner in which the musical elements described in the model interact with and shape formal structures. Also, not all aspects of the model pertain to every operatic work; leitmotifs, for example, will not be explored in this case study, but will be reserved for future examination.

First-Level Investigation

The first level of dramatic investigation focuses on fundamental aspects of the drama: the characters and their personality traits, the stated objectives of the characters within the operatic plot, and the dramatic events that occur. These elements of Mozart's trio are summarized in Figure 2.4, which lists the characters and their roles, and gives a translation of the libretto for this scene.

The drama of the trio breaks into three large sections:
1. the presentation of the three characters' initial reactions to the preceding recitative through to Susanna's fainting episode and the attempts to revive her;
2. the placating of Susanna, followed by an interruption of the dramatic narrative in the form of the story about Barbarina, and, ultimately, the revealing of Cherubino;
3. the summation of events as the Count's anger is rekindled by Cherubino's presence.

The primary level of musical investigation explores the purely intra-musical aspects of the operatic work, what Edward T. Cone (1974) calls "the musical persona." The result is the identification of purely structural aspects of the music: melody, harmony, formal articulations, etc. ...[19] A summary of the structural organization of the trio can be seen in Figure 2.5.[20]

---

[19]   What Tarasti 1994 refers to as *isotopies*.

[20]   The careful reader may prefer to consult a score. Excerpts of essential thematic material are, however, provided in Example 2.1.

Characters:
1) <u>Cherubino</u>: The Count's adolescent pageboy. He has taken a fancy to every woman in the castle. (Played by a woman.)
2) <u>Susanna</u>: The maid of the Countess. She is engaged to Figaro, the Count's valet. She sympathizes with Cherubino and would like nothing to do with either the Count or Basilio.
3) <u>Count</u>: The head of the castle. Prone to fits of anger. He would like his relationship with Susanna to go *much* further.
4) <u>Basilio</u>: The castle gossip and music teacher. He is a rather unsavory character, who provides comic relief. He is manipulative, witty, and supposedly serves the Count, but in reality he delights in mischief.

Synopsis:
This scene takes place in Susanna's chambers, where Cherubino, the count's adolescent page, is hiding, for the Count has arrived to arrange a tryst with Susanna. Then Basilio, the court gossip *and* music teacher, arrives so that the Count, too, must hide. Basilio wants to discuss rumors about Cherubino's interest in the Countess, making the Count furious, and motivating him to storm out of his hiding place. In the scene, the Count decides to throw Cherubino out of the castle after which Susanna faints, perhaps as a ruse to draw the men's' attention away from Cherubino's hiding place. Basilio and the Count revive Susanna (taking unlicensed liberties in the process), and she continues to protest the Count's decision. In response, the Count describes how he had recently found Cherubino in Barbarina's room and then discovers that Cherubino has been hiding in Susanna's room the entire time. The Count is angry (ironically accusing Susanna of infidelity), Susanna is distraught, and Basilio is delighted with the new grist for the rumor mill.

Libretto and translation

COUNT: Cosa sento! Tosto andate, E scacciate il seduttor.	What do I hear? Go at once and send the seducer away.
BASILIO: Il mal punto son qui giunto! Perdonate, o mio signor.	My presence is ill-timed. Pray excuse me, my lord.
SUSANNA: Che ruina, me meschina! Son oppressa dal dolor.	Unhappy me, I'm ruined! I'm overcome with misery.
BASILIO AND COUNT: Ah, già svien la poverina! Come, oh Dio! Le batte il cor!	Ah! The poor child's fainted! Lord, how her heart beats!
BASILIO: Pian pianin su questo seggio. SUSANNA: Dove sono? Cosa veggio? Che insolenza, andate fuor.	Gently, Gently, on to this seat. Where am I? What's going on? How dare you! Go away!
COUNT: Siamo qui per aiutarvi. Non turbarti, o mio tesor.	We're only helping you; Do not be alarmed, my dear.
BASILIO: Siamo qui per aiutarvi, É sicuro il vostro onor. Ah del paggio quel ch'ho detto era solo un mio sospetto!	We're only helping you; Your honor is quite safe. What I said about the page was only my suspicion.
SUSANNA: É un'insidia, una perfidia, non credete all'impostor.	It's a plot, it's quite untrue; Don't believe this deceiver.
COUNT: Parta, parta il damerino	That young fop must go.
ALL: COUNT: Poverino! Ma da me sorpreso ancor.	Poor boy! I've found him out again.

Figure 2.4   Level-one dramatic investigation; plot and character overview

COUNT:	
Da tua cugina l'uscio ier trovai rinchiuso,	Yesterday I found your cousin's door
Picchio, m'apre Barbarina puarosa fuor dell'uso.	locked; I knocked, and Barbarina opened it
Io dal muso insospettito, guardo, cerco in ogni sito,	more flustered than usual.
Ed alzando pian pianino il tappeto al tavolino,	My suspicions aroused by her appearance, I
Vedo il paggio!... Ah, cosa veggio!	looked and searched every corner, and very
	softly lifting the tablecloth, there I saw the
	page!...Ah, what do I see?
SUSANNA:	
Ah, crede stelle!	All is lost!
BASILIO:	
Ah, meglio ancora!	Better and better!
COUNT:	
Onestissima signora! Or capisco come va.	You Paragon of virtue! Now I see how it is.
SUSANNA:	
Accader non può di peggio; Giusti Dei! Che mai sarà?	Nothing worse could happen. Heavens,
	what's to happen?
BASILIO:	
Così fan tuttele belle! Non c'è alcuna novità.	Every woman's alike! There's nothing new
	about it.

Figure 2.4 Concluded

A number of useful observations may be made exclusively on the basis of level-one analysis:

4. The trio can be easily divided into four thematic areas, each of which returns at some point in the scene, typically sung by the same character or characters.
5. The thematic areas are musically distinct (see Example 2.1). The first theme (2.1 a) is sentential with dotted rhythms configured in an *ascent* to tonic followed by a descending-third sequence leading to the cadence. This is immediately juxtaposed with a theme (2.1 b) that *descends* to the supertonic through a third sequence that travels at twice the speed of the previous theme, while smoothing out its dotted rhythms. The material in 2.1c is characterized by its move to f-minor as well as its faster melodic rhythms, numerous anticipations, and dissonant melodic leaps. The final thematic material (2.1 d) is also sentential, but starts as a unison canon between the two male voices. The cadential material includes a chain of applied dominants.
6. The trio's tonal/thematic structure divides into three large sections. The first starts in the key of B♭, and closes in the dominant, F. The second starts with a move to g-minor, which is interrupted by the return of earlier themes in E♭ (IV). The section ends with a long expansion of the home dominant (in the form of an accompanied recitative). The third section recalls thematic material from the previous two sections, but all in the tonic.

SECTION 1

	Measure #s Tonal Strategy:	Comments/Function
Introduction	(mm. 1–3) V of B♭	Standing on the dominant
A	(mm. 4–15) B♭: V–I	Count: Sentential ♭ (Presentation+Cadential) Ascent from D to B♭/Dotted Rhythms
B	(mm. 16–23) B♭: I–V	Basilio: Descent from F to B♭, then G to C. Smoothing of dotted rhythms
C	(mm. 23–42) B♭: V -> fm: V-> FM: I(!)	Susanna (with interjections from the Count and Basilio): Modulatory, increased rhythmic activity, dissonant leaps, anticipations
D	(mm. 42–57) F: I–V–I	Imitation between Basilio and Count: Sentential (with double presentation), "One-More-Time" *

SECTION 2

E	(mm. 57–69) gm: V	Susanna: Modulatory
D' (in IV)	(mm. 70–84) E♭: I–V–I	Imitation between Basilio and Count
Fragments of B', E', A' (starts in IV)	(mm. 85–100) E♭: 16 -> B♭: V	Basilio/Susanna/Count
Interruption	(mm. 101–128) B♭: I–V -> gm: V	Count:
B"	(mm. 129–146) gm: -> B♭: V	Count (not Basilio): Modulatory

SECTION 3

A'	(mm.147–155) B♭: I–V–I	Count
C'	(mm.155–167) B♭: V–I	Basilio (with interjections by Count and Susanna)
D" (In I)	(mm.168–175) B♭: I–V–I	Imitation is left out—all three characters sing
B	(mm.175–182) B♭: I–V	Basilio (Identical to earlier material)
C'	(mm.182–190) B♭: I–V	All characters from this point forward
D"	(mm.191–201) B♭: I–V–I	
Coda	(mm. 201–221) B♭ (PAC)	

*The "One-more-time" technique, wherein a complete repetition of cadential material is motivated by an evaded cadence, is discussed at length in Janet Schmalfeldt "Cadential processes: The evaded cadence and 'one more time' technique," *Journal of Musicological Research*, Vol. 12 (1992): 1-52.

Figure 2.5   Summary of the structural organization of musical sections in the Act I Trio from Mozart, *The Marriage of Figaro*

Second-Level Investigation

At the secondary level of investigation, I will focus on *denotative*, as opposed to *connotative*, meaning. *Denotative* meanings are the most obvious and direct meanings for their signs, typically called *icons*. *Connotative* meanings, discussed in level 3, are removed by some intermediate semiotic relationship from their signs and are typically established through a second-order cultural or personal association. For example, a canine growl may denote *dog*, but it may also connote *danger*. A *pragmatic* approach to the same sign (as in level 4) would examine the context of the sign, noting that a wagging tale and a nearby toy creates a dissonance between the sign's *connotative* meaning and its context, leading the interpreter to understand the dog's behavior as playful mock aggression. Although some scholars have suggested that music has no universal *denotative* or *iconic* function, I have adopted a broader view of *denotation*, viewing musical icons as a sort of *hypoicon*, in Peirce's own terms, and following Umberto Eco's assertion that all icons require cultural context.[21] These same signs will also have *connotative* meanings, which are established by culturally defined, second-order associations.[22]

In Mozart's trio, I wish to focus on two elements of the music that have *denotative* meaning, *topics* and *gestures*, especially in conjunction with a third element that has *denotative* meaning, formal *type*.[23] *Topics* constitute direct musical references to extra-opus musical styles or genres.[24] For example, the Count's opening theme (in fact, much of the Count's music throughout the opera) may suggest the *march* style by invoking musical characteristics of the eighteenth-century march (Example 2.1a).[25] The relationship is one of *iconicity*, wherein specific musical similarities, such as the dotted rhythms and symmetrically spaced rolled thirds, relate the signifier, the Count's theme, to a generic perception (*token*) of the signified, the musical march. The *march* itself has certain stylized meanings (*connotations*), which are mentioned on level 3. Basilio's theme (Example 2.1b) also suggests *march*, although his includes smoother rhythms and is infused by a *lamento* descent. Susanna, on the other hand, is initially characterized by a *bourrée* upbeat pattern (recalling her first two scenes in the opera), but this quickly falls to the more insistent dotted rhythms of the Count and Basilio's interjections, which she later adopts. Her music also acts as a pitch-specific foreshadowing of Barbarina's act-IV cavatina (see Example 2.2), although there it is recast in a distinctly *pastoral* 6/8 (this connection is discussed below). Finally, the imitation of Basilio by the Count (Example 2.1d), recalls the *strict* or *learned* style.[26]

---

[21]   See Eco 1984.

[22]   Raymond Monelle has also posited first-order meanings that rely on a cultural foundation, such as the musical imitation of natural sounds or extra-opus musical quotations. See Monelle 1992.

[23]   Note that the fourth element in the model, leitmotif, does not play a significant role until later opera, although precursors to the leitmotif certainly are present as early as Monteverdi's *Orfeo*.

[24]   The study of borrowed musical styles and meanings stems from early notions of music and rhetoric. See Mattheson 1739. However, Ratner 1980 first coined a theory of "topics." Agawu 1991 and Hatten 1994 have promoted the use of topics to investigate meaning in Classical music. Several recent studies have attempted to adapt topics to other repertoires. See, for example, Floyd 1995.

[25]   Icons are one of three types of signs defined by Peirce. The iconic relationship is one of similarity between signifier and signified (a picture is the most common kind of icon in the visual medium). Topics are literally *hypoicons* in that they relate iconically to other stylized music, which themselves have symbolic meaning. Ultimately these meanings are connoted by the topic, as discussed in level 3.

[26]   See Ratner 1980, 23–4.

Example 2.1 Four themes/thematic areas of the first-act Trio from Mozart, *The Marriage of Figaro*

Example 2.1 Concluded

L'ho per - du - ta, me me - schi - na! ah chi sa do - ve sa -

rà, ah chi sa do - ve sa - rà?

Example 2.2 Mozart, *The Marriage of Figaro*, Barbarina's Cavatina, Act IV, mm. 9–15

Musical gestures are also iconic, but rather than referring by similarity to other music, they relate to physical motion by way of *metaphor*. Here, I rely on the work of Lakoff and Johnson. They see *conceptual metaphors* as an essential element of human communication. I have already employed this type of metaphor on numerous occasions in this essay, describing both the Count's ascending line and Basilio's descending melody in terms of a MUSIC AS MOTION metaphor, wherein the perception of gradually higher frequencies over time is mapped onto a physical ascent. These types of *metaphors* have been accepted by western-musical society for many centuries, and thus I view them as *denotative* properties of music. Secondary *connotations* of these *metaphors* will be explored below.

Finally, and, perhaps, most significantly, I view an association between the musical investigation in level one and formal structural types to be an *iconic* or *denotative* relationship.[27] Here, again, I return to the semiotic categories of *type* and *token*. Peirce believed that *types* were inferred at the level of cognition, while *tokens* were specific perceptible entities. In other words, a formal type can be seen as a generic, sociologically developed category that may see specific musical manifestation in the form of a *token*.[28] Several features of the trio suggest a sonata-form *type* wherein a full repeat of the secondary-thematic material in the development recalls a Haydnesque monothematicism (see Example 2.1).[29]

---

[27] There are many other *denotative* aspects of operatic music (see Burton's list of m-tools: 1995, 7). Note that in a letter to his father (September 26, 1781), Mozart himself describes the denotative meanings of remote key changes in *Die Entführung aus dem Serail*. Discussed in Kivy 1988, 59–60.

[28] Charles S. Peirce was the first to define the semiotic categories of *type* and *token*. He claimed that *types* were inferred at the level of cognition, while *tokens* were specific perceptible entities. A third category, *tone*, has largely been dismissed by recent semioticians. See especially volume three of *The Collected Writings of Charles Peirce 1931–1958*. My use of the terms is informed by Hatten 1994.

[29] The "monothematic" sonata is particularly common in Haydn, where it typically manifests a strong similarity between the first and secondary thematic areas of the exposition. Thus, the recapitulation of the secondary thematic area is often substantially altered, with the

The *rhetorical* units of sonata formal design reflect the dramatic structure of the trio.[30] Both the musical score and the libretto clearly divide into three *rhetorical* units: an *exposition*, with an establishment of three distinct themes (the last of which is in the dominant) and an introduction of the three primary plot elements; a *development* in which earlier musical and dramatic ideas are developed in new key areas; and a *recapitulation* in which nearly all of the *exposition* materials return in the home key, although the *ordering has been altered*. Indeed, an altered version of the tonic-key secondary theme (with the first half replaced by new material) returns before the arrival of the second Main Theme (Basilio's music). One might be tempted to ask at this point, "if elements of the recapitulation are altered, how can this level of investigation identify this as a sonata *type* at all?" The answer to this lies in the most generic characteristics of the sonata *type* and the boundaries that are drawn to distinguish it from other formal *types*. Charles Rosen suggests one such boundary for *recapitulations*:

> … the one fixed rule of sonata recapitulation: material originally exposed in the dominant must be represented in the tonic fairly completely, even if rewritten and reordered, and only material exposed in the tonic may be omitted.[31]

The trio's recapitulation certainly falls within the confines of Rosen's generously drawn boundary. James Hepokoski disagrees with the extent of Rosen's axiomatic flexibility, but still believes that the reordering of *exposition* material in the *recapitulation* is possible, if not normative (that is, this kind of alteration is restricted to *tokens*):

> Incomplete S- [secondary group] … spaces within recapitulations are surely to be understood as non-normative. Unless we are prepared to assert that compositional practice, at bottom, is arbitrary, we must presume that each instance responds reactively to local conditions generated earlier in the work … Hence as an initial axiom of analysis one should suspect that any incomplete recapitulatory S- or C- space emerges under a larger narrative purpose … It is our hermeneutic task to reconstruct this purpose.[32]

---

first half of the phrase replaced by new material. Here, the main themes are quite different from the secondary theme, but the secondary theme appears in the subdominant key as the "core" of the development. This is reminiscent of sonata-rondo procedures, where a subdominant, "interior" theme typically occurs in the development. The alteration of the secondary theme in the recapitulation, however, is modified in accordance with Haydn's typical "monothematic" practice. For musical examples, see Haydn, Symphony No. 100 in G, i; String Quartet in E♭, Op. 50/3, i; String Quartet in C, Op. 64/1, i.

[30]   Levarie 1952 (57–61) first identified this trio as a sonata form with altered recapitulation. His analysis, though brief, is quite intriguing.

[31]   Rosen 1972, rev. ed., 1997, 72.

[32]   Hepokoski 2002, 130.

On a *typological* level, then, the music and drama of the trio are sonata-like, but the dissonances between sonata *type* and Trio *token* add an unexpected twist to the tripartite *romance narrative* introduced earlier.[33] Investigative levels 3 and 4 (below) will take on the "hermeneutic task" of "reconstructing" the purpose for the twist.

The *denotative* meanings of the drama are also examined at level two, associating elements of the libretto and its characters with familiar aspects of the culture that is represented *within* the plot (but not its *connotations* for the historical period in which the work was written or in which the audience members are living). Also, the identification of the *type* of drama (comedy, tragedy) at this level will lead to certain expectations that may or may not be met in the investigation of the *token* in level three. Although there is much that could be said about the *denotative* aspects of the drama, I will restrict the commentary to two observations:

1. It is only in the audience's locating of the story in feudal Spain, and in their—at least passing— familiarity with what has happened in Beaumarchais' previous play in the trilogy, *Le Barbier de Séville*, that they can fully understand the dissonance between the Count's desire to restore his feudal rights with Susanna and the arrangement he made with the Countess in return for her agreement to marry him. The understanding of the story *within* its setting also clarifies Susanna's precarious position as a servant in the castle.

2. Basilio's sycophantic behavior towards the Count, needling of Susanna, and ironic repetition of his suspicions about Cherubino after the page's discovery identifies him as a distinctly *buffo* character. Susanna, too, is immediately recognizable as an incarnation of the woman servant from *La serva padrona*, again associating her *type* with the *buffo* characters of earlier operas.

I will explore the connotations of these conclusions later on.

---

[33]   Several numbers from Mozart's operas suggest the sonata type. Schachter 1999, for example, discusses sonata-form aspects of *Don Giovanni*. In *Figaro*, sonata form principles also seem to shape the opening duet of Act I, as well as the Act II finale. Demonstrating a much finer boundary for sonata type than either Hepokoski 2002 or Rosen 1972, Webster 1991 (115–16) cites Susanna's aria, "Venite inginocciatevi" from the second act of *Figaro* as the only example of a sonata form in Mozart's Viennese operas. He classifies the aria as "sonata form with tonal return section," but he cites the lack of a first-theme return as problematic.

Third- and Fourth-Level Investigation

Level three focuses on the *connotational* meanings of the elements of music and drama suggested above. This is essentially a *pragmatic* undertaking – that is, it requires an examination of the relationship between a sign and its context.[34] The meanings that will have a significant bearing on interpretation at this level are derived from *marked* or foregrounded events and interactions.[35] The *connotational* dimensions of the drama relate it to the broader context, allowing the drama to comment on the creator's (or even, perhaps, the audence's) own sociological milieu.[36] The *connotations* of this work's drama are made clear from the facts that the play upon which it was based was initially banned by King Louis XVI, and that Emperor Joseph II placed a number of obstacles in the way of the opera's German production in Vienna. Indeed, the work is quite revolutionary in its configuration of Susanna as the central figure—a witty and resourceful servant who wins out against the surprisingly un-buffa Count. Its setting in Spain was seen as a weak attempt at passing the work below the gaze of the court, who objected to its exultation of the proletariat. The audience may best understand the opera when its "buffa" characteristics are played against the seriousness of the Count's angry desires. Indeed, it is the dissonances between the "comic" *type* and the *Figaro token* that are most worthy of exploration in the drama.

Level three also attempts to interpret such dissonances in the music, seeking out those moments that are *marked* because the expectations of formal *type* and the actual manifestation of the *token* do not agree.[37] This is summarized later on in Example 2.8. In addition, level three investigates the second-order meanings of the *topics* and *gestures* identified in level two. In other words, this level explores the meanings connoted by the particular style or genre that is evoked by a *topic* and interprets gestural *metaphors*, such as MUSIC IS MOTION, in terms of an additional *metaphor*, such as CHANGING EMOTIONAL STATE IS MOTION. This would allow one to interpret the Count's rising musical line in terms of his growing anger.[38]

---

[34]   *Pragmatics* is a field that covers many aspects of the non-semantic dimension of language. See Levinson 1983.

[35]   I borrow this usage of the term *marked* from Hatten 1994, who adapted it from Russian linguist Roman Jakobson. See Jakobson 1963 (580–92).

[36]   Panofsky 1955, 30.

[37]   Meyer 1956 discusses the way meaning is created when musical expectations are either met or thwarted. Burton makes the thwarting of expectation a key feature of her analytical approach to opera. She claims that musical elements, what she calls "m-tools," that do not follow the listener's expectations are actually "illustrative musical tools," which express "verbal or textural content" (1995, 5, 9).

[38]   Leitmotifs fall outside the scope of this project. Suffice it to say that they create *connotative* meanings when they interact with plot elements and/or each other. This essentially falls under the purview of the fourth level.

At this point, rather than reciting the results of level-three analysis only to summarize them again in relation to the drama, I would like to turn directly to level four, where drama and music are integrated with four possible outcomes. The music can:

- *paraphrase* or correspond with the meaning of the drama
- *polarize* or define an ambiguous dramatic content
- *contradict* or *ignore* the drama
- *supplement* the drama, frequently in the form of a subnarrative or subtext[39]

Figure 2.6 summarizes the level-four investigation of the trio in detail.

The thematic material of the trio's exposition both *paraphrases* and *supplements* the drama by setting the three characters with contrasting material (refer back to Example 2.1). The Count's main theme is a tonic-affirming, *march*-like ascent, demonstrating his strident and regal nature, and reflecting his growing anger. In addition, it suggests a staging wherein he strides out from his hiding place, marching between comments. Basilio's smooth and descending alteration of the *march* with its augmentation of the descending-third sequence suggests an attempt to placate the Count's anger, while playfully imitating his material. Basilio's use of intervening applied harmonies (including a deceptive resolution) *polarizes* his character, giving the first indication of Basilio's insincerity, despite his initial apologies to the Count.

Susanna interrupts Basilio at a half-cadence with her breathless and distraught music. She attempts to seize control of the situation by motivating a change to f-minor and by replacing the *march* with her own *bourrée*, and when this fails she faints (or at least pretends to do so). Her foreshadowing of Barbarina's Cavatina (which, incidentally, was written prior to the trio), may relate to the growing concerns about her virtue (refer back to Example 2.2). Barbarina sings an identical melody, also in f-minor, but with a suggestive text, "I have lost it … ." Just what she has lost is never stated explicitly, but the audience can easily make out the double entendre, linking the poor girl's virtue with the Count's "pin," which she had been asked to deliver.[40] The relationship between the two women's virtue is made even more explicit when the Count later reveals that he has found Cherubino hiding in Barbarina's room. One might wonder what both males were doing there in the first place.

The imitation of the second theme (Example 2.1d) has the Count following Basilio's lead, *contradicting* the expected order, solidifying our understanding

---

[39]   Noske 1977 (316) has developed similar categories. He identifies a musico-dramatic sign as one that "stresses, clarifies, invalidates, contradicts, or supplies an element of the libretto."

[40]   This is not the first time that such a suggestive allusion has been made—note the references to "pini" in the third-act duet "Sull'aria".

Typical Features of Late 18th-Century Sonata Form		Sonata Form *Type* vs. *Token* Act I Trio from Mozart's *Le Nozze di Figaro*		
EXPOSITION:				
		Measure #s Tonal Strategy:	Comments/Function:	Dramatic events/Role of music:
	Intro:	(mm. 1-3) V of B♭	Standing on the dominant; beginning of *march*	Count *marches* out of hiding. (*Supplement*)
MT	MT:	(mm. 4-15) B♭: V-I	Count: Sentential (Presentation+Cadential) Continuation of *march* connotes militaristic anger/regal stature Ascent from D-B♭/Dotted Rhythms. Rising Anger/Forward motion. Descending-third sequence towards cadence.	"What do I hear? Go at once and send the seducer packing." Pauses allow Count to continue an accusatory advance towards Basilio and Susanna. (*Paraphrase/supplement*)
(MT2)^Σ	MT2:	(mm. 16-23) B♭: I-V	Basilio: Descent from F-B♭, then G-C. Borrows F-D opening minor third from Count. Smoothing of Count's dotted rhythms. Gesture connotes obsequious/placating behaviour. Descending-thirds now twice as slow and include intervening secondary harmonies (including deceptive resolution)—a reflection of Basilio's insincerity/manipulative nature. Basilio has not finished speaking when Susanna interrupts.	"My presence is ill-timed. Pray excuse me, my lord." (*Contradict/Polarize*) A literal reading of the libretto at this point would suggest that Basilio is about to leave. This is not, however, what is suggested by the music.
Transition	Trans:	(mm. 23-42) B♭: V -> fm: V -> FM: I (!)	Susanna (with interjections from the Count and Basilio): Mode change, increased rhythmic activity, dissonant leaps, anticipations. She is breathless and distraught. Attempt at *bourrée* rhythm (from the opening duets of Act I), but interrupted by *march* interjections. Stands on new dominant in an attempt to control the direction of the conversation. (questions about virtue: see Barbarina's Cavatina)	"Unhappy me, I'm ruined! I'm overcome with misery." (*Paraphrase/supplement*) Susanna faints (or, at least, pretends to; after all, she does finish her phrase). This is motivated by staging in which Cherubino is about to be discovered.
ST	ST:	(mm. 42-57) F: I-V-I	Imitation between Basilio and Count: Sentential (with double presentation). Continuation with sequence of applied chords (suggests swooning). "One-More-Time" repetition. Basilio takes the lead in the *learned style*. Is he "teaching" the count to be mischievous?	"Ah! The poor child's fainted! Lord, how her heart beats!" (*Supplement*)

Σ Formal elements in parenthesis are somewhat less common in 18th- century sonata forms. Terms are drawn from William Caplin's, *Classical Form* (Oxford University Press, 1998). The understanding of sonata forms in James Hepokoski and Warren Darcy's work also applies, especially since the articulation of the *medial caesura* is so clear in this excerpt, but Caplin's approach to developmental procedures allows for clearer codification of the trio's middle section.

DEVELOPMENT:

Precore (Transitional)	Precore (Trans.)	(mm. 57-69) gm: V	Susanna modulates abruptly and stands on the new dominant. She borrows the Count's dotted rhythms, connoting insistence. Codetta material is reinterpreted as the beginning of a transitional precore.	"Where am I? What's going on? How dare you! Go away!" (*Paraphrase*) The Count and Basilio are about to place Susanna on the chair where Cherubino is hidden. The sudden key change/insistence is motivated by a need to keep them away from the chair.
Core	Core	(mm. 70-84) E♭: I-V-I	Imitation between Basilio and Count: ST in IV They repeat ST material to explain the physical "liberties" they took during the previous material. The move to IV (cantus mollis) connotes attempts to placate Susana or an insincere piety.	"We're only helping you; Your honor is quite safe." (*Polarize/supplement*)
(False Retransition)	False Retrans.	(mm. 85-100) E♭: I6 -> B♭: V	Basilio: MT2 material Basilio attempts to take control of the situation, irking the Count's anger again. Drama cannot end now, however, as Cherubino has yet to be found. Susanna thus interrupts and stands on the dominant.	"What I said about the page was only my suspicion." "It's a plot, it's quite untrue" (*Contradicts*, while *paraphrasing* the apparent drama)
	False Recap.	(mm. 101-128) B♭: I-V -> gm: V	Count: MT1 material followed by cadenza-like recit.	"That young fop must go." "Yesterday I found... Barbarina... more flustered than usual. ...I looked and searched every corner, and..."
Retransition	Retrans.	(mm. 129-146) gm: -> B♭: V	Basilio's MT2: (But with an extension and with the Count singing) The Count has now become the gossip! In fact, he has taken Basilio's lead again (as in the ST).	"very softly lifting the tablecloth, there I saw the page!...Ah, what do I see?" (*Supplement*)

RECAPITULATION:

MT	MT	(mm.147-155) B♭: I-V-I	Count's Theme:	"You Paragon of virtue! Now I see how it is."
	Trans.	(mm.155-167) B♭: V-I	Susanna's theme is altered by Basilio into laughter.	"Every woman's alike! There's nothing new about it." (*Paraphrase/supplement*)
	ST!	(mm.168-175) B♭: I-V-I	Imitation is left out—All three characters sing. Play on earlier discussion of Susanna's "virtue"	No new text. (*Supplement*)
(MT2)	MT2!	(mm.175-182) B♭: I-V	Basilio (Identical to earlier material) Irony: what was previously "only a suspicion" is now apparent!	"What I said about the page was only my suspicion." (*Supplement*)
Transition	Trans(2)	(mm.182-190) B♭: I-V	Transition material repeated. Now in the "correct" spot. Remainder of recapitulation is uninverted.	
ST	ST(2)	(mm.191-201) B♭: I-V-I		
Coda	Coda	(mm. 201-221) B♭: (PAC)	Descent to tonic—calming of emotions. Also, Susanna ends with the Count and Basilio's opening F-D third; she has lost this round, but she will come out ahead.	(*Paraphrase/supplement*)

Figure 2.6   Typical features of late eighteenth-century sonata form (applied to the Act I Trio from Mozart, *The Marriage of Figaro*)

of Basilio's subservience as disingenuous, and employing the *learned style* in an ironic fashion as the two men attempt to revive Susanna, while taking liberties with her personal space.[41] It is here that the narrative of the trio veers from its Cherubino-bashing course. Remember that the Count was motivated by his anger for Cherubino when he initially left his hiding place, thus starting the trio. Once more, however, he has turned to his primary goal of the opera: challenging Susanna's virtue. Basilio, on the other hand, has been focused on Susanna's interactions with both Cherubino and the Count since the outset, juxtaposing his "mere suspicions," in his main-theme material, with the physical liberties of the secondary theme (ST). This is the conflict that will see its dramatic (and musical) resolution in the recapitulation as Basilio's doubts about Susanna and Cherubino appear to be confirmed. As promised, Mozart provides a twist on Abrams *romance narrative*, replacing a more normative Count vs. Susanna conflict with a surreptitious side character, who initially seems allied with the Count, but whose objective (to discover all three of the other characters in compromising positions) is the only one achieved in the scene.[42] Now that the essential dramatic and musical elements have been established, the exposition can give way to the development.

It is Susanna's response to the men's wandering hands that motivates the beginning of the development. She adopts the Count's dotted rhythms and attempts, again, to change key areas, this time to g minor. The men return instead to the secondary-theme material in E♭ as the *core* of the development, attempting to explain the liberties taken in the original ST, but now invoking the *cantus mollis* in a placating or pious twist.[43] Ultimately this *polarizes* the dramatic content, clarifying stage directions that are sketchy at best and requiring the two characters literally to challenge Susanna's virtue, and then comment upon that challenge.

Mozart's sonata *type* is ready to recapitulate, since it would seem that all of the drama for the trio has already occurred. Hence, mm. 85–101 includes two false starts at recapitulation.[44] In this case, the formal structure must succumb

---

[41] Some performances are quite explicit here.

[42] In some ways, the plot twist brings the scene closer to Abram's archetypal narrative, which, in its biblical origins, typically plots good against evil. Since the Count repents in the end of the opera, it is Basilio, who has no other motivation than ill will, who exhibits the most serpentine qualities of maleficence.

[43] Harmonic motion toward the flat side of the circle of fifths was seen as a mutation towards the "soft" hexachord, which has long been associated with pastoral or pious thoughts. Webster 1990 (210) claims that the key of E♭ is reserved for "deeply-felt utterances" throughout Mozart's operas.

[44] For a very thorough treatment of the concepts of false recapitulation and precursory recapitulation, see Bonds 1988. In Bonds's terms, these instances in the trio would be seen as weighted towards the precursory recapitulation paradigm, since what follows is true recapitulation, not more development (the Count's cadenza-like recitative seems to be an aside to the musical narrative's formal design). For this analysis, however, I have construed any attempts at recapitulation that do not actually lead to full recapitulation as false, following the lead of Ratner 1980, 229.

to the requirements of the drama (effectively *supplementing* the drama), and the Count, employing Basilio's theme as he adopts the role of gossip, recounts the story of finding Cherubino with Barbarina in a cadenza-like recitative. It is the actual discovery of Cherubino that finally motivates a complete recapitulation, as the Count returns to his initial angry theme.

The trio's recapitulation *token* departs from sonata *type* in two essential manners. First, the first half of the secondary material is substantially altered, leaving only the "swooning," chromatically tinged continuation of the second half. The appearance of the entire secondary theme in the development seems to have alleviated the trio's need for a musical return to a dramatic subject (the challenge of Susanna's virtue, followed by assurances that it has been kept intact) that is no longer relevant. Indeed, the validity of concerns about Susanna's virtue is quite readily apparent. The second sign of sonata *deformation* (in Hepokoski's terms), is the inverted appearance of Basilio's theme (MT2) *after* the recapitulation of the secondary material, fundamentally *contradicting* the earlier drama and supporting the ironic plot twist discussed above.[45] Basilio disassociates his material from the Count's, achieving thematic independence and "markedness."[46] The heightened emphasis of the theme lends ironic significance to his repetition of an earlier statement, "what I said about the page was only my suspicion," even though what was before "only a suspicion" is now (apparently) true. This exposes Basilio's character as manipulative and deceitful. In addition, it reveals him as one of the two truly *comic* characters in the drama. A "corrected" recapitulation of the remaining musical materials follows, leaving Basilio with the final say as the other two characters' materials fall aside. As stated earlier, Basilio is the only character who has achieved his objective in this scene (as reflected by his manipulation of Susanna's earlier material into a new "laughter" motive).

---

[45]   In his axioms concerning partial recapitulations, Hepokoski claims that: "... incomplete S-spaces [secondary thematic material] ... within recapitulations will have produced the missing modules, in the tonic, in the development." Here, however, a complete restatement of the secondary material in the development in the key of the subdominant provides thematic balance, while clearly indicating "sonata-deformational practice," by avoiding final tonal resolution; this "deformation" seems contrived out of dramatic necessity. A similar situation can be seen in the first movement of Haydn's G-minor quartet, Op. 20, no. 3, where only the second half of an unusually "loose-knit" (in Caplin's terms) secondary theme is recapitulated, with portions of the first-half material appearing in the key of E♭ (VI) in the development. Hepokoski's comments about this movement apply surprisingly well to Mozart's trio: "[this] is an extravagantly capricious piece, a paragon of purposeful disorder and distraction." See Hepokoski 2002, 140–43.

[46]   Hatten 1994 comments on the ability of material to become strategically *marked*: "Strategic (thematic) markedness goes beyond the markedness of style in just this sense— any material can be thematically foregrounded by becoming a subject, or even the premise, for a musical discourse" (118).

Conclusion

Sonata-form principles play an essential role in the trio's musical and dramatic narrative. Through the cracks between formal *type* and *token* the analyst can shine a hermeneutic light, "reconstructing" narrative process (in Hepokoski's words) and its purposes. The investigative model explored in this essay is the key to this "reconstruction," moving methodically through the practice of critical analysis, while avoiding the *mimetic* limitations of earlier operatic studies. In its integrationist approach to drama and music it takes a holistic view of the operatic work, while maintaining a hierarchy of investigation that leads to strongly supported and opaquely developed interpretations. This essay takes only the initial steps towards a much needed study of operatic formal structures, but its discoveries may ultimately lead to a new understanding of musical, structural, and dramatic narrative as it is manifested in the operatic work.

Bibliography

Abbate, Carolyn. 1989. "Opera as Symphony: A Wagnerian Myth." In Carolyn Abbate and Roger Parker, eds, *Analyzing Opera: Verdi and Wagner*, Berkeley: University of California Press, 92–124.

——. 1991. *Unsung Voices: Opera and Musical Narrativity in the Nineteenth Century*, Princeton: Princeton University Press.

Abrams, Meyer H. 1971. *Natural Supernaturalism: Tradition and Revolution in Romantic Literature*, New York: W.W. Norton.

Agawu, V. Kofi. 1991. *Playing with Signs: A Semiotic Interpretation of Classic Music*, Princeton: Princeton University Press.

Bonds, Mark Evan. 1988. "Haydn's False Recapitulations and the Perception of Sonata Forms in the Eighteenth Century," PhD dissertation, Harvard University.

Burton, Deborah. 1995. "An Analysis of Puccini's *Tosca*: A Heuristic Approach to the Unifying Elements of the Opera", PhD dissertation, University of Michigan.

——. 2004. "Orfeo, Osmin and Otello: Towards a Theory of Opera Analysis." *Studi Musicali* 33/2: 359–85

Caplin, William Earl. 1998. *Classical Form: A Theory of Formal Functions for the Instrumental Music of Haydn, Mozart and Beethoven*, New York: Oxford University Press.

Carter, Tim. 1990. *W.A. Mozart: "Le Nozze die Figaro"*, Cambridge: Cambridge University Press.

Cherlin, Michael. 1983. "The Formal and Dramatic Organization of Schoenberg's *Moses und Aron*", PhD dissertation, Yale University.

Cone, Edward T. 1979. *The Composer's Voice*, Berkeley: University of California Press.

——. 1982. "Schubert's Promissory Note." *19th-Century Music* 5/3: 233–41.

Darcy, Warren, and James Hepokoski. 2006. *Elements of Sonata Theory: Norms, Types, and Deformations in the Late-Eighteenth-Century Sonata*, New York: Oxford University Press.

Eco, Umberto. 1984. *Semiotics and the Philosophy of Language*, London: Macmillan Press.

Floyd, Samuel A. Jr. 1995. *The Power of Black Music*, New York: Oxford University Press.

Gombrich, Ernst. 1960. *Art and Illusion: A Study in the Psychology of Pictorial Representation*, New York: Pantheon Books.

Haimo, Ethan. 1995. *Haydn's Symphonic Forms: Essays in Compositional Logic*, New York: Oxford University Press.

Hatten, Robert. 1994. *Musical Meaning in Beethoven: Markedness, Correlation, and Interpretation*, Bloomington: Indiana University Press.

Hepokoski, James. 2002. "Beyond the Sonata Principle." *Journal of the American Musicological Society* 55/1: 91–154.

Jakobson, Roman. 1963. "Implications of Language Universals for Linguistics." In *Roman Jakobson: Selected Writings II*. The Hague: Mouton Press.

Kivy, Peter. 1988. *Osmin's Rage: Philosophical Reflections on Opera, and Text*, Princeton: Princeton University Press.

Korsyn, Kevin. 1994. Review of *Wordless Rhetoric: Musical Form and the Metaphor of the Oration* by Mark Evan Bonds. In *Music Theory Spectrum* 16/1: 124–33.

Lakoff, George, and Mark Johnson. 1980. *Metaphors We Live By*, Chicago: Chicago University Press.

Lehrdahl, Fred, and Ray Jackendoff. 1983. *A Generative Theory of Tonal Music*, Cambridge: Cambridge University Press.

Levarie, Sigmund. 1952. *Mozart's* Le Nozze di Figaro*: A Critical Analysis*, Chicago: University of Chicago Press.

Levinson, Stephen. 1983. *Pragmatics*, Cambridge: Cambridge University Press.

Mathes, James. 2006. *An Introduction to Musical Form, Style, and Genre*, Upper Saddle River, NJ: Prentice Hall.

Mattheson, Johann, 1739. *Der vollkommene Capellmeister*, Hamburg.

Meyer, Leonard. 1956. *Emotion and Meaning in Music*, Chicago: University of Chicago Press.

Mitchell, W.J. Thomas. 1986. *Iconology: Image, Text, Ideology*, Chicago: University of Chicago Press.

Monelle, Raymond. 1992. *Linguistics and Semiotics in Music*, London: Hardwood Academic Publishers.

Noske, Frits. 1977. *The Signifier and the Signified: Studies in the Operas of Mozart and Verdi*, The Hague: Nijhoff.

Panofsky, Erwin. 1939. *Studies in Iconology: Humanistic Themes in the Art of the Renaissance*, New York: Oxford University Press.

——. 1955. *Meaning in the Visual Arts*, Garden City, NY: Doubleday.

Peirce, Charles S. 1931–58. *The Collected Writings of Charles Peirce*, ed. Charles Hartshorne, Paul Weiss, and Arthur Burks. Cambridge, MA: Harvard University Press.

Platoff, John. 1984. "Music and Drama in the Opera buffa Finale: Mozart and His Contemporaries in Vienna, 1781–1790," PhD dissertation, University of Pennsylvania.

Ratner, Leonard. 1980. *Classic Music: Expression, Form, and Style*, New York: Schirmer Books.

Rosen, Charles. 1972, rev. ed., 1997. *The Classic Style: Haydn, Mozart, Beethoven*, New York: W.W. Norton.

——. 1980, rev. ed. 1988. *Sonata Forms*, New York: W.W. Norton.

Rousseau, Jean-Jacques. 1768. *Dictionnaire de Musique*, Paris.

Schachter, Carl. 1999. "Structure As Foreground: 'Das Drama des Ursatzes.'" In Carl Schachter and Heidi Siegel, eds, *Schenker Studies II*, Cambridge: Cambridge University Press, 298–314.

Schmalfeldt, Janet. 1992. "Cadential processes: The evaded cadence and 'one more time' technique," *Journal of Musicological Research* 12: 1–52.

Shaftel, Matthew. 2003. "Translating for GOD: Schönberg's Moses und Aron," *Journal of the Arnold Schönberg Center* 5: 309–329.

Tarasti, Eero. 1994. *A Theory of Musical Semiotics*. Bloomington: Indiana University Press.

Tovey, Donald Francis. 1927. "Some Aspects of Beethoven's Art Forms." *Music and Letters* 8/2: 131–55.

Warburg, Abby. 1999; originally published in 1932. *The Renewal of Pagan Antiquity: Contributions to the Cultural History of the European Renaissance*, trans. David Britt. Los Angeles: Getty Research Institute for the History of Art and the Humanities.

Webster, James. 1990. "Mozart's Operas and the Myth of Musical Unity." *Cambridge Opera Journal* 2/2: 197–218.

——. 1991. "The Analysis of Mozart's Arias." In Cliff Eisen, ed., *Mozart Studies* (New York: Oxford University Press), 101–199.

Wittkower, Rudolph. 1977. *Allegory and the Migration of Symbols*, New York: Thames and Hudson.

Chapter 3

Mahler's Third Symphony and the Dismantling of Sonata Form

William Marvin

Between 1992 and 2006, James Hepokoski and Warren Darcy developed a taxonomy for describing and measuring normative procedures in eighteenth-century sonata compositions, which they refer to as Sonata Theory. Further, they have profitably explained many post-Beethoven works in terms of "sonata deformation," whereby compositions are understood as either in dialogue with normative sonata form while deviating from it, or as belonging to one or more families of deformational strategies that were common enough to be recognizable by contemporary audiences.

One central aspect of Darcy and Hepokoski's procedure is the analysis of each work in relation to rigorously defined generic norms.[1] In the case of nineteenth-century works entitled "Symphony," we are confronted with an overwhelming expectation of "sonata form" for the first movement: no matter how far the conventions of that form are stretched, a listener will be compelled to hear the movement in dialogue with significant traits of sonata organization. This contrasts with the expectations a listener has for a symphonic poem, in which other formal strategies would be more likely and less disruptive of the listener's understanding of the work.[2]

Mahler's Third Symphony (1896) provides a fascinating test case for Sonata Theory. The opening movement presents an extreme case of deformational strategy. The movement is anomalous in terms of length (an enormous 875 measures, lasting over 33 minutes in performance); in terms of its tonal organization, beginning in d minor and ending in F major; and in terms of its thematic organization, being highly episodic in some ways, but thematically unified in areas where contrast would be expected. This chapter unfolds in three stages. First, I will present a brief summary of the relevant aspects of Sonata Theory. Second, I will offer a reading of Mahler's movement, demonstrating how rhetorical sonata structure is maintained while tonal structure is subverted. Finally, I will speculate on the

---

[1]   Sonata Theory resonates strongly with the implicative model advocated by Leonard B. Meyer (1956, 1973, 1989) in that a "competent listener" is defined by Hepokoski and Darcy (1997, 2006) as one whose set of expectations is formulated through the analysis of a large corpus of compositions, using a consistent method.

[2]   See Hepokoski 1992a for an extended discussion of this distinction.

implications of such procedures as they relate to a hierarchical theory of tonality such as Schenker's. My reading of the form in this movement will be related to an interpretation of hermeneutic elements of the work.[3]

Sonata Theory: A Brief Overview

It is not possible in this limited space to do justice to the wealth of detail or rich implications of Sonata Theory. My goal here is to present terminology that may not be familiar, thereby elucidating the ensuing analysis.

Figure 3.1 lists Hepokoski and Darcy's five sonata types, and then offers a schematic of a normative "Type 3" sonata form. Note first that the Introduction and Coda are bracketed in the diagram. This indicates that they are optional and, more significantly for the theory, that they lie outside of normative sonata "space." Most of this diagram should look familiar from other post-Marxian descriptions of sonata form. Hepokoski and Darcy's refinements include the medial caesura, a structural cadence that divides the exposition into two large areas: P TR ' S/C. The labeling of the structural cadences at the end of the S zone represents a further innovation; these perfect authentic cadences represent Essential Expositional Closure (EEC) and Essential Sonata Closure (ESC), respectively.

Hepokoski and Darcy view each moment in sonata form as an opportunity for the composer to choose from various defaults, with those most common providing generic norms, and others further down the list creating additional expressive options. The most remote options are understood as deformations of the form, although the concept of deformation is historically fluid: procedures considered deformations in 1780 might become high-level defaults in 1810. Further, Sonata Theory asserts clear rhetorical functions for each section of a sonata. For example, an exposition is a promissory structure that leads to a tonal zone other than tonic and attains it through EEC. A recapitulation, by contrast, is a structure of accomplishment, whose central mission is to achieve ESC at the end of the S zone.

Hepokoski and Darcy contrast their two-part expositional model with a description of the continuous exposition, in which there is no medial caesura to mark the beginning of an S zone. In this rhetorical category, the secondary key emerges through *Fortspinnung* techniques and it becomes meaningless to divide the Exposition into the traditional zones of P, TR, S, and C. Although less common than the two-part exposition, this model successfully describes numerous eighteenth-century works, and the procedure is resurrected in the exposition of the first movement of Mahler's Symphony No. 1.

---

    [3]   A shorter version of this chapter was presented at the Thirteenth Biennial International Conference for Nineteenth-Century Music at Durham, England on July 7, 2004. I would like to thank Matthew Brown, Julian Horton, and Kevin Swinden for their perceptive comments and suggestions.

Type 1: Sonatas without development

Type 2: Sonatas where the recapitulation begins with S rather than P

Type 3: The normative "textbook" sonata

Type 4: Sonata-Rondo mixtures

Type 5: Concerto-Sonata adaptations

Type 3 Sonata Form:

[Introduction]

Exposition

Primary Zone P: TONIC

Transitional Zone TR; ends with Medial Caesura

Secondary Zone S; ends with EEC. NOT TONIC

Closing Zone C. NOT TONIC

Development

Recapitulation

Primary Zone P: TONIC

Transitional Zone TR; ends with Medial Caesura

Secondary Zone S; ends with ESC. TONIC

Closing Zone C. TONIC

[Coda]

(from Hepokoski and Darcy 1997 and 2006)

Figure 3.1   Hepokoski and Darcy's five sonata types, and Type 3 outlined
             Source: from Hepokoski and Darcy 1997 and 2006

For nineteenth-century repertoire, Hepokoski and Darcy's deformational strategies allow listeners and composers to make intertextual connections. Nevertheless, it appears that the theory has evolved over time; the listings of deformational strategies in their numerous articles differ from each other and overlap.[4] Further, other authors have suggested their own terminology and categories of deformational procedures that may or may not be accepted by Hepokoski and Darcy; one such example is the "tragic reversed recapitulation" as described by Timothy Jackson.[5] For these reasons, I do not attempt to offer a complete list of deformational strategies, but suggest a few that will be useful in my examination of the first movement of Mahler's Third Symphony; these can be found in Figure 3.2.

For convenience, I have arranged Figure 3.2 in three broad categories: rhetorical deformations, tonal deformations, and combinations of the two. Most of the deformational procedures listed here are self-explanatory, but three involve new or unusual terminology. "Rotational form" is defined as a process in which a referential set of materials is presented, followed by a series of "rotations," in which the referential materials are restated, normally in the same order, but with developments and/or omissions. A normative eighteenth-century Type 3 sonata contains four rotations: the exposition, its repeat, the development (usually developing P, then S, material), and the recapitulation. There are many possibilities for non-alignment of the normative sonata sections and a series of thematic rotations, creating numerous subcategories of deformational strategy.[6] Breakthrough, or *Durchbruch*, is a term coined by Theodor Adorno, in which "an unforeseen inbreaking of a seemingly new (although normally motivically related) event in or at the close of the 'developmental space' radically redefines the character and course of the movement and typically renders a normative, largely symmetrical recapitulation invalid."[7] My own extensions of this concept will be offered in the analysis below. Finally, the idea of "fantasy projection" is defined by Darcy as an interpolated, tonally remote episode inserted into a normative rotational presentation. While related to *Durchbruch*, the difference seems to be that a fantasy projection is parenthetical within a more normative outer structure, while a breakthrough event derails normative structural procedures in the ensuing music.

---

[4]   Books and articles that present listings of deformational strategies include Darcy 1994, 1997, 2001, and Hepokoski 1992a, 1992b, 1993, 1996a, and 2002a.

[5]   See Jackson 1996 for a description of this procedure.

[6]   Hepokoski and Darcy 2006 provides more detailed description of rotational norms and deformations.

[7]   Hepokoski 1993, 6.

Rhetorical Deformations:

    1. Loosely knit discursive exposition (Liszt, Faust Symphony first movement;

    Strauss, Also sprach Zarathustra, Ein Heldenleben; Mahler, Symphony No. 2/v)

    2. Written out repeat of the exposition (Mahler, Symphony No. 2/i)

    3. Tableau-episodic developments (Liszt and Strauss, tone poems; Wagner,

    Siegfried Idyll)

    4. Rotational Form, giving rise to various strophic/sonata hybrids (Schubert,

    Symphony 8/i; Schumann, Symphony 4/iv)

Tonal Deformations:

    1. Tonal plan deformation of exposition (Tchaikowsky, Symphony No. 4/i, Saint-

    Saens, Symphony No. 3/i)

    2. Non-resolving recapitulations.

    3. The redemption paradigm - minor to Major. Within movement or postponed to

    last; delay of redemption until coda (outside sonata space) is common

Tonal and Rhetorical Deformations:

    1. Breakthrough deformations (Adorno)

    2. Fantasy Projections

Figure 3.2   Nineteenth-century deformational strategies in Mahler's Third Symphony, first movement.
Source: from Hepokoski 1993, 1996a, 2002a, Darcy 1997, 2001

Mahler's Third Symphony as Sonata

In the case of Mahler's Third Symphony, the tonal problem seems paramount: how can a sonata form begin in d minor and end in F major? Such a procedure is quite familiar throughout the nineteenth century in songs and piano character pieces but it is virtually unprecedented in symphonically organized movements. This observation calls into question whether the movement can be analyzed in relation to sonata form at all: after all, part of the traditional definition of P and S requires a monotonal reference for the movement in question. In response to this concern, I offer two preliminary arguments in favor of a sonata analysis. First, as suggested above, this is the opening movement of a symphony without programmatic title, and as such carries a generic expectation of sonata form. Second, the rhetoric of the piece is in keeping with sonata form: the largest sections of exposition, development, and recapitulation are quite obvious, with the recapitulation presenting a normally ordered, albeit abbreviated, rotation of the exposition's material. While the tonal procedure in this work is undoubtedly abnormal, the movement is most productively understood as a sonata where tonality does not behave as the defining generator of musical form.

This last observation has profound implications, for it directly contradicts statements by Heinrich Schenker that form is a property that emerges directly from tonal procedures. This paper is not the place to offer a thorough critique of Schenker's theory of musical form, but it seems clear that musical form in general, and sonata form in particular, can be meaningfully defined in many works that do not observe the laws of tonality as they are codified by Schenker. My analysis explores formal organization as a prerequisite to examining tonal concerns in this movement—an important, though little recognized, aspect of Schenkerian practice.

The tonal anomalies in this movement have misled analysts, and the published literature is filled with dubious readings. In many of these, the opening 272 measures are relegated to the category of Introduction, and the movement is viewed as a sonata in F major, with a monothematic exposition modulating from F major to D major.[8] Support for such analyses comes from readings of Mahler's programmatic descriptions of the movement, along with interpretations of programmatic marginalia in Mahler's sketches, the autograph, and Willem Mengelberg's copy of the score.[9]

That such analyses are untenable is demonstrated easily enough by examining the recapitulatory moment. There can be no doubt that the recapitulation begins in m. 643, with the horn theme that opened the movement returning at pitch.[10] Further, the vast majority of the opening material not only recurs in order, but also remains in d minor/major. Sonata analyses that assign the opening material outside of expositional space create nonsense of the simplest and most obvious rhetorical gesture in the piece; it is the recapitulation of this material in its original key that confirms our understanding of sonata form in this expansive work.

Example 3.1 presents thematic incipits for important landmarks in the movement. The labels include my assignments of Sonata Theory functions, as well as the programmatic monikers described above, deriving from Mahler's autograph

---

[8]   These analyses include Newlin 1947, Bekker 1969, Mitchell 1975, Floros 1985 [1993], Zenck 2001, and Brown 2003.

[9]   For descriptions of the primary source material, see Franklin 1977, 1991, 1999, and Williamson 1980.

[10]   Stephen Hefling correctly identifies this as the point of recapitulation, but misidentifies the key as F major (see Hefling 1996, 394–5).

materials. Readers may find it helpful to refer back to this thematic catalogue in relation to the formal diagrams that follow.

Example 3.1   Thematic landmarks in Mahler's Third Symphony, first movement

Figure 3.3 presents a detailed description of the exposition, with taxonomic labels derived from Hepokoski and Darcy's work. The chart indicates two "expositions," a procedure familiar from the first movement of Mahler's Second Symphony, and one that is derived both from the normative classical exposition with repeat, and from the "double exposition" found in classical concerto adaptations of sonata form (Hepokoski and Darcy's "Type 5" Sonata). Rhetorically and tonally, the first exposition is a failure; while the motion away from P is convincing enough to establish a rotation, the thematic material collapses before it can truly establish S, fading to percussion in the remote key of D♭ major. Each exposition is divided in half rhetorically, with P material and S material on either side of the "medial caesura." I use this latter term cautiously for three reasons: a) there is no transition (TR) in my view of the form; b) although the "cadences" that mark the end of P material clearly round off the respective passages in d minor, they do not represent classically formed PACs or IACs;[11] c) S material is defined primarily through contrast in gesture and affect to that of P material, NOT through the clear establishment of a contrasting key. Such a procedure broadens Hepokoski and Darcy's definition of the caesura; it is clear that a rhetorical break occurs at this point in the music, but it is not a traditional cadence. In some sense, given the problematic nature of S itself in the second exposition, it may be productive to think of this exposition as some type of hybrid between the two-part and continuous exposition models.

Also essential to understanding the form is my labeling of the opening 26 measures as "P0." While the horn fanfare in d minor clearly marks the recapitulation later in the movement, it does not represent the gestural or thematic material that fully defines the P zone, and it is excised in the rotations of the second exposition and development. Indeed, the horn fanfare is thematically quite close to the march material that characterizes S. (Compare "*Der Weckruf!*" and "Summer March" in Example 3.1). Mahler's procedure here clearly derives from works such as Beethoven's Third or Fifth Symphonies, in which the opening measures mark P, but do not fully embody the main theme of P.

A closer analysis of the second exposition reveals an extreme crisis in its construction as well, and this will have a significant impact on our understanding of the recapitulation. In the first exposition, P is presented as a small ternary structure, with the *Trauermarsch* accompaniment providing a recognizable point of departure. In the second exposition, this accompaniment returns to mark the beginning of a new rotation, but a "new" development of P occurs with the trombone melody introduced in m. 166. This trombone melody appears in classical period structure, the antecedent phrase concluding with a half cadence in m. 177, with dominant expansion derived from the "*O Mensch*" melody first heard as P0b. The consequent phrase hints at a redemptive motion to D major, but collapses back to d minor as the P1 theme returns in the trumpet over plagal closure to the P zone.

The rotation continues with a repeat of the "Pan Sleeps" and "*Wanderlied*" motives. "*Wanderlied*" is abbreviated here, and the "Herold" motive announces C major instead of D♭. This provides the dominant to the expected classical S key of F major. However, S has difficulty establishing itself: the harmony continuously sidetracks to neighboring a-minor and d-minor chords, suggesting either unstable elements in F, or possibly that P is unwilling to relinquish its tonal sphere of influence. Further, the hypermeter of summer's march has some difficulty

---

[11]   Agawu 1997, 222–5, discusses elements of cadential intensification in Mahler's work. Here, Mahler seems to be de-emphasizing traditional cadential roles at a point of articulation.

EXPOSITION 1: mm.1–163

    1–131 P material

    1 P0 a Horn Fanfare *Der Weckruf*!

    11 P0 b *O Mensch*! (4th movement)

    27 P1 Trauermarsch

    27 (a), 83 (b), 110 (a′); b and a' comprise a single tonal motion

    131 Medial caesura

    132–163 S material

    132 S0 *Pan schläft + Wanderlied*

    148 *Der Herold!*

    150 (S1) March rhythm

EXPOSITION 2: mm.164-362

    164–224 P material

    164 P1 *Trauermarsch* with trombone solo

    164 (trombone ant.), 184 (trombone cons.), 209 (a″)

    224 Medial caesura

    225-362 S material

    225 S0 *Pan schläft + Wanderlied*

    237 *Der Herold!*

    239 (S1) March rhythm + fragments

    273 S1 March in F
    315 F major established? 4-bar hypermeter

    331 D major *Durchbruch*

    351 cadential approach

    362 EEC, immediately undone by $\hat{5}$–$\flat\hat{6}$ and glissandi

Figure 3.3   Mahler's Third Symphony, form of the exposition (mm. 1–362)

establishing four-bar groups, with extra two-bar patterns disrupting it enough to call into question the success of this march. F major and four-bar hypermeter seem to settle in at m. 315, only to be tonally crushed by the trombone entrance at m. 331 in a triumphant D major. From this point forth, F major disappears, and the exposition achieves EEC in D major at m. 362.

The hermeneutic element here can still be related back to Mahler's program: if the S group represents "summer marching in," then either the movement represents a full annual cycle (since summer will march in again in the recapitulation), or there must be a failure in the exposition (the reading espoused here). My interpretation of the tonal drama of this exposition is that S represents a problematized attempt to achieve the expected key of F major which fails in measure 331. I identify this D-major interruption as an example of tonal *Durchbruch* in the sense that the remainder of the movement cannot sustain such an anomalous tonal event: normative sonata discourse cannot reasonably be maintained once the exposition has concluded in the original tonic (from a tonal standpoint, d minor to D major is not an acceptable tonal conflict upon which an exposition can be built). Upon reaching EEC in measure 362, Mahler initiates a $\hat{5}-\flat\hat{6}$ *fortissimo* harmonic scream, including harp glissandi, as if horrified that he has closed in the wrong key. The development ensues back in tonic with a despairing return to P material.

One of the most convincing aspects of Hepokoski and Darcy's analyses is their demonstration that pieces that end unexpectedly often foreshadow problems through anomalous procedures in the exposition.[12] This movement is no exception to this rule, as the above analysis has shown: not only does it end in the "wrong" key, but also the exposition fails to achieve tonal contrast. In asserting first that the movement begins on the tonic of d minor, and secondly that the exposition attempts to establish a new tonality of F and fails, we are confronted with a catastrophic situation within the opening third of the movement, one from which the sonata form, viewed in conventional terms, cannot recover. At the same time, we can understand the exposition as successfully establishing a conflict or problem in need of resolution: The S group needs to get to F major and stay there to resolve the needs of the program. Programmatically, our assumption is that summer has not yet arrived at the end of the exposition; projecting to the end of the movement, when summer marches in successfully, we will feel triumph over the failed attempt of the exposition, but we will also feel a sense of unease in that the movement has ended off-tonic.

Figure 3.4 provides a brief outline of divisions in the development, indicating derivation of thematic and tonal materials from what has come before. In keeping with the character of the exposition and Mahler's implicit programmatic associations, the development is constructed from fairly discreet episodes, but also exhibits clear rotational structure. The unexpected return to d minor at the

---

[12]   For the most extensive discussion of this aspect of the theory, see Hepokoski 2001/02, and 2002b, especially the analysis of Haydn String Quartet Op. 64/3, first movement.

DEVELOPMENT

362 return of P1(a) d minor (cf. m. 58 ff.)

398 P1(b)

424 Trombone ant. B♭ minor/major; cf. Exposition 2, m.164

440 Oboe cons.

453 (455) *Pan schläft* + *Wanderlied* D major

478 Summer attempts to march while Pan sleeps

492 G♭ Fantasy Projection derives from *Wanderlied* + Summer march

530 B♭ minor – E♭ minor (cf. mm. 247 ff.)

539 *Das Gesindel!*

583 C major P0/S [*Die Schlacht beginnt!*]

603 D♭/G♭ [*Der Südstorm!*] *Der Herold*

635 "Retransition"

Figure 3.4   Mahler's Third Symphony, form of the development (mm. 362–642)

beginning of the development, along with the *Trauermarsch* material, helps listeners to recognize the rotational procedure here, and thematic material returns largely in the same order familiar from the expositions. Two elements of the development are most notable within my Sonata Theory reading. First is the self-contained episode in the remote key of G♭ major, with the Summer March music counterpointed against the *Wanderlied* material and incorporated into the *Wanderlied*'s orchestration and hermeneutic affect. I label this inserted passage as a fantasy projection due to its transfiguring character and remote tonality. Perhaps more surprising initially is the labeling of the snare drum fanfare at m. 635 as the retransition. Clearly the military figure announces the return of the *Weckruf* theme, and yet there is no dominant harmony, and traditional harmonic interruption is avoided. Further reflection reveals that the catastrophe of the exposition's tonal trajectory renders interruption an invalid procedure here, and Mahler's use of percussion as a rhetorical alternative is a brilliant solution that provides the necessary announcement before the recapitulation.

The recapitulation is outlined in Figure 3.5. While P0 is slightly expanded in this presentation, P1 is radically compressed, with the trombone solo from Exposition 2 overlapping the opening *Trauermarsch* melodic material from Exposition 1. The antecedent phrase of the trombone solo is very similar to its initial presentation, but the consequent presents a redemptive motion to D major, only hinted at the first time. The medial caesura is marked by a long-held fermata in m. 736. At this point, Mahler eschews the "Pan Sleeps" and "Herold" themes (surely Pan is awake by now, and Summer needs no annunciation at this point in the movement), and the march rhythm establishes itself, along with the familiar counterpointing of the *Wanderlied* and Summer themes. Once again, there is some initial difficulty in establishing four-bar hypermeter and F major, but this is resolved clearly by m. 800, whereupon the music continues to build up in regular 4- and 8-bar hypermetric groups. F major is further established by the elimination of mediant neighbor chords and finally by the convincingly brighter orchestration of that key, with the cadential melodies presented a third higher than the disruptive D-major statements of the exposition. In sum, the work achieves ESC in F major at m. 857, but all is not resolved: F major has been programmatically convincing, but remains tonally incorrect. The familiar negative $\hat{5}$–$\flat\hat{6}$ contrapuntal gesture initiates the coda, which bombastically reaffirms F as the off-tonic ending for this astonishing movement.

The "failure" of sonata form in this movement has significant implications for our interpretation of the succeeding movements. (In spite of the first movement having been composed last, a listener must evaluate tonal processes in the chronological order in which they are presented within the completed work.) A hearing of the movement as beginning in tonic and ending in the mediant makes sense of the large two-part division of the work, with the first movement itself representing part 1 and the remaining five movements comprising part 2.[13] Figure 3.6 identifies the tonic keys for each movement in the symphony, and a quick perusal reveals a closely knit tonal network around the harmonic centers D and F, with D eventually achieving victory in the final movement. This results in a global application of the "redemption paradigm" familiar from Beethoven's Fifth Symphony and innumerable other nineteenth-century works. Further, such associations with the succeeding movements allow the listener to interpret the first movement as programmatically closed, but tonally open, and sense the classical tonal resolution of the entire work only in the last movement.

---

[13]   Early performances of the work included an intermission at the end of the first movement; see Franklin 1991, 38.

RECAPITULATION

643–736 P material

643 P0 a horn fanfare *Der Weckruf!*

655 P0 b *O Mensch!* (fourth movement)

671 P1 *Trauermarsch*

683 Trombone ant.

703 Trombone cons. redemptive D major

736 Medial caesura

737–857 S material

737 March rhythm and fragments

778 March established

800 F major and 4-bar hypermeter established

846 Cadential approach

857 ESC, immediately undone by $\hat{5}$ – $\flat\hat{6}$ and glissandi [*Schrei!*]

CODA

857 $\hat{5}$ – $\flat\hat{6}$ and glissandi [*Schrei!*]

867 F recovered

875 *Schluß*

Figure 3.5   Mahler's Third Symphony, form of the recapitulation (mm. 643–857) and coda (mm. 857–875)

I   D minor → F major

II   A major (V of d)

III   c minor → C major (V of F)

IV   d minor; begins and ends on A (V)

V   F major

VI   D major

Figure 3.6   Mahler's Third Symphony, tonalities of each movement

Mahler's Third Symphony and Schenker's Tonal Theory

That Heinrich Schenker's theory of tonality would accommodate the first movement of Mahler's Third Symphony uncomfortably at best should be obvious. While I will not attempt a Schenkerian reading of the movement here, I do believe that Schenkerian definitions of tonal norms still have much to tell us about Mahler's music and other tonally open works of the nineteenth century. I will discuss two aspects of Schenkerian theory in relation to Mahler's work: the distinction between tonality and monotonality, and hierarchical vs. associational elements in Schenker's theory.

In claiming that a single *Ursatz*, in combination with a set of transformational rules of counterpoint and *Stufen* succession, generate tonal compositions, Schenker's theory provides a powerful model for discussing pieces that are monotonal, to borrow a term from Arnold Schoenberg. While Schenker's auxiliary cadence, a topic first described in *Der freie Satz* and discussed widely in the published literature, provides a compelling model for describing many pieces and movements that begin and end in different keys, it is clearly not applicable to the first movement of Mahler's Third Symphony.[14] An auxiliary cadence reading would assert that the movement is in F major, opening off-tonic on the submediant. Given my description of tonal events within the movement and the conclusion of the symphony in D major, such an interpretation of the first movement seems inappropriate, and Schenker's theory does not provide models for explaining works or movements that end off-tonic. An attempt to apply Schenker's approach to Mahler's Third Symphony would require either: a)

----

[14]   See *Der freie Satz* section 244. The most extended secondary discussion of the auxiliary cadence is found in Burstein 1988 and 2006; see also Marvin 2002, 138–54 for further discussion.

generation of all six movements from a single *Ursatz* across the entire symphony (a solution unprecedented in Schenker's own work, and one that has not received widespread acceptance in the subsequent literature); or, b) abandonment of the *Ursatz* as the generative background of the work (a solution which could call into question the theoretical underpinnings of Schenker's theory). While Schenker did not provide sufficient evidence of how his theory would approach pieces that are clearly tonal, but not monotonal, there are options for analysis using his method even when the piece in question is not classically monotonal.[15]

Since Schenker's death in 1935, there have been several attempts to address the distinction between tonal and monotonal compositions. In 1947, Dika Newlin coined the term "progressive tonality" in order to describe a broad category of pieces that begin and end in different keys. The term has been utilized in nineteenth-century research by Graham George, Deryck Cooke, Robert Bailey, Christopher Lewis, Patrick McCreless, and others, including, most recently, Boyd Pomeroy; several of these authors have also invoked models of "directional tonality" and the "double-tonic complex" as specific cases within the umbrella category of "progressive tonality."[16] All of these forms of tonality are defined independently of Schenker's theory, as I have shown elsewhere.[17] While the auxiliary cadence can be viewed as a subset of "progressive tonality," there are serious methodological problems involved in asserting progressive tonality as a single organizational category within Schenker's theory.

The question of hierarchy vs. association has also arisen in discussion of tonally open works such as the first movement of Mahler's Third Symphony. In examining Schenker's views on the subject, a surprising fact emerges: it is possible to assert both hierarchical relationships and associational relationships within an analysis, as long as a distinction between the two is maintained. Hierarchical relationships, or those that can be defined through the laws of counterpoint and *Stufen* succession, are essential to an understanding of the work's tonal generation. Associational relationships include many types of pitch relationships that are not derivable from counterpoint or *Stufen* analysis. Schenker makes numerous observations of this type throughout his mature writings, but he is quite careful to avoid asserting the same level of explanatory value to these connections. Of the many clear examples of this distinction that might be drawn from Schenker's writings, I select one: Schenker's discussion of Beethoven's quotation of thematic material in *Fidelio* within the Leonore Overture No. 3 represents a cross-movement association that cannot be understood as hierarchically derived from his tonal theory. The

---

[15]   Schenker's own analysis of portions of Stravinsky's Piano Concerto provide one model for analysis of tonally problematic work (Schenker 1996, 17–18; see also Krebs 1981, 1985, 1991, and 1996 for alternative backround readings in works by Schubert and Chopin).

[16]   See George 1970, Bailey 1977, Cooke 1980, McCreless 1982, Lewis 1984, Pomeroy 2004.

[17]   See Marvin 2002, 22–8.

discussion further indicates that the quotation has its own hierarchical meaning within the Overture, deriving from a chromatic passing tone, yet also maintains the associational reference to foreshadowing the key of Florestan's aria.[18]

The Mahler analysis presented above presents interesting challenges for this distinction: at one level, D must be considered the hierarchical tonic for the entire symphony, but a Schenkerian analysis of the first movement in terms of D is problematic because the movement is hierarchically incomplete in that key. Further, the conflict between D and F throughout all six movements creates rich associational relationships that cut across any hierarchical tonal relationships within the movements. Finally, these associational conflicts have been hinted at within the first movement itself, as the above analysis asserts, with elements of d minor subverting the establishment of F major in the "Summer March" theme. While this essay has left these tonal problems unresolved, I hope that it has demonstrated that accurate formal and hermeneutic analysis is a necessary prerequisite to tonal interpretation in this repertoire.

Bibliography

Agawu, Kofi. 1997. "Prolonged Counterpoint in Mahler," in *Mahler Studies*, ed. Stephen E. Hefling. Cambridge: Cambridge University Press, pp. 217–47.

Bailey, Robert. 1977. "The Structure of The Ring and its Evolution." *Nineteenth Century Music* 1/1, pp. 48–61.

Bekker, Paul. 1969. *Gustav Mahlers Sinfonien*. Berlin: 1921. Reprint ed. Tutzing: Hans Schneider.

Brown, A. Peter. 2003. *The Symphonic Repertoire IV: The Second Golden Age of the Viennese Symphony*. Bloomington: Indiana University Press.

Burstein, L. Poundie. 1988. "The Non-tonic Opening in Classical and Romantic Music." PhD dissertation, City University of New York.

——. 2006. "Schenker's Concept of the Auxiliary Cadence," in *Essays from the Third International Schenker Symposium*, ed. Allen Cadwallader (Hildesheim: Georg Olms), pp. 1–36.

Cooke, Deryck. 1980. *Gustav Mahler: An Introduction to his Music*. London: Faber Music.

Darcy, Warren. 1994. "The Metaphysics of Annihilation: Wagner, Schopenhauer, and the Ending of the Ring." *Music Theory Spectrum* 16/1, pp. 1–40.

——. 1997. "Bruckner's Sonata Deformations," in *Bruckner Studies*, ed. Timothy L. Jackson and Paul Hawkshaw (Cambridge: Cambridge University Press), pp. 256–77.

——. 2001. "Rotational Form, Teleological Genesis, and Fantasy-Projection in the Slow Movement of Mahler's Sixth Symphony." *19th-Century Music* 25/1, pp. 49–74.

---

[18]   See Schenker 1979, Fig. 62/2 and discussion on p. 64.

Floros, Constantin. 1985. *Gustav Mahler III: Die Symphonien*. Wiesbaden: Breitkopf und Härtel. English trans. by Vernon Wicker as *Gustav Mahler: The Symphonies*. Portland: Amadeus Press, 1993.

Franklin, Peter R. 1977. "The Gestation of Mahler's Third Symphony." *Music & Letters* 58/4, pp. 439–46.

———. 1991. *Mahler: Symphony No. 3*. Cambridge Music Handbooks. General Editor: John Rushton. Cambridge: Cambridge University Press.

———. 1999. "A Stranger's Story: Programmes, Politics, and Mahler's Third Symphony," in *The Mahler Companion*, ed. Donald Mitchell and Andrew Nicholson (Oxford: Oxford University Press), pp. 171–86.

George, Graham. 1970. *Tonality and Musical Structure*. New York: Praeger Publishers.

Hefling, Stephen E. 1996. "Mahler: Symphonies 1–4," in *The Symphony 1821–1914*, ed. D. Kern Holoman, Studies in Musical Genres and Repertoires VI, series ed. R. Larry Todd (New York: Schirmer Books), pp. 369–416.

Hepokoski, James. 1992a. "Fiery-Pulsed Libertine or Domestic Hero? Strauss's Don Juan Revisited," in *Richard Strauss: New Perspectives on the Composer and His Work*, ed. Bryan Gilliam (Durham, NC: Duke University Press), pp. 135–75.

———. 1992b. "Structure and Program in Macbeth: A Proposed Reading of Strauss's First Symphonic Poem," in *Richard Strauss and His World*, ed. Bryan Gilliam (Princeton: Princeton University Press), pp. 67–89.

———. 1993. *Sibelius: Symphony No. 5*. Cambridge: Cambridge University Press, esp. pp. 1–9 and 19–30.

———. 1994. "(En)gendering Sonata Form: Masculine-Feminine." *The Musical Times* 135/1818, pp. 494–9.

———. 1996a. "The Essence of Sibelius: Creation Myths and Rotational Cycles in Luonnotor," in *The Sibelius Companion*, ed. Glenda Goss (Westport, CT: Greenwood Press), pp. 121–46.

———. 1996b. "Elgar," in *The Symphony 1821–1914*, ed. D. Kern Holoman, Studies in Musical Genres and Repertoires VI, series ed. R. Larry Todd (New York: Schirmer Books), pp. 327–44.

———. 1996c. "Sibelius," in *The Symphony 1821–1914*, ed. D. Kern Holoman, Studies in Musical Genres and Repertoires VI, series ed. R. Larry Todd (New York: Schirmer Books), pp. 417–49.

———. 2001/02 "Back and Forth from Egmont: Beethoven, Mozart, and the Nonresolving Recapitulation." *19th-Century Music* 25/2–3, pp. 127–54.

———. 2002a. "Beethoven Reception: The Symphonic Tradition," in *The Cambridge History of Nineteenth-Century Music*, ed. Jim Samson. Cambridge: Cambridge University Press, pp. 424–59.

———. 2002b. "Beyond the Sonata Principle," *Journal of the American Musicological Society* 55/1, pp. 91–154.

Hepokoski, James, and Warren Darcy. 1997. "The Medial Caesura and Its Role in the Eighteenth-Century Sonata Exposition." *Music Theory Spectrum* 19/2, pp. 115–54.

———. 2006. *Elements of Sonata Theory: Norms, Types, and Deformations in the Late-Eighteenth-Century Sonata*. New York: Oxford University Press.

Jackson, Timothy L. 1996. "The Tragic Reversed Recapitulation in the German Classical Tradition." *Journal of Music Theory* 40/1, pp. 61–111.

Krebs, Harald. 1981. "Alternatives to Monotonality in Early Nineteenth-Century Music." *Journal of Music Theory* 25/1, pp. 1–16.

———. 1985. "The Background Level in Some Tonally Deviating Works of Franz Schubert." *In Theory Only* 8/8, pp. 5–18.

———. 1991. "Tonal and Formal Dualism in Chopin's Scherzo, Op. 31." *Music Theory Spectrum* 13/1, pp. 48–60.

———. 1996. "Some Early Examples of Tonal Pairing: Schubert's 'Meeres Stille' and 'Der Wanderer'," in *The Second Practice of Nineteenth-Century Tonality*, ed. William Kinderman and Harald Krebs. Lincoln: University of Nebraska Press, pp. 17–33.

Lewis, Christopher Orlo. 1984. *Tonal Coherence in Mahler's Ninth Symphony*. Ann Arbor: UMI Research Press.

Marvin, William M. 2002. "Tonality in Selected Set Pieces from Richard Wagner's *Die Meistersinger von Nürnberg: A Schenkerian Approach*." PhD dissertation, Eastman School of Music.

McCreless, Patrick. 1982. *Wagner's Siegfried: Its Drama, History, and Music*. Ann Arbor: UMI Research Press.

Meyer, Leonard B. 1956. *Emotion and Meaning in Music*. Chicago: University of Chicago Press.

———. 1973. *Explaining Music: Essays and Explorations*. Berkeley: University of California Press.

———. 1989. *Style and Music: Theory, History and Ideology*. Berkeley: University of California Press.

Mitchell, Donald. 1975. *Gustav Mahler: The Wunderhorn Years*. London: Faber and Faber.

Newlin, Dika. 1947. *Bruckner-Mahler-Schoenberg*. New York: King's Crown Press.

Pomeroy, Boyd. 2004. "Tales of Two Tonics: Directional Tonality in Debussy's Orchestral Music." *Music Theory Spectrum* 26/1, pp. 87–118.

Schenker, Heinrich. 1979. *Free Composition (Der freie Satz)*, trans. and ed. Ernst Oester. New York: Longman.

———. 1996. "Further Considerations of the Urlinie: II," in *The Masterwork in Music: A Yearbook* Volume 2 (1926), ed. William Drabkin, trans. John Rothgeb. Cambridge: Cambridge University Press, pp. 1–22.

Williamson, John. 1980. "Mahler's Compositional Process: Reflections on an Early Sketch for the Third Symphony's First Movement." *Music & Letters* 61/3–4, pp. 338–45.

Zenck, Claudia Maurer. 2001. "Die 'dünne Hülle' über dem Kopfsatz der Dritten Symphonie," in *Gustav Mahler und die Symphonik des 19. Jahrhunderts*, ed. Bernd Sponheuer and Wolfram Steinbeck. Frankfurt am Main: Peter Lang, pp. 81–99.

Chapter 4

Motivic Design and Coherence in the First Movement of Schubert's "Arpeggione" Sonata D. 821

Evan Jones

As territories ripe for plunder, sonata forms have proven to be particularly effective tableaux for the illustration of motivic relationships, and have therefore taken on a special role in the scholarly study of motive. Most motivic studies of Classical-era sonata forms over the last thirty years have followed (and extended) one of two theoretical models. Heinrich Schenker's conception of the "concealed repetition" (*verborgene Wiederholungen*) of musical motives—also termed "motivic parallelism" (*motivischer Parallelismus*)—informed many of his analyses after 1920, but was formally expressed as a component of his theory of structural levels only in 1935.[1] Arnold Schoenberg defined his notion of a "basic shape" (*Grundgestalt*) as the germinal musical material sounding at the outset of a piece and generating all subsequent content, but never provided an analysis of a complete piece to illustrate his ideas.[2] Within the last three decades, these concepts have inspired renewed scholarly attention to sonata forms by Haydn, Mozart, and Beethoven—establishing a canon of analytical practices to parallel the privilege accorded to those composers and their works. Charles Burkhart's pivotal study of motivic parallelism (in, among other works, the first movements of Mozart's K. 330 and K. 545 and Beethoven's op. 2 no. 1) prompted a great resurgence of interest and activity within the Schenkerian community; analyses by David Beach, Roger Kamien, John Rothgeb and others further expanded a Schenkerian understanding of motivic relationships in Classical sonata forms.[3]

---

[1]   Schenker 1979, 98–100 and Fig. 119. Schenker's earlier references to this idea are surveyed in Burkhart 1978, 168–73 and Cadwallader and Pastille 1992, 119–35. See also Cohn 1992 for an important discussion of contradictions between Schenkerian theory and practice regarding motivic relationships.

[2]   Schoenberg 1967, 8; Schoenberg 1995, 226–7. Carpenter 1983 provides a useful introduction to the concept of *Grundgestalt*. Schiano 1992 traces in more detail the evolution of this concept in Schoenberg's teachings and in the writings of his students.

[3]   Motivic parallelisms in Classical-era sonata forms are identified in (among many other sources) Burkhart 1978, Beach 1983, Kamien 1983, Rothgeb 1983, Beach 1987, and Cadwallader and Pastille 1992.

Schoenberg's theoretical premise afforded his student Patricia Carpenter and her student Severine Neff an entirely different perspective on motivic development in the first movements of Beethoven's opp. 57 and 95 and in several later pieces.[4] Notwithstanding several attempts to integrate these two traditions—most notably by David Epstein—the theories seem to have resisted any kind of synthesis.[5]

With respect to the music of Franz Schubert, however, such a bifurcation of methodology has been all but effaced, as scholars have pioneered a host of new approaches to the motivic analysis of his music. To be sure, the inherited models have lost none of their relevance: the Schoenbergian view is ably and productively represented among Schubert studies,[6] and Schenker's concept of motivic parallelism is most clearly and archetypally illustrated in Schubert's songs.[7] As David Beach and Gordon Sly have shown in a compelling series of articles, Schubert's sonata forms are no less coherently crafted: their analyses demonstrate a motivic unity that underlies Schubert's innovative harmonic language and extended formal plans.[8] But Schubert's music can be, and has been, understood as "coherent" in many ways. In an influential pair of studies, Edward T. Cone

---

[4]   Carpenter 1983 and Carpenter 1984 contain the Beethoven analyses; Carpenter 1988a, Carpenter 1988b, Neff 1993, and Carpenter 1997 present equally revealing analyses of works by Schubert and Brahms. Elsewhere (Jones 2003) I have discussed the "cartographic" character of Carpenter's analyses and some other music-theoretical models.

[5]   Epstein 1979 features a chapter on the first movement of Beethoven's Symphony no. 3 and extended illustrations and discussions of other sonata forms by Haydn, Mozart, Beethoven, Schumann, and Brahms. Burkhart 1978, 146–7 and Rothgeb 1983, 40–42 argue that the motivic segmentation practiced by Schoenberg and Schoenbergians does not conform to a correct Schenkerian understanding. More recent efforts toward "Schenkerian-Schoenbergian" strategies include Clemens 1998 and Boss 1999.

[6]   Carpenter 1988b analyzes Schubert's Impromptu op. 90 no. 3; Neff 1993 provides a comprehensive motivic treatment of Schubert's "Der Wegweiser." Sobaskie 2005b cites Schoenberg's notion of the "tonal problem" (and identifies its eventual solution) in Schubert's C-major Quintet D. 956.

[7]   Burkhart 1978, McNamee 1985, Krebs 1988, and Stein 1989 all identify various instances of motivic parallelism in Schubert's "Erlkönig." Schachter 1983 discusses the connection between motivic design and poetic imagery in four songs by Schubert, including a detailed examination of concealed motivic repetition in "Nacht und Träume."

[8]   Beach 1993 contrasts conflicting Schenkerian interpretations of the first movements of Schubert's G-major Quartet D. 887, C-major Quintet D. 956, and the "Trout" Quintet D. 667. Beach 1994 discusses the motivic derivation of distant harmonic juxtapositions in the first movements of the G-major Quartet and the C-major Quintet, as well as in the *Quartettsatz* D. 703. Beach 1998 explores aspects of modal mixture in another extensive examination of the first movement of the G-major Quartet and several shorter pieces. Sly 1995 explicates the "tonal architecture" of the first movement of Schubert's Violin Sonata D. 408 by juxtaposing graphs of motivic design and voice-leading structure on adjacent staves. Sly 2001 contrasts conflicting readings of the first movements of Schubert's B♭-major Trio D. 898 and Symphony no. 4 D. 417, which feature off-tonic recapitulations.

proposed that a certain pitch class or harmonic event can serve as a "promissory note," singled out by some means at the beginning of the piece and signifying by its persistent recurrence in new musical settings (or spellings) a continuing element of dramatic import.[9] Other scholars have similarly traced the journeys of particular pitch classes through Schubert's songs and sonata forms within the contexts of Schenkerian, Schoenbergian and transformational theory.[10] Moreover, the capacity of "motives" in almost any musical parameter to exert a palpable presence throughout a piece has been widely investigated.[11]

The analysis that follows, then, proceeds from an environment of expanding assumptions about the motivic character of Schubert's music, and specifically an

---

[9]   Cone 1982 identifies E♮/F♭ as a promissory note in Schubert's *Moment Musical* in A♭ op. 94 no. 6 (D. 780)—specifically symbolizing, in Cone's view, the composer's awareness of his own syphilitic infection. Cone 1984 considers several of Schubert's sonata-form movements from a similar perspective.

[10]   Here are a few such sources that concern Schubert's music. Lewin 1982 divines the answer to a lovelorn protagonist's questions in the eventual emergence of an "icy G♯" in "Auf dem Flusse." Schachter 1983 highlights a recurring role played by F×/G♮ at different structural levels of "Nacht und Träume." McCreless 1990 understands an enigmatic F♭ chord within the B♭-major tonality of "Pause" as anticipating the E-major key of the poet's demise later in the same song cycle. Beach 1994, 4–5 identifies a recurring role for D♯/E♭ in the first movement of the C-major Quintet, suggesting that "the motive E♮–E♭–E♮ may be considered as a basic motive—a generating source, if you will" (5). Laitz 1996 finds parallels to textual content in the treatment of ♯5̂/♭6̂ (for Laitz, the core of the "submediant complex") in a number of songs. In an engaging exploration of hexatonic organization in the first movement of the Sonata D. 960, Cohn 1999 traces three particular semitonal pitch-class motives in both local and large-scale contexts, assigning each one a role in the overall modulatory plan of the movement. Finally, Schmalfeldt 2003 finds another semitonal pitch-class motive, F–E, operating "as a chief protagonist within the music drama" of the first movement of the A-minor Sonata D. 845, and featured throughout the piece in other keys as well. These studies identify motivic elements that are continuous without being prolonged in the Schenkerian sense, but the apparent incompatibility with a strict Schenkerian reading seems only to heighten the impact of the analysis, as if confirming the actorial status of the highlighted element.

[11]   I will again mention only sources relevant to Schubert's music. McCreless 1977 and Schachter 1987 explore the intersection of pitch and metric/rhythmic structures in the *Moment Musical* op. 94 no. 2 and in "Wandrers Nachtlied" D. 768, respectively. Epstein 1979, 99–100 identifies "a nuance of unusual autonomy" involving an accent followed by a diminuendo, which "assumes aspects of an integral motive" in the first movement of the "Unfinished" Symphony D. 759. Also in the first movement of the "Unfinished," Kurth 1999 describes a continuing conflict between simple triple meter and compound duple meter as an "agonistic discourse." Agawu 1984 proposes a framework of local and global "highpoints" (often coinciding with registral climaxes but depending also on other parameters) in "Der greise Kopf." Hatten 1993 ascribes motivic status to gestures, rhythmic figures, and aspects of instrumental resonance in the first movement of the Sonata D. 959. Other studies of gesture in Schubert include Sobaskie 2003 and Sobaskie 2005a.

interest in the roles of motivic parallelism and motivic pitch classes within the context of sonata form. Although the piece to be explored, the first movement of the Sonata for Arpeggione and Piano D. 821, is hardly his most innovative from the perspective of tonal structure, its motivic design rewards close study.[12] In the interests of clarity, some observations concerning motives in domains other than pitch will be withheld from the main body of the text and mentioned only briefly in the notes; the reader may consider these comments as more tightly or loosely connected to the main arguments, depending on the breadth of one's motivic interests.[13] Even within the main argument, however, it proves crucial to refer to certain rhythmic, registral, textural, gestural, and proportional aspects of the music that seem to participate in the motivic picture of the piece. A fully integrated, unified description of these numerous factors is not the goal of this study; but if we do not seek unity, we may yet hope to find coherence—to discover that observed musical entities and properties "cohere" to each other in reinforcement of their mutual significance.

Example 4.1 reproduces the opening phrase of the piece.[14] A sense of containment, even confinement, is suggested by the remarkably proscribed melodic range (A4–F5), the regularity of the harmonic rhythm, the tightly woven web of melodic motives, and the overall symmetry of the phrase. The opening four melodic notes provide a kernel of closure, departing from and returning to the tonal center; from a motivic standpoint, however, they represent more than

---

[12]   The term "arpeggione" seems to have originated with the sonata's publication in 1871 rather than with the invention of the instrument nearly fifty years earlier in Vienna by Johann Georg Staufer. (The instrument was originally known as the "Bogen-guitarre," the "guitarre d'amour" or the "guitarre-violoncell.") Schubert composed the sonata in November 1824—the same year as the *Moment Musical* no. 6, in which Cone 1982 finds such deep motivic significance; the same year as the A-minor Quartet D. 804 in which Rast 2003, 81 finds the composer "confront[ing] his own mortality as never before" through self-quotation; and only six months before his A-minor Sonata D. 845, in which Schmalfeldt 2003, 52 finds motivic design of "haunting obsessiveness—of the kind, for example, that thoughts of death might bring…". A motivic approach to this work is thus well warranted.

[13]   My own interest in this piece arose from the experience of preparing and performing it on the cello—several times with Norman Carey, who I would like to thank for his inspired collaboration. Unlike the groundbreaking dialogue staged between Analyst and Performer in Schmalfeldt 1985, and the fusion of the two personalities into a single insightful voice in Schmalfeldt 2003, this study will not explicitly address a performer's thought process or physical experience. At least for this author, however, the preparation of this essay has completed the experience of performing, inasmuch as it has afforded the opportunity to pursue some intuitions about the piece that predated any serious analytical scrutiny on my part.

[14]   Note that the arpeggione part transposes down an octave (an explanatory "8" has been added to the clef). Also, since this piece is performed today on a variety of string, wind, and brass instruments, I will refer generically to the soloist or the solo part in my discussion.

merely an ornamented upper-neighbor figure. Although the C5 in m. 1 could be characterized as an escape tone, it anticipates the chordal third of the returning tonic harmony in m. 2; its slightly premature sounding can be heard as the result of rhythmic displacement. From this perspective, the surface configuration of A4–B4–C5 can be heard as a stepwise passage between two chordal members a third apart, even though the C is dissonant during its actual sounding. The melodic succession at the cadence (mm. 8–9) invites a parallel description: C5 again sounds as a dissonance against the dominant harmony at the end of m. 8, but its membership in the cadential six-four on the previous beat adumbrates the acoustic offense. Among several other factors, the retrograde relation between the opening and closing melodic gestures contributes to the audible symmetry of the phrase; m. 9, in particular, is a particularly close approximation of m. 1 in retrograde.[15]

Example 4.1   Schubert, "Arpeggione" Sonata D. 821, opening phrase

Example 4.2 sketches the opposition of these two framing gestures, along with several other stepwise thirds in the phrase. Notwithstanding its chromatic character, the expressive descent from E5 to C5 over mm. 5–6 prefigures the continuing descent from $\hat{3}$, leading subsequently to melodic closure. Another instance of this motive at the end of m. 6 connects the root and the third of the Neapolitan harmony, articulating a pervasive rhythmic figure comprised of three eighth-note upbeats that is deployed eight times over mm. 2–7.[16] Moreover, the weakness of the V–I motion into m. 6 (due to the suspension on the downbeat in the right

---

[15]   See Newbould 1992 concerning an exceptional instance of a musical palindrome in Schubert's melodrama *Die Zauberharfe*.

[16]   This recurring three-upbeat figure recalls Robert Hatten's identification of a characteristic rhythmic-textural motive in Schubert's Sonata D. 959. Hatten 1993, 44 writes: "One especially important gesture involves two sound events separated by a lift, with the first given less weight and duration than the second. Described in such neutral fashion, the gesture can be analyzed independently of any intervallic, melodic, harmonic, or even fixed

hand and the silence in the left) encourages the hearing of a larger stepwise third descending in the bass from C3 in mm. 3–4 through B2 and A2 in mm. 5–6.[17] Taken together with the opening A2, this succession reflects the melody in mm. 8–9 (and, in retrograde, the opening melodic gesture as well) on a larger scale.

Example 4.2   Schubert, "Arpeggione" Sonata D. 821, some stepwise thirds in the opening phrase

The neighboring aspect of the opening gesture, however, is impossible to ignore, and is emphasized by the answering melodic gesture of the E5–F5–E5 melody in mm. 3–4. Over the course of the movement, these two pitch classes give the "neighbor motive" the greatest meaning.[18] The E5–F5–E5 line is set in particular relief in mm. 3–4 not only by its own shadow an octave lower but by the harmonic support below, in which yet another upper neighbor (C3–D3–C3) is articulated.

Contributing further to the salience of the neighboring contour, F5 is the highest pitch of the phrase (and, with one exception, the highest pitch of the first 60 measures). Schubert's dynamic markings in this phrase only enhance the prominence of this neighbor figure; the first of several swells is specified in m. 3, to reinforce the melodic peak. The second such marking (mm. 6–7) coincides with a return to F5 in the melody, which is supported again by an upper-neighboring figure in the bass—this time D3–Eb3–D3. The third such marking (m. 8) coincides with an E–F–E neighbor in the bass rather than the melody, supporting a chromatic neighbor figure (E4–D#4–E4) in the alto line. While the neighbor motive assumes unquestionable surface-level importance in this opening phrase and throughout the movement—as exemplified by the material at the end of the first tonal area in mm. 22–25 (see Example 4.7) and the beginning of the second tonal area (see Example 4.10)—its significance at deeper levels of "concealed repetition" will soon be explored.

---

durational manifestations." In conjunction with later rhythmic events in this movement, the three-upbeat figure accrues a similar degree of motivic autonomy.

[17]   This hearing is also encouraged by the absence of an intervening E3 between G#2 and A2 at the corresponding place (mm. 14–15) in the second phrase—which recasts the first phrase fairly faithfully, following the soloist's entrance.

[18]   As mentioned in note 10, Schmalfeldt 2003 follows the same two pitch classes through Schubert's A-minor Sonata D. 845—perhaps a significant coincidence, given the close dates of their composition.

Although the doubly iterated F5 might be heard as another element of the symmetry of the opening phrase, its return in m. 7 sounds anything but redundant. Instead of enjoying consonant support between downbeats, as in m. 3, the climactic pitch now appears on a downbeat and supported by a dissonance in the bass, as an applied V⁴₂ expands a Neapolitan harmony. This expansion is surely the most remarkable point in the phrase—the hiatus in rhythmic action and the conceptual distance of the applied dominant sonority from the home key conspire to create a moment of apparent unguardedness within the otherwise businesslike opening phrase, as if hinting at something of substance. Returning to F5 so portentously in m. 7 highlights its transformation from a dissonance to a consonance—against which the bass line, in turn, now dissonates—and rekindles the relevance of the upper melodic register. Since this second F5 arrival is articulated so much more substantially than the first, and since it is itself embellished in a manner so similar to the E5 in mm. 3–4, a deeper-level connection is suggested, encompassing the earlier E–F–E neighbor figure in a nested fashion. Example 4.3 sketches the emergence of a hidden repetition of the surface E5–F5–E5 neighbor from mm. 3–4 at a larger scale, as indicated by the beaming. Since this larger E–F–E neighbor figure is completed by the lower-octave Es in mm. 8–9 rather than in the same register, it is perhaps to be expected that the motivic element will return in the forsaken register before too long.

Example 4.3   Schubert, "Arpeggione" Sonata D. 821, some neighbor figures in the opening phrase

Something of the composer's phraseological strategy becomes clear if we hear this important Neapolitan expansion as coinciding with a phrase expansion, and if we take the second phrase as a further expansion of the first. As diagrammed in Example 4.4, the expansion of the Neapolitan harmony in mm. 6–7 can be heard as coinciding with a phrase expansion. By omitting m. 7, the top system in Example 4.4 reshapes the opening phrase into a symmetrical, and more obviously sentential, eight-bar phrase.[19] That this bowdlerization is musically meaningful is supported

---

[19]   Even Schubert's original phrase projects a clear sentential character, including the fragmentation at the beginning of the continuation phrase predicted by Caplin 1998. (Caplin would not identify mm. 1–9 as a phrase, but that is my preference based on the absence of an interior cadential arrival.) We will soon note an instance of nested sentential organization extending over the entirety of the first tonal area (see note 24).

by Schubert's more substantial expansion of the same harmonic and contrapuntal structure in the second phrase, in which the soloist reprises the opening melody. Example 4.5 juxtaposes the second phrase (mm. 10–22) against the first, and supplies annotations concerning their comparison. As the second phrase begins, the bass voice retains the tonic pitch for four downbeats (mm. 10–13) instead of two downbeats (mm. 1–2) before moving to C—thus doubling its length and preparing the listener for several upcoming phrase expansions. The first such expansion occurs in m. 15, in which the half-measure of tonic from m. 6 expands to a full measure in length—again a factor of two—thus delaying the Neapolitan triad that was to follow by half a measure. Only the weakest possible reference is now permitted to the Neapolitan harmony above the D3 that is attained in the bass in m. 16; sounding as yet another dissonant incomplete neighbor, C5 now precedes a fleeting B♭4, which yields immediately to A4. Instead of then progressing toward cadential closure as before (mm. 6–9), the harmonic motion is diverted quickly back to an unstable tonic (m. 17) without a cadence. As a result, the derivation of the second phrase from the first must be reassessed to reflect an even larger expansion of the half-measure tonic harmony in m. 6, corresponding to three full measures (mm. 15–17) in the second phrase. Example 4.5 indicates the initial impression with question marks and dotted lines, and the revised hearing with solid lines and renumbered measures.

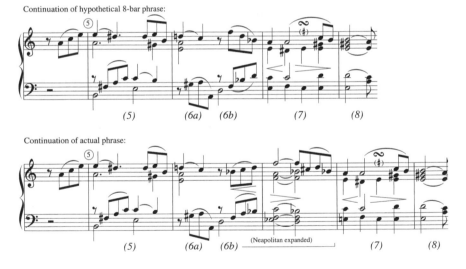

Example 4.4   Schubert, "Arpeggione" Sonata D. 821, derivation of opening phrase from a normative eight-bar structure. Continuation of hypothetical and actual phrases shown, with hypermetric numbering.

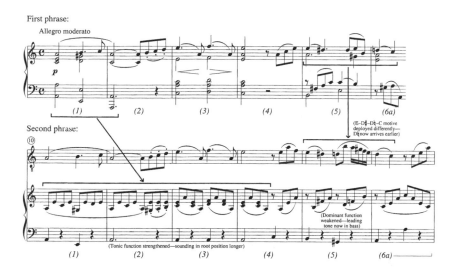

Example 4.5 Schubert, "Arpeggione" Sonata D. 821, derivation of second phrase (measures 10–22) from first phrase. Larger parenthesized numbers correspond to Example 4.4; smaller numerals (at bottom) indicate surface metric grouping.

As if recognizing the misdirection that has occurred, the soloist's swooning arpeggio in m. 17 serves to clean a metaphorical slate as it rounds out an eight-measure subphrase.[20] Regaining the relation to the model of the first phrase, the Neapolitan is redeployed in much more spectacular fashion in mm. 18–20, and is embellished by the same metrically accented applied V^4_2 as before. The insistent reiteration of the applied harmony in mm. 19–20 accomplishes (yet again) a two-fold expansion of the Neapolitan harmony from mm. 6–7 (six beats) to mm. 18–20 (twelve beats).[21] As a result of this expansion, the second phrase seems to fall into a straightforward, metrically square 4 + 4 + 4 division. Example 4.5, however, suggests a more irregular, asymmetric derivation from the first phrase, which was itself explained in Example 4.4 as a perturbation of an underlying eight-measure structure. Although the larger parenthesized numerals in Example 4.5 conflict with the regularity of the surface metric grouping, they represent and coincide with the structural relationship between the two phrases; they explain how m. 21 might be heard as metrically strong (rather than the end of a group of four measures) and they appropriately describe m. 22 as an elision (even though the four-measure groups on the surface continue undisturbed).

The manner in which the second phrase deviates melodically from the first phrase reveals a dramatic instance of registral expansion in concert with the phrase expansion. The melodic similarity between the two phrases highlights the soloist's ascent from E4 to A4 in m. 13 as the first departure from the model of the first phrase. Even though F5 remains the highest pitch heard to this point, the soloist has transgressed a previously established upper boundary defined with respect to the melody itself (the limit of a minor sixth above the first note) rather than the particular register being used. As the soloist continues to leap farther and farther beyond the earlier melodic limit, the reprise of the melody is quickly infused with a virtuosic character. Not merely for show, however, these leaps in fact serve a motivic purpose. Example 4.6 illustrates a pattern of pitch symmetry established by the successively larger leaps. Within the more bravura contour, the E–D♯–D♮–C descent returns (from mm. 5–6) as one of several contrapuntal components in mm. 14–15. The three diatonic tones of this descent are each answered in a higher register, reflecting the stepwise contour of the lower line in inversion. These upper-octave tones spell out an elongated, embedded copy of the original stepwise-third

---

[20]   This kind of extended arpeggio is a significant and frequent textural trope in this piece. Gutmann 1979 suggests that the preponderance of such arpeggios might explain Schubert's use of the term "arpeggione." (See note 12.) Geiringer 1979 draws attention to the composer's sensitivity to the resonance of the instrument's six open strings (E2–A2–D3–G3–B3–E4) as observed in the construction of arpeggios and chords, and even in the key of the piece.

[21]   The repetitive alternation of the Neapolitan and its applied dominant in these measures also recalls a familiar rhythmic pattern—a downbeat articulation followed by a longer rhythmic value on the second beat—that was previously heard in a melodic context in mm. 5, 6, 8, 15, 16, and 18.

motive (A4–B4–C5) at exactly the same pitch level as the motive was first heard in m. 1.

Example 4.6 Schubert, "Arpeggione" Sonata D. 821, symmetrical layout of melodic minima/maxima in second phrase

Unlike the three tones of this upper-octave motivic statement, the E5 on the downbeat of m. 17 precedes its inversional reflection, the A3 at the end of the measure, as shown in Example 4.6. With the Neapolitan as harmonic support in the following measure, the soloist then attains F4 and F5, both echoing the memorable F5 arrival in m. 7. Although the soloist's F4 in m. 18 is approached by the largest leap yet, and is the longest note yet heard, it sounds much less climactic than the corresponding high F on the downbeat of m. 7, since the soloist's more expansive treatment of the melody has already vaulted much higher. The registral transfer of the F4 in m. 18 up to the F5 in m. 20 serves several purposes: it reestablishes the role of high F as highpoint, it continues the recent trend of successively higher melodic peaks, and it allows the soloist to participate in the true upper boundary of the pitch range to this point (F5). It also gives meaning to the E5 in m. 17 as the initiation of an upper-octave elongation of the E–F–E neighbor motive—following and complementing the upper-octave elongation of the A–B–C ascent in mm. 13–16. The immediate destiny of the F5 in m. 20 is, of course, a prompt registral "un-transfer" back down to F4, resolving to the completion of the neighbor figure, E4, on the downbeat of m. 21. But the F5 also follows another, slightly longer-range trajectory within its own register. Example 4.7 illustrates the resumption of the upper octave with the soloist's E5–F5–E5 in m. 22, the first of a flurry of surface neighbor figures with which the first tonal area concludes. Thus, the soloist's upper-octave neighbor figure finds secondary completion in its appropriate register.

Example 4.7 Schubert, "Arpeggione" Sonata D. 821, end of first tonal area

Example 4.8 sketches some of the motivic interrelationships discussed so far.
This example conveys a deliberately incomplete picture of the content of the first
22 measures; it includes only those iterations of the stepwise third motive and the
neighbor motive that involve their normative pitch classes, specifically A–B–C
and E–F–E (stemmed downward and upward, respectively). In many respects,
these two phrases embody a process akin to refraction or recursive generation.[22]
The surface embellishments of E5 in mm. 3–4 and E4 in mm. 12–13 are nested
within deeper-level upper neighbors spanning nearly the entirety of each phrase.
Hidden repetitions of the stepwise third motive that begins and ends each phrase
are also identifiable in the bass voice and, in the second phrase, among the tones
attained by upward leap in the solo part. The soloist then articulates a six-measure
elongation of the E–F–E motive in a similar manner, striking each pitch at the
apex of an upward melodic gesture. This statement of the E–F–E motive could
well be heard as a refraction of its prior appearances—transposed and elongated,
as if projected onto an angled musical surface. As such, its initial tone (the E5 in
m. 17) might be heard as one of several articulations of a continually resounding,
motivically meaningful tone, fastened to the fabric of the first two phrases with

---

[22]   Along these lines, Burkhart 1978 refers to "motivic nesting," while Kamien 1983
refers to "progressive motivic enlargement." Sly 1995 provides some similar illustrations
of nested motives, displayed separately from his voice-leading graphs.

semitonal neighboring embellishments at multiple levels. (Indeed, the multi-level importance of this E–F–E figure continues to resonate through the remaining measures of the principal tonal area; both E4 and E5 are embellished repeatedly with complete and incomplete upper neighbor tones in mm. 22–25, and E persists as a melodic drone through mm. 26–28.)[23] As indicated by the series of nested schematic beams in the example, the consistency and self-similarity of the motivic content of these phrases evokes a nested design of some depth.[24]

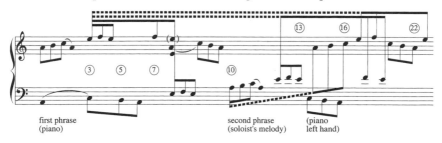

first phrase
(piano)

second phrase
(soloist's melody)

(piano
left hand)

Example 4.8   Schubert, "Arpeggione" Sonata D. 821, occurrences of A–B–C and
             E–F–E motives in first two phrases

The first tonal area culminates with a final melodic leap up to the highest pitch yet, A5, in mm. 29–30, and with the pianist's descent to A1, the lowest pitch yet sounded.[25] Comparing the first and last downbeats of the section (mm. 1 and 30), the registral space of the piece is heard to double, from a range of two octaves (A2–A4) to four octaves (A1–A5). The symmetry of this registral expansion emphasizes the importance of register as a vehicle for projecting different contrapuntal copies of motives—already observed with reference to the concealed motivic repetitions in mm. 13–20. Further, the registral transfer of the opening

---

[23]   The immediate onset of the accompanimental "oom-pah" figuration in m. 23 (coinciding with the final tone of the soloist's opening phrase) and the soloist's apparent obsession with the memory of the high E only underscore the character of this material as "resonance" of a kind.

[24]   Recalling that the opening nine-measure phrase and its modified repetition both exhibit sentential organization, it is conceivable that those two phrases could together comprise the "presentation" component of a larger sentence structure, of which the "continuation" component would extend from mm. 22 to 30. These last nine measures of the first tonal area also evoke the sentential model, with mm. 22–25 as presentation and mm. 26–30 as continuation. Finally, the presentation component of this later nine-measure sentence itself subdivides into two sentential structures—each eight beats long, concluding on the downbeats of mm. 24 and 26.

[25]   A1 was previously heard in m. 2, doubling at the lower octave what would seem to be the "genuine" bass line an octave higher, since the octave doubling immediately evaporates and the remaining bass line dips below A2 only rarely throughout the rest of the section.

melodic tone to an unprecedented height at the end of the section is suggestive of its motivic significance; the pitch-class association between the opening A4 and the (quietly) climactic A5 in m. 29 emphasizes its ostensible continuity over that span as a motivic element and highlights its potential to initiate even deeper-level motivic statements.

The texture of both performers' parts brings the ensuing transitional passage (reproduced in Example 4.9) to the fore. While the soloist again offers arpeggiated flourishes, the pianist's chordal texture recalls the accompanimental rhythm noted earlier—three upbeats followed by a downbeat—and extends it by a factor of two. Both the dominant and tonic harmonies in mm. 31–34 receive a rhythmic articulation of seven upbeats followed by a downbeat, with afterbeats sounding in mm. 32 and 34. Destined to recur at several later points in the movement, this "seven upbeats" figure can be heard as a longer version of the previous "three upbeats" figure (or possibly as the concatenation of two consecutive statements of the "three upbeats" figure). Another motivic elongation is completed by the pianist's afterbeats: the highest pitches in each of the afterbeat chords, F5 and E5, are sure to stand out, due to their relative height and to the *fz* markings on the two chords. The motivic significance of these two local highpoints is hard to miss, especially in the context of the soloist's heavy concentration of high Es in mm. 22–28. Continuing the succession of nested motivic statements at larger and larger scales that we have identified, this latest iteration of the E–F–E motive actually survives the demise of the first tonal area (eulogized with plagal cadences in mm. 29–30) and finds its completion as the music moves into the relative major.

Momentarily preserving the symmetry of the registral plan outlined earlier, the soloist resumes at the end of m. 30 with an upbeat on A3—the precise center of the A1–A5 span and the opening A2–A4 span, and also the pitch with which the soloist began in m. 10. The stepwise ascent from this A3 through B3 and C4 on the downbeats of mm. 31 and 33 not only facilitates the requisite modulation to the relative major but also realizes a yet-larger projection of the opening A–B–C motive, in counterpoint with the pianist's simultaneous completion of the E–F–E motive just described. Previously heard at double-size in mm. 13–15, the A–B–C motive is now articulated at quadruple-size; its elements succeed each other at a two-measure interval, as compared to a half-measure interval in m. 1 or a one-measure interval in mm. 13–15.[26] Its scope is even larger if we understand its first element (the pitch-class A) to encompass conceptually the first 30 measures, including all previous statements of the motive, and its third element (the pitch-class C) to encompass the rest of the exposition. Just as the primary tonal center of the piece initiates the melody in the opening measures of the piece, the subordinate theme group proceeds melodically from C, the new tonic pitch, as shown in Example 4.10. Schubert could hardly have articulated the stepwise melodic line

---

[26]   This quadrupling of scale is enabled by the soloist's rhythmic diminution (by a factor of two) of the "seven upbeats" gesture, heard in sixteenth notes at the ends of mm. 31 and 33.

in mm. 29–34 (linking these two successive tonal centers) more forcefully. The relationship of this line to earlier, nested iterations of the A–B–C motive suggests an intriguingly symbiotic connection between the tonal form of the movement and its motivic structure. We may legitimately consider whether some aspect of the predictability of the overall tonal trajectory—the heritage of minor-mode first-movement form—may have "motivated" even the opening melodic gesture of the piece.

Example 4.9 Schubert, "Arpeggione" Sonata D. 821, transition within exposition

The "seven upbeats" rhythmic gesture recurs at three pivotal moments later in the movement. One of these is the point in the recapitulation that parallels mm. 31–34, which will be discussed presently. More ominously, the gesture resurfaces at two parallel points within the second theme group in both the exposition and recapitulation, leading into the closing material and coinciding with the deployment of a particular harmonic motive. Examples 4.11a and 4.11b provide the relevant excerpts from the score; Example 4.11a concludes the 13-measure phrase begun in Example 4.10, and Example 4.11b concludes a similar 13-measure phrase. The two diminished-seventh chords in mm. 49 and 166, respectively, support prominent melodic highpoints in the solo part and receive the loudest dynamic indications within spans of over 20 measures. (As can be seen in Example 4.9, the earlier occurrence of this diminished-seventh chord in m. 35 involves a similar confluence of accent and pitch height in the soloist's part, although the same chord's reappearance at the corresponding point in the recapitulation, m. 153, does not.) The coincidence of these textural markers with the return of the "seven upbeats" motive serves to highlight these two chords as memorable and mutually referential events. The enharmonic equivalence of these two chords only deepens their interconnection; they function as vii°7/V in both keys (C major, then A major) and are spelled the same except for the change of E♭ to D♯. We will soon recognize some ramifications of this enharmonic pun elsewhere in the movement.

Example 4.10   Schubert, "Arpeggione" Sonata D. 821, beginning of second tonal area

By virtue of its obsessive repetition throughout the rest of the secondary tonal area in the exposition and the parallel measures in the recapitulation, the diminished-seventh chord takes on a continuing importance. In what is arguably the most dramatic passage in the entire exposition—given in Example 4.12—the soloist plunges precipitously from a climactic F5 down nearly three octaves to a low F♯2, and then enjoys an arpeggiated ascent of nearly four octaves to E♭6. The diminished-seventh in question is sounded at both the lowest and highest points of this manic, oceanic contour (mm. 59 and 61), serving to prepare and then to ornament the cadential six-four. Thereafter, a long-sought dominant arrival is denied its resolution not once but twice, as the harmonic motion detours back to the same diminished-seventh in mm. 63 and 67. All four of these appearances are faithfully recapitulated in mm. 176–184, allowing the same pitch-class set to participate in and to frustrate cadential expectations in the new key. Through its sheer frequency and its repeated frustration of cadential closure, this diminished-seventh harmony gains a substantial motivic significance.

Example 4.11   Schubert, "Arpeggione" Sonata D. 821,   (a) prominent diminished-seventh articulation (measure 49) within second tonal area in exposition; (b) enharmonically reinterpreted diminished-seventh chord (measure 166) within parallel passage in recapitulation.

Example 4.12   Schubert, "Arpeggione" Sonata D. 821, recurrence of same diminished-seventh chord (measures 59, 61, 63, 67) toward end of exposition

Notwithstanding this harmony's "fearful symmetry," there would seem to be a certain precedence among its constituent tones as deployed in the score. In the exposition, pitch-class E♭ gains a particular melodic prominence, beginning with the soloist's searing, soaring arrival on E♭5 in m. 49 (Example 4.11a). A similar ascending gesture precedes the next such arrival, that of E♭6 in m. 61, which exceeds the highest previously heard pitch—the A5 in mm. 29–30—by another half an octave.[27] Finally, the repeated recall of the m. 49 arrival in mm. 63 and 67 (Example 4.12) sets the melodic pitch-class E♭ in clear relief. (Over the last 12 measures of the exposition—between the downbeats of mm. 60 and 72, that is—the soloist's only departures from the diatonic C-major scale are, in fact, to the pitch-class E♭.) When they return in the recapitulation, of course, these high-register melodic arrivals are reduced from high E♭s to high Cs, sounding within the context of A major as fatalistic harbingers of the inevitable modal shift back to A minor in the coda. The transposition to A major (down a minor third in pitch) at once robs the melodic peaks of some of their spectacle and deepens the impact of the accompanying bass line—which now features emphatic D♯s in octave doubling, as shown in Example 4.13.

Example 4.13   Schubert, "Arpeggione" Sonata D. 821, recurrence of same diminished-seventh chord (measures 178, 180, 184) toward end of recapitulation

---

[27]   Somewhat incredibly, by m. 61 the pianist has still not exceeded the pitch height of the opening E5–F5–E5 neighbor figure; these remain the pianist's highest-sounding pitches through the first 70 measures of the piece—virtually the entire exposition.

In light of the outer-voice salience of this pitch class in the latter stages of both the exposition and the recapitulation, we might also consider the significance of the fact that the first melodic departures from the key of A minor in both of the first two phrases of the movement (first in the piano, then in the solo part) were to D♯ (mm. 5 and 14). In both cases, the introduction of D♯ resulted in an intriguing and memorable chromaticization of the stepwise-third motive in descending form.[28] We also noted the momentarily expansive, deliberate character that marked the prominent half-note neighboring motion to and from the bass-voice E♭3 in m. 7, the dynamic accent on the immediately subsequent alto-voice D♯4 neighbor tone in m. 8, and the insistence with which the bass voice reiterates the E♭3 neighbor in mm. 18–20 (see Examples 4.1 and 4.5). At least in retrospect, the density with which this pitch class is highlighted in the opening two phrases would seem to be related to its later prominence.

In particular, the fact of its deployment in two different enharmonic guises and its participation in so many subsequent dramatic moments pegs the D♯/E♭ as a "promissory note," to borrow Cone's term for a persistent and narratologically significant chromatic tone. This pitch class is specially positioned at the beginning of the piece in at least two ways. First, it represents the furthest extreme in both "sharpward" and "flatward" directions (along a line of fifth-related tones) attained by any pitch in the first 40 measures.[29] Second, until we arrive at the first of the diminished-seventh chords containing this pitch class in m. 35, we encounter not a single chromatic passing tone (between two diatonic pitches a tone apart) other than the passing D♯ in m. 5 and its reprise in m. 14. As has been seen, however, the scarcity of chromatic motion to that point receives generous compensation once the new key is attained. The bass line in mm. 35–39 (Example 4.9) and mm. 48–51 (Example 4.11a) passes chromatically upward from F to A; this local deceptive gesture is recalled again following each of the cadential evasions noted in mm. 63 and 67 (Example 4.12). Although such a common bass succession might not ordinarily seem motivically significant, these chromatic passing tones are the only chromatic pitches in the bass voice in the entire second key area. Due to the exclusion of other bass-voice chromaticism, this recurring figure accrues motivic status, and could be taken to represent an inversion of the descending chromatic passing line from the opening phrases—not only in its direction but in the register

---

[28]   See notes 9 and 10 concerning Cone 1982 and related studies. Samarotto 2004 and Wen 2004 discuss the musical meaning of passages in which the ascending impetus of ♯4 is deflected downwards—as with the melodic D♯s in mm. 5 and 14.

[29]   Schachter 1994 observes that the "space" on the line of fifths of the Prelude to Bach's E♭-major suite for solo violoncello, BWV 1010, is similarly bounded by a passing D♭ at the beginning and a prominent low-C♯ near the midpoint. Recognizing the hermeneutic significance of such enharmonic events, Schachter reads the transformation from falling D♭ to rising C♯ as representative of Christ's resurrection.

in which it sounds.[30] One might also cite the recurring chromatic descent in the pianist's right hand in mm. 51, 65 and 69 as another related gesture, and thus as further testimony to the continuing motivic significance of the "stepwise third" idea and its chromaticization.

Paving the way for the transposed return of the secondary theme in the recapitulation, a new transitional phrase (Example 4.14) recalls earlier motivic material in several striking ways while preserving the rhythmic and textural character of the original transition. The familiar "seven upbeats" motive returns, now five times in a row (mm. 149–153) instead of just twice (in Example 4.9); it might not be coincidental that its first appearance in the recapitulation drives home a diminished-seventh chord, although not the same one that we have noted elsewhere. Whereas the soloist articulated an expanded form of the A–B–C motive in the transition in the exposition, the E–F–E motive is featured this time around. The vii°$^4_3$ in m. 149 yields obliquely to a dominant seventh in the following measure via the completion of the E–F–E motive, which the soloist's part projects especially clearly. Thereafter, a reference in m. 153 to the prominent Neapolitan arrivals in the opening theme prepares a three-measure dominant pedal, above which a chromatic texture writhes. One particular strand of this upper-voice maelstrom enjoys an intriguing connection to a contrapuntal component in the opening theme. Example 4.15 provides a pair of explanatory sketches. Each melodic strand features an E–D♯–D♮ segment and a B♭–A–G♯ segment, joined in each case by a diatonic scale degree a whole tone away from the nearest note in the two segments, and concluding with a cadentially appropriate semitonal resolution. The two-semitone segments themselves, however, sound in opposite order. To observe that (as pitch-class segments) the two lines are each other's tritone transposition is to disregard obviously crucial diatonic meaning. But it is not meaningless to recognize an interesting motivic affinity between the two different, motivically significant scale-degree successions ($\hat{5}$–♯$\hat{4}$–♮$\hat{4}$ and ♭$\hat{2}$–$\hat{1}$–$\hat{7}$) despite the difference in diatonic interval sizes.

---

[30]   In a similar vein, Forte 1980, 459 states an interest in how "chromatic elements, expressed in the detail of melodic lines and in their interaction, contribute to a unified and organic whole." It is relevant here to note that Forte's use of the term "chromatic" in his article denotes any half step, and that the first word of his title, "Generative Chromaticism in Mozart's Music," denotes the derivation of later chromatic events from "kernel elements given at the beginning of the music" (460). The particular "kernel elements" that Forte follows through Mozart's A-minor Rondo K. 511 include what I might call a "five upbeats" motive and a significant turn motive that is sometimes shortened to just an F–E dyad.

Example 4.14   Schubert, "Arpeggione" Sonata D. 821,   transition within
recapitulation

Example 4.15   Schubert, "Arpeggione" Sonata D. 821, transpositionally related
lines (with six of seven pitch classes in common) in opening
phrase and in transition within recapitulation

Example 4.16 reproduces an extended excerpt from the end of the development,
which includes both the most harmonically ambitious passage of the movement and
the passage of greatest harmonic stasis. In several respects, the dominant expansion
in mm. 110–123 anticipates the transition in the recapitulation, which was just
discussed. The E–F–E motive is similarly prominent in both passages—sounding
in the pianist's left hand and in the solo part through mm. 110–114, and again at

the top of the soloist's arpeggiated gesture in mm. 121–123. The soloist realizes closely related contours in mm. 117–122 and mm. 149–152; in fact, the soloist's flourish in mm. 148–150 is very nearly the retrograde of the one in mm. 121–123. And the chords in mm. 117–120 are struck with the same "tolling" syncopation as is the pedal bass tone in mm. 155–156. The similarity of syncopation here is itself motivically suggestive. Both instances of this "tolling" texture serve to expand the dominant harmony; we have also observed an association between the "seven upbeats" motive and a diminished-seventh chord quality. Given the close functional relationship between dominant and diminished-seventh harmonies, the tolling textures could conceivably be heard as motivically derived from the "seven upbeats" motive.[31]

The extract in Example 4.16 begins in F major, the same key in which the development itself begins 27 measures earlier (although Schubert attains a stable D minor tonality in the middle). At the largest possible scale, then, the movement refers to the opening E–F–E motive as the focus on F over the course of the development is inevitably succeeded by the dominant preparation for the return to A minor.[32] The modal change from F major to F minor in m. 103 is perhaps not an obvious move to make toward the E-major goal only seven measures later, but its necessity will soon be understood.[33] A wrenching chromatic sequence takes us from the dominant in F minor at the end of m. 104 to a D minor triad in m. 108, after which D then passes upwardly and triumphantly through D♯ to E (in the pianist's right hand, mm. 109–110). This finally permits an upward resolution of that chromatic tone, reversing the opening E–D♯–D♮ gesture and forecasting the repeated confirmations of its upward potential in the recapitulation (Examples 4.11b and 4.13).

Moreover, the success of the D♯–E ascent is anticipated in the sequence itself. While mm. 106–107 appear to accomplish an enharmonic reinterpretation, as D♭ and F♭ are respelled as C♯ and E, this is only a notational convenience to prevent the difficulty of wandering into double- and triple-flats. The harmonic succession is simply a chromatic "5–6" motion—exactly the same relationship as between the C-major and A♭ dominant-seventh chords in mm. 104–105. (Without this

---

[31] More generally, following Hatten 1993, a class of "resonant" phenomena might be proposed to include not only the tolling syncopations and the "seven upbeats" motive but the "super arpeggios" identified by Geiringer 1979, the obsessive character of the section mentioned earlier in note 23, the upward octave transfer of the A–B–C motive in mm. 13–16, and perhaps other instances of concealed repetition as well.

[32] We might locate the front end of this large-scale E–F–E motive in the final cadence of the exposition—not shown—which features pizzicato chords in the solo part with E4 as the highest pitch. Moving abruptly to F major as the development begins, the soloist proceeds to arpeggiate the new tonic triad in a figuration with F4 as the highest pitch.

[33] See Epstein 1979, 45 and Sobaskie 2005b regarding the succession of E-major and F-minor tonalities (and their motivic significance) in the second movement of Schubert's C-major Quintet D. 956.

Example 4.16   Schubert, "Arpeggione" Sonata D. 821, retransition

respelling, the passage would have arrived on an F♭-major sonority in m. 110, more precisely reflecting the route taken. The darkening of the F-major triad to F minor in mm. 101–103 thus represents the first "flatward" step in this direction.) The real enharmonic reinterpretation is located between mm. 104 and 106: the note E in m. 104 moves down an augmented prime (a chromatic inflection rather than a diatonic step) to E♭ in m. 105, which then moves up a minor second (a diatonic step) to F♭ in m. 106.[34] In addition to its other roles in this movement, then, pitch-class 3 thus serves as a contrapuntal intermediary directly between the two loci (E and F♭) of perhaps the most striking and the most "Schubertian" harmonic progression in the piece.

Motivic analyses have been most typically employed in the effort to discover and document the unity of musical works. But an analysis like the foregoing, which traces multiple strands of motivic recurrence in pitch, rhythm, and other parameters, might seem to indicate disinterest in unity, or actually to be seeking disunity. While the above analysis is not explicitly grounded in a single theoretical methodology, and is therefore not constrained to describe the piece as unified according to set criteria, its coherence may yet be considered. One certainly could not argue that the identification of motives in several domains unifies a piece to any greater degree than, for instance, a thoroughgoing analysis of pitch motives. The coherence of the analysis, however, can be described in terms of the ideological bent, the common element or orientation that aligns its component statements.

After introducing a formal model of perception that admits of multiple, possibly contradictory perception-statements, and applying it with great sensitivity to a passage from Schubert's song "Morgengruß," David Lewin warns us to "mistrust anything that tells you not to explore an aural impression you have once formed; mistrust anything that tells you not to listen any more to music that once gripped you, as soon as you have heard one thing going on (or two things, or three, four, ..., five hundred ... things)."[35] Although one might not expect an analysis of focused and singular purpose to emerge immediately by following this strategy, a constant attention to that which "grips" will coherently (and invaluably) convey the analyst's own perspective. If there is a unifying thread to the density of motivic observations recounted herein, it is an interest in finding relationships that reflect and participate in the dramatic momentum of the form itself. The exposition attains the second tonal area via a concealed repetition of the opening A–B–C motive; the development realizes the E–F–E motive writ large; and the downward-passing D♯ later dons the cloak of E♭, catalyzes the chromaticism in the retransition,

---

[34]   Such issues are explored in chapter 3 of Jones 2002 under the rubric of "diatonic drift," although this sonata is not mentioned there. Also see Lewin 1991 regarding a similar tonal disjunction in a passage from Schubert's G-major Quartet D. 887.

[35]   Lewin 1986, 359–60. Along related lines, Lewin 1991 cautions against "the Platonic THE"—the tacit assumption that musical objects under discussion have only a single description.

and receives the reward of a leading tone's proper ascending resolution.[36] These processes may not completely coincide with each other (or with the rhythmic, registral, and textural associations that have been noted) within any one theoretical system, but it is hoped they may be heard to "cohere" on their own terms.

Bibliography

Agawu, Kofi. 1984. "On Schubert's '*Der Greise Kopf*'." *In Theory Only* 8/1: 3–21.

Beach, David. 1983. "A Recurring Pattern in Mozart's Music." *Journal of Music Theory* 27/1: 1–29.

———. 1987. "Motivic Repetition in Beethoven's Piano Sonata Op. 110; Part I: The First Movement." *Intégral* 1: 1–29.

———. 1993. "Schubert's Experiments with Sonata Form: Formal-Tonal Design versus Underlying Structure." *Music Theory Spectrum* 15/1: 1–18.

———. 1994. "Harmony and Linear Progression in Schubert's Music." *Journal of Music Theory* 38/1: 1–20.

———. 1998. "Modal Mixture and Schubert's Harmonic Practice." *Journal of Music Theory* 42/1: 73–100.

Boss, Jack F. 1999. "'Schenkerian-Schoenbergian Analysis' and Hidden Repetition in the Opening Movement of Beethoven's Piano Sonata Op. 10, No. 1." *Music Theory Online* 5/1.

Burkhart, Charles. 1978. "Schenker's 'Motivic Parallelisms'." *Journal of Music Theory* 22/2: 145–75.

Cadwallader, Allen, and William Pastille. 1992. "Schenker's High-Level Motives." *Journal of Music Theory* 36/1: 117–48.

Caplin, William E. 1998. *Classical Form: A Theory of Formal Functions for the Instrumental Music of Haydn, Mozart, and Beethoven*. New York and Oxford: Oxford University Press.

Carpenter, Patricia. 1983. "*Grundgestalt* as Tonal Function." *Music Theory Spectrum* 5: 15–38.

———. 1984. "Musical Form and Musical Idea: Reflections on a Theme of Schoenberg, Hanslick, and Kant." In Edmond Strainchamps and Maria Rika Maniates, eds, *Music and Civilization: Essays in Honor of Paul Henry Lang* (New York: W.W. Norton), 394–427.

———. 1988a. "A Problem in Organic Form: Schoenberg's Tonal Body." *Theory and Practice* 13: 31–64.

———. 1988b. "Aspects of Musical Space." In Eugene Narmour and Ruth A. Solie, eds, *Explorations in Music, The Arts, and Ideas: Essays in Honor of Leonard B. Meyer* (Stuyvesant, NY: Pendragon Press), 341–73.

---

[36] The cloak metaphor is Lewin's (1986, 389–90).

———. 1997. "Tonality: A Conflict of Forces." In James M. Baker, David W. Beach, and Jonathan W. Bernard, eds, *Music Theory in Concept and Practice* (Rochester, NY: University of Rochester Press), 97–129.

Clemens, Jon. 1998. "Combining *Ursatz* and *Grundgestalt*: A Schenkerian-Schoenbergian Analysis of Coherence in Hugo Wolf's *Italienisches Liederbuch*." PhD diss., University of Cincinnati.

Cohn, Richard. 1992. "The Autonomy of Motives in Schenkerian Accounts of Tonal Music." *Music Theory Spectrum* 14/2: 150–70.

———. 1999. "As Wonderful as Star Clusters: Instruments for Gazing at Tonality in Schubert." *19th-Century Music* 22/3: 213–32.

Cone, Edward T. 1982. "Schubert's Promissory Note: An Exercise in Musical Hermeneutics." *19th-Century Music* 5/3: 233–41.

———. 1984. "Schubert's Unfinished Business." *19th-Century Music* 7/3: 222–32.

Epstein, David. 1979. *Beyond Orpheus: Studies in Musical Structure*. Cambridge, MA: MIT Press.

Forte, Allen. 1980. "Generative Chromaticism in Mozart's Music: The Rondo in A Minor, K. 511." *Musical Quarterly* 66/4: 459–83.

Geiringer, Karl. 1979. "Schubert's Arpeggione Sonata and the 'Super Arpeggio'." *The Musical Quarterly* 65/4: 513–23.

Gutmann, Veronika. 1979. "Arpeggione: Begriff oder Instrument?" In Otto Brusatti, ed., *Schubert Kongress Wien 1978. Bericht* (Graz: Akademische Druck- und Verlagsanstalt): 233–48.

Hatten, Robert S. 1993. "Schubert the Progressive: The Role of Resonance and Gesture in the Piano Sonata in A, D. 959." *Intégral* 7: 38–81.

Jones, Evan. 2002. "Pervasive Fluency: A Contrapuntal Definition of Stability and Transience in Tonal Music." PhD diss., University of Rochester.

———. 2003. "The Cartography of Musical Space." In Mike Silver and Diana Balmori, eds, *Mapping in the Age of Digital Media: The Yale Symposium* (West Sussex: Wiley Academy), 64–79.

Kamien, Roger. 1983. "Aspects of Motivic Elaboration in the Opening Movement of Haydn's Piano Sonata in C♯ Minor." In David Beach, ed., *Aspects of Schenkerian Theory* (New Haven, CT: Yale University Press), 77–93.

Krebs, Harald. 1988. "Some Addenda to McNamee's Remarks on '*Erlkönig*'." *Music Analysis* 7/1: 53–8.

Kurth, Richard. 1999. "On the Subject of Schubert's 'Unfinished' Symphony: *Was bedeutet die Bewegung?*," *19th-Century Music* 23/1: 3–32.

Laitz, Steven. 1996. "The Submediant Complex: Its Musical and Poetic Roles in Schubert's Songs." *Theory and Practice* 21: 123–65.

Lewin, David. 1982. "*Auf dem Flusse*: Image and Background in a Schubert Song." *19th-Century Music* 6/1: 47–59.

———. 1986. "Music Theory, Phenomenology, and Modes of Perception." *Music Perception* 3/4: 327–92.

———. 1991. "Some Problems and Resources of Music Theory." *Journal of Music Theory Pedagogy* 5/2: 111–32.

McCreless, Patrick. 1977. "Schubert's Moment Musical No. 2: The Interaction of Rhythmic and Tonal Structures." *In Theory Only* 3/4: 3–11.

——. 1990. "Schenker and Chromatic Tonicization: A Reappraisal." In Hedi Siegel, ed., *Schenker Studies* (Cambridge: Cambridge University Press), 125–45.

McNamee, Ann K. 1985. "The Role of the Piano Introduction in Schubert's Lieder." *Music Analysis* 4/1–2: 95–106.

Neff, Severine. 1993. "Schoenberg and Goethe: Organicism and Analysis." In Christopher Hatch and David W. Bernstein, eds, *Music Theory and the Exploration of the Past* (Chicago: Chicago University Press), 409–33.

Newbould, Brian. 1992. "A Schubert Palindrome." *19th-Century Music* 15/3: 207–214.

Rast, Nicholas. 2003. "'*Schöne Welt, wo bist du*?': Motive and Form in Schubert's A Minor Quartet." In Brian Newbould, ed., *Schubert the Progressive: History, Performance Practice, Analysis* (Aldershot: Ashgate), 81–8.

Rothgeb, John. 1983. "Thematic Content: A Schenkerian View." In David Beach, ed., *Aspects of Schenkerian Theory* (New Haven, CT: Yale University Press), 39–60.

Samarotto, Frank. 2004. "Sublimating ♯4̂: An Exercise in Schenkerian Energetics." *Music Theory Online* 10/3.

Schachter, Carl. 1983. "Motive and Text in Four Schubert Songs." In David Beach, ed., *Aspects of Schenkerian Theory* (New Haven, CT: Yale University Press), 61–76.

——. 1987. "Rhythm and Linear Analysis: Aspects of Meter." *Music Forum* 6: 1–59.

——. 1994. "The Prelude from Bach's Suite No. 4 for Violoncello Solo: The Submerged *Urlinie*." *Current Musicology* 56: 54–71.

Schenker, Heinrich. 1979. *Free Composition*, trans. and ed. Ernst Oster (New York: Longman).

Schiano, Michael Jude. 1992. "Arnold Schoenberg's *Grundgestalt* and Its Influence." PhD diss., Brandeis University.

Schmalfeldt, Janet. 1985. "On the Relation of Analysis to Performance: Beethoven's Bagatelles Op. 126, Nos. 2 and 5." *Journal of Music Theory* 29/1: 1–31.

——. 2003. "On Performance, Analysis, and Schubert." *Per Musi: Revista de Performance Musical* 5–6: 38–54.

Schoenberg, Arnold. 1967. *Fundamentals of Musical Composition*, ed. Gerald Strang and Leonard Stein (London: Faber and Faber).

——. 1995. *The Musical Idea and the Logic, Art, and Technique of its Presentation*, trans. and ed. with a commentary by Patricia Carpenter and Severine Neff (New York: Columbia University Press).

Sly, Gordon. 1995. "The Architecture of Key and Motive in a Schubert Sonata." *Intégral* 9: 67–89.

——. 2001. "Schubert's Innovations in Sonata Form: Compositional Logic and Structural Interpretation." *Journal of Music Theory* 45/1: 119–50.

Sobaskie, James William. 2003. "Tonal Implication and the Gestural Dialectic in Schubert's A Minor Quartet." In Brian Newbould, ed., *Schubert the Progressive: History, Performance Practice, Analysis* (Aldershot: Ashgate): 53–79.

——. 2005a. "A Balance Struck: Gesture, Form, and Drama in Schubert's E flat Major Piano Trio." In Xavier Hascher, ed., *Le style instrumental de Schubert: sources, analyse, contexte, évolution* (Paris: Publications de la Sorbonne), 115–46.

——. 2005b. "The 'Problem' of Schubert's String Quintet." *Nineteenth-Century Music Review* 2/1: 57–92.

Stein, Deborah. 1989. "Schubert's Erlkönig: Motivic Parallelism and Motivic Transformation." *19th-Century Music* 13/2: 145–58.

Wen, Eric L. 2004. "More on ♯4̂ to ♮4̂: Further Thoughts on Frank Samarotto's Article 'Sublimating ♯4̂'." *Music Theory Online* 10/4.

Chapter 5

Reading Mozart's Piano Sonata in D Major (K. 311) First Movement

Neil Minturn

The opening movement of Mozart's Piano Sonata, K. 311, unfolds a beautiful and subtle formal drama that strains against traditional notions of sonata form. My aim in studying the aberrant formal characteristics of Mozart's movement is to illuminate and delight in the rhetoric and charm of the music, rather than to defend any particular theory of sonata form.

Most of Mozart's sonata-form movements follow the "Standard Model" of exposition, development, and a recapitulation that presents first and second tonal areas, in order, in the tonic. K. 311/i does not. It is atypical in that it features a reversed, subdominant recapitulation. Indeed, as we will see below, the movement was regarded as so unusual that at least one traditionally minded editor did his best to correct Mozart's missteps by re-composing parts of the work. As absurd as that may sound, it does underline just how startling Mozart's departures from normative sonata procedures were seen to be. Even from our vantage point, informed as it is by the expanded purview of sonata form provided by recent and exciting research, the movement is still striking. Yet the piece is highly attractive and highly esteemed: several of my professional pianist friends tell me that K. 311 is their favorite Mozart piano sonata. I cannot help but believe that much of its attraction derives precisely from its unusual handling of sonata form.

This essay begins by outlining the Standard Model, and surveying how this model is represented in our pedagogy. It then explores some of the unusual aspects of Mozart's sonata and their interpretation from the point of view of the Standard Model as well as that of some recent research. Finally, it turns to works of Haydn, Beethoven, Schubert, and Mozart himself for commentary on sonata form. As William Butler Yeats reminds us in *Sailing to Byzantium*, "Nor is there singing school, but studying / Monuments of its own magnificence." The music itself is arguably the best textbook ever written on sonata form.[1]

---

[1]   Yeats 1928.

The Standard Model

A typical summary of the Standard Model would run roughly as follows: Sonata form comprises an exposition with first theme/first tonal area (FTA) in the tonic, a transition, the second theme/second tonal area (STA) away from the tonic, and often closing material and/or codetta; a development that draws on the motivic/thematic material of the exposition, and retransition; and a recapitulation that reprises the exposition essentially entirely in the tonic key. *Engaging Music: Essays in Music Analysis* is a collection of writings whose collective goal is to provide models of analytical work for students. Its editor, Deborah Stein, has brought together a group of contributors who are leaders in the field. We may be confident, then, that definitions of our discipline's central ideas given in its glossary are representative of the discipline's views and of how we wish students—our future musicians and scholars—to understand them. The entry for sonata form reads as follows:

> **Sonata form** A tripartite, full-movement form that became a hallmark of the classical style. This form contains (1) an **exposition** (consisting of a main theme or theme-group, a transition, a new-key secondary theme or theme-group, and a closing theme or **codetta**); (2) a **development** (usually featuring unstable, sequential repetitions and then a **retransition** leading to the dominant of the home key); and (3) a **recapitulation** (a modified version of the exposition, in which the secondary-theme materials now return in the original key, thus resolving tonal conflict) … .[2]

The Standard Model regards sonata form primarily as a succession of events. An outline of this view is given in Figure 5.1.[3] The leftmost column lists the large-scale tripartite division. The middle column provides detail about each section of the form. The rightmost column offers selected insights from William Caplin's *Classical Form* and the work of James Hepokoski and Warren Darcy.[4]

My own view is that the essence of sonata form is harmonic structure—or, more precisely, harmonic drama. The frequent marked contrast in character between FTA and STA material ought to be understood in terms of rhetorical emphasis, clarifying the more fundamental harmonic structure. Simply that FTA and STA normally express different themes must be regarded as rhetorical; the monothematic sonata is evidence that such contrast is not required.

---

[2]   Stein 2005, 332.

[3]   Rosen 1980 also gives an outline of the Standard Model in Chapter I, "Intro-duction."

[4]   See Hepokoski and Darcy 1997, Caplin 1998, Hepokoski 2001–02, Hepokoski 2002, and Hepokoski and Darcy 2006.

		Caplin/Hepokoski & Darcy
Exposition	First Tonal Area (FTA) • establishes tonic • possibly includes more than one theme, hence it is often referred to as a First Theme Group	FTA themes often feature "tight-knit" organization (Caplin)
	Transition • connects FTA to STA • usually involves an increase in rhythmic activity and an increase in harmonic instability • may be modulating or non-modulating. The modulating transition aims at the dominant of the new key, either V/V or V/III	
	Second Tonal Area (STA) • establishes a new tonic, in a major-mode sonata the STA is in the dominant and in a minor-mode sonata the STA is in the mediant • possibly includes more than one theme, hence it is often referred to as a Second Theme Group • may include a clear closing section, • may include a codetta	STA themes often feature "loose" organization (Caplin) The Essential Expositional Close (EEC) often occurs at the end of the STA, preceding the closing and the coda or codetta (Hepokoski & Darcy)
Development	• Fragments, sequences, reharmonizes motivic material from the exposition. • The retransition aims at V/tonic in order to prepare a return to the original tonic	Development usually closes on a standing on the dominant (Caplin)
Recapitulation	• Restates material from the exposition, in order, and puts non-tonic material into the tonic (in particular, the recapitulation restates material from the STA in the tonic). FTA, recapitulated • possibly includes some modification, especially a shortened presentation	
	Transition, recapitulated • Since all the material from the STA is in tonic, the transition will not prepare a move to a new key. Hence the restated transition at this point is often referred to as a "false transition."	
	STA, recapitulated • Like the FTA, the recapitulated STA may be modified; if the movement is in the minor mode, the STA may occur in the parallel major (=transposed [major] mediant). Coda • The movement often ends with a coda, a rhetorical signal that helps to mark the end of the recapitulation as essentially different from the end of the exposition.	As in the exposition, the Essential Structural Close (ESC) often occurs at the end of the STA, recapitulated, and before both the closing section and the coda. (Hepokoski & Darcy)

Figure 5.1   Outline of the Standard Model of sonata form

The Pedagogy of Sonata Form

Our pedagogy propagates the Standard Model. For better or worse, most theory textbooks, when they treat form, almost without exception teach sonata form according to the Standard Model, occasionally including certain qualifications. It has been my experience that most musicians do, in fact, carry the Standard Model as their conception of sonata form.

Robert W. Ottman, in *Advanced Harmony: Theory and Practice*, claims that "sonata-allegro … is usually considered a variety of an ABA form."[5] He emphasizes the rounded structure of exposition-development-recapitulation and elaborates by saying that the exposition is "based on two themes" and that the recapitulation features "the return of the themes from A."[6] The exceptions to normal sonata-form structure that Ottman points out involve a non-standard key for the second tonal area.

Stefan Kostka and Dorothy Payne's *Tonal Harmony* shows a standard diagram of sonata form (exposition-development-recapitulation). It then presents form diagrams for three pieces: Mozart K. 525/i, Beethoven Op. 2, No. 1/i, and Beethoven Op. 14, No. 2/i.[7] Each example is well-behaved, conforming to the Standard Model.

The Standard Model given in *Music in Theory and Practice*, by Bruce Benward and Gary White, is qualified. Benward and White point out that it is an "outline [that is] … simply a point of departure—few examples actually adhere to this form."[8] They offer the monothematic sonata and the subdominant recapitulation as examples of departures from the outline.

In *Techniques & Materials of Tonal Music*, William Benjamin, Michael Horvit, and Robert Nelson slightly refine the Standard Model.

> The development section develops the material of the exposition, and possibly new material as well … . [T]he recapitulation … normally contains the material of the exposition, although with some modifications. The recapitulation normally remains in the tonic key.[9]

By explicitly discussing "normal" structure, they implicitly recognize the possibility of deviation.

Harmony in Context, by Miguel Roig-Francoli, provides one of the lengthier discussions of sonata form.[10] Additionally, Roig-Francoli cites the article of Hepokoski and Darcy, "The Medial Caesura and its Role in the Eighteenth-Century Sonata Exposition," though its contents do not figure in his discussion.[11] Roig-Francoli mentions the monothematic sonata and, like Benjamin, Horvit, and Nelson, allows that a recapitulation may not remain in the tonic throughout. He analyzes Mozart's K. 309/i and Beethoven's Op. 2, No. 1/i, both reasonably well-behaved, and Beethoven's Op. 53/i, a movement featuring both a second tonal area in the mediant major rather than the dominant, and a substantial coda.

---

[5]   Ottman 2000, 112.

[6]   Ibid., 112.

[7]   Kostka and Payne 2004, 333–4.

[8]   Benward and White 1993, 127.

[9]   Benjamin, Horvit, and Nelson 1998, 267.

[10]   Roig-Francoli 2003, 769–77.

[11]   Hepokoski and Darcy 1997.

As noted above, the Standard Model tends to value placement over quality, viewing sonata form as a series of events. Thus, for example, in the Standard Model's view, the "first theme group" is, above all, the first event(s) to occur in the tonic. None of the cited textbooks discuss deviations in order, such as a reversed recapitulation or a recapitulation that deletes the thematic material from the FTA. Save for the occasional mention of the monothematic sonata and the emphasis Roig-Francoli places on Op. 53/i's coda, the textbooks view departures from the Standard Model harmonically, as in the cases of a STA in the mediant major in a major-mode movement, or a subdominant recapitulation.

When applied too rigidly, when viewed as an inviolable template, or when conceived as a lifeless mold to be filled with content, the Standard Model is misleading at best and simply wrong at worst. However, its widespread acceptance is not unearned. The Standard Model is a compact, efficient, and reasonably successful explanation of what is arguably the most important and most highly developed tonal form. In the subsequent discussion of K. 311/i we will use the Standard Model to play against Mozart's music.

Mozart's Piano Sonata in D Major, K. 311, First Movement

Figure 5.2 displays the form outline of K. 311/i. The leftmost column shows the standard three-part, ABA' form that underlies the Standard Model. The middle column shows FTA, transition, and STA. The rightmost column shows details of phrase structure. Indents, asterisks, and repeated measure numbers show elisions. For example, the indented "*24–8" is aligned with a further indented "*28–32" to show the elision at m. 28.

Exposition

As Figure 5.2 makes clear, the exposition of K. 311/i follows the Standard Model in its tonal plan. The FTA establishes D major and then blends into a nonmodulating transition concluding in m. 16. The STA establishes A major with a parallel interrupted period over mm. 17–24. Closing material leads to a perfect authentic cadence (PAC) in m. 37 before mm. 38–39 tag on two extra measures. Caplin describes this type of exposition in *Classical Form* (1998).

In this pattern, the home key is destabilized in two stages. First, a nonmodulating transition brings a half cadence (HC) in that key, and then the subordinate theme brings an internal HC in the new key. Full confirmation occurs at the end of the subordinate theme. A variant arises if the main theme is periodic, in which an antecedent brings a HC before the PAC ending the theme. In this form, all five of the primary cadential goals occur in the exposition.[12]

---

[12] Caplin 1998, 197. The five cadential goals are (1) HC in the home key, (2) PAC in the home key, (3) HC in the home key, (4) HC or dominant arrival in subordinate key,

Exposition	FTA	1-4: phrase 1, ends on IAC
		*4-7: phrase 2, ends on PAC (main theme)
	Transition, dependent and non-modulating	*7-16: phrase 3, a dependent, nonmodulating transition, ends on HC (V/A)
	STA In A major, the key of the dominant	17-20, ends on HC (interruption) 21-24, mm. 17-24 = PIP (second theme) [EEC] *24-8, closing 1 28-32, closing 2, PAC in 32 *32-6, closing 2 |*36-9|, PAC in 37, two-meas. tag in mm. 38-9
Development		40-57, based on mm. 38-9
Recapitulation	STA (closing), recapped in subdominant	58-62, closing 2 in G, the subdominant *62-6, closing 2 in G
	Transition	*66-78, transition, based on mm. 11-16, ends on V/I
	STA (second theme), recapped	79-82, ends on HC (V/I) 83-6, ends on HC (V/i), mm. 79-86 based on mm. 17-24
	STA (closing), recapped in tonic	87-91, closing 1, in tonic *91-5, closing 2, in tonic *95-9, closing 2, in tonic [ESC]
	FTA, recapped	*99-112, ends on PAC in m. 112; comprises subphrases over mm. 99-102, 102-5, 105-7, 107-10, 111-12; all in tonic.

Figure 5.2   Form of Mozart, Piano Sonata in D Major, K. 311/i

In K. 311/i, the HC at the end of the nonmodulating transition occurs in m. 16. The subordinate theme, mm. 17–24, is, in fact, periodic and its HC (in the key of the dominant) occurs in m. 20. The main theme, mm. 1–7, is periodic in a qualified sense. It does comprise two parallel phrases. However, one must allow for the elision at m. 4 (more on this below). Further, mm. 1–7 do not form the more common parallel interrupted period, but rather what Douglass Green calls a period with repeated harmonic movement, since the first cadence, at m. 4, is an imperfect authentic cadence (IAC) rather than a HC.[13] Thus, K. 311/i does not fulfill all five of the exposition's primary cadential goals.

(5) PAC in subordinate key (196). The presence of all of these cadential goals is not necessary.

[13]   Green 1979, 62.

Caplin shows how sensitivity to quality, "mode of behavior," or, to use his term, "function" can refine our notion of sonata form.[14] He views form in classical music not simply as a succession of events defined thematically and harmonically, but as

> a set of formal processes (e.g., repetition, fragmentation, extension, expansion) and a set of formal types (e.g., sentence, period, small ternary, sonata, rondo). Along the way, a host of concepts associated with harmony, tonality, and cadence are introduced and examined.[15]

The "host of concepts" will suggest that, for example, not only do the FTA and STA occur at certain points within the form, but also that they are characterized by certain behaviors, independent of both key and order.

Following Caplin's approach, it should be possible to study components of a piece and to determine salient aspects of the missing context as well as their proper order. Imagine that we are trying to distinguish the FTA from the STA in a well-behaved recapitulation. Because the key signature would match the tonic of both passages, it would not aid in distinguishing between FTA and STA. In Caplin's view, not only is the first theme group the first event(s) in the tonic, it is also characteristically a stable phrase or period structure:

> The main theme of a sonata exposition is most often constructed as one of the conventional theme-types described in part II of this study—sentence, period, hybrid, or small binary. A significant minority of main themes are nonconventional in their organization ... .[16]

The main theme is typically "tight-knit." It is familiar, regular, and comfortable, in contrast to the characteristically loose organization of thematic material in the STA.

> ... in the classical repertory, subordinate themes are, with rare exceptions, more loosely organized than their preceding main themes.[17]

Caplin contrasts tight-knit and loose organization:

> Tight-knit organization is characterized by harmonic-tonal stability, cadential confirmation, unity of melodic-motive material, efficiency of functional expression, and symmetrical phrase groupings. Loose organization is characterized by harmonic-tonal instability, evasion or omission of cadence,

---

[14] Caplin 1998, 9.

[15] Ibid.

[16] Ibid., 197.

[17] Ibid., 97.

diversity of melodic-motivic material, inefficiency or ambiguity of functional
expression, and asymmetrical phrase groupings ... .[18]

Thus, tight-knit and loose organizations are behavioral qualities. It is in this sense
that one usually ought to be able to distinguish between FTA and STA.

Caplin affirms the idea that the FTA and the STA are contrasting, and points to
the specific means of accomplishing that contrast. Caplin's insight applies even to
a monothematic sonata such as the first movement of Haydn's Sonata No. 36 in
C♯-Minor (Hob. XVI: 36). The theme of the FTA is based on an arpeggiated tonic
triad that yields, in the second measure, to a static G♯, expressed rhythmically as
a motive one might label "dit-dit-dit." The same motivic material occurs in the
STA, in E major, but now the arpeggio is sequenced for four measures after which
a fifth measures ushers in dit-dit-dit on the note B. Dit-dit-dit itself is developed
sequentially and chromatically; a deceptive move in m. 24 evades an authentic
cadence in the new tonic. Thus, loose organization easily distinguishes the STA
from the FTA even though both sections rely on identical motivic material.

The FTAs of Mozart's String Quartets, K. 458/i and 464/i are stable period
structures. In them, the composer establishes a tonic harmony as well as a "tonic"
hypermeter. The STAs of the same movements, while not lacking in regular
hypermeter, are far more discursive, featuring sequential and quasi-developmental
passages more akin to the STA of Haydn's C♯-Minor Sonata than to their own
FTAs.

K. 311/i, however, does not behave as we might expect. One of its aberrant
characteristics is the FTA's tendency toward loose organization. K. 464/i, for
example, begins with a 16-bar theme comprising four four-bar hypermeasures. K.
311/i also begins with a 16-bar group, strongly suggesting powers-of-two phrase
lengths and, thus, some sort of metric regularity. But, as the rightmost column
of Figure 5.2 shows, this is not the case: the phrase and grouping structure is
irregular. Measures 1–4, a four-bar phrase, are elided with mm. 4–7, another four-
bar phrase. Similarly, mm. 4–7 are elided with mm. 7–16, a ten-bar phrase. Thus,
mm. 1–16 do not contain four four-bar phrases. Instead, they contain two four-bar
phrases and a ten-bar phrase. Elisions condense 18 underlying bars into 16.

Compounding the complication and irregularity is the vexing problem of how
to read m. 4. Example 5.1 shows mm. 1–7. For one authoritative interpretation of
this passage, we turn to Alfred Brendel, who, in his 2003 Philips recording, makes
a slight decrescendo into the downbeat of m. 4 to conclude a first phrase. He then
plays the third beat of m. 4 at a louder dynamic, marking it as the beginning of
a second phrase.[19] I find Brendel's interpretation hard to resist. The end of m. 3
clearly cadences into m. 4. Abetting the ii⁷–V⁷ cadential progression is the melodic
structure. Example 5.1 uses arrows to show the down/up contour in m. 3, beat 3
repeating in the more relaxed, slower moving notes that drive into m. 4. Yet, at the

[18]   Ibid., 17
[19]   Brendel 2003.

same time, the close parallelism of m. 1 and m. 4 is difficult to deny: if m. 1 is a beginning, should not m. 4 also be a beginning? Should a performer bring out this parallelism in some way?

Example 5.1 Mozart, Piano Sonata in D Major, K. 311/i, measures 1–7

Christopher Hasty addresses this passage in his book *Meter as Rhythm.*[20] Hasty hears the first four beats as a legitimate measure in the sense that we can distinguish the qualities of beat 1 and beat 3—strong and semi-strong, respectively—and we can hear beats 2 and 4 as weak. Helping us to hear in this way is the emphatic chord on the downbeat of m. 1, which sounds like a clear beginning. But m. 1, beat 3 is also the beginning of a legitimate measure. In fact, the third beat of each of mm. 1, 2, 3, and 4 initiates an event in the right hand, as though Mozart had misnotated the music, shifting the music by a half measure.

There is evidence, however, suggesting a proper notation. The activity of the left hand tends to favor interpreting the music as notated. In particular, the left hand's arrival at the downbeat of m. 2, its subsequent rest through the remainder of the measure, and the onset of eighth-note activity at the downbeat of m. 3 all suggest a proper notation. Hasty himself states, "I believe [reading the downbeat of m. 4 as the beginning of a new phrase] is preferable [to reading a half-measure displacement]."[21]

Hypermetric structure is made ambiguous at best by the potential half-measure shift and by overlaps.[22] If one were to conduct quadruple hypermeter with one beat equal to the notated measure, recalibrating would be required at m. 4 in order to take account of the phrase that begins there. A similar recalibration would be required at m. 7. William Rothstein calls the phenomenon "overlap with metrical reinterpretation."[23] By contrast, overlap without metrical reinterpretation would be the case when five-bar groups (or phrases) were overlapped in four-bar hypermeter. Overlap with metrical reinterpretation invariably involves some sort of a surface

---

[20]   Hasty 1997.

[21]   Ibid., 204–205.

[22]   I will not be observing the distinction made by Lerdahl and Jackendoff 1983 between overlap and elision. See, for example, their discussion on p. 58. For Lerdahl and Jackendoff, *overlap* refers to the situation "in which an event or sequence of events is shared by two adjoining groups" while in the case of *elision* harmonic content, but not the specific melodic content, is shared between two groups.

[23]   See Rothstein 1989, 52–6.

irregularity while overlap without metrical reinterpretation usually involves some sort of underlying irregularity (to the extent that a five-bar phrase can be construed as irregular).

The third phrase, mm. 7–16, settles into regular two-bar hypermeter, in Hasty's terms, "a clear two-bar measure supported by the distinction strong/weak."[24] This phrase is a dependent, nonmodulating transition, whose target is V/I (rather than V/V, as would be the case for a modulating transition). The third phrase also restores $\hat{3}$, which first arrived at the downbeat of m. 4. Specifically, the subphrase of mm. 7–10 brings in F♯3 in m. 10. A voice exchange from m. 10 to m. 11 then lifts F♯ into the melodic line at the downbeat of m. 11. The transitional function of the third phrase is especially clear in mm. 13–16, which contain the standing on the dominant that typifies the ends of transitions.

The STA begins with a parallel interrupted period in mm. 17–24, thereby delivering the regularity that, over mm. 1–7, the FTA failed to do. The harmonic structure of the period, sketched in Example 5.2, is reasonably straightforward, featuring a $\hat{5}$-line and a voice exchange prolonging $\hat{3}$.

Beginning in m. 24, five-bar groups overlap in quadruple hypermeter, a regularity that continues through to the end of the exposition. Such seamlessness is a common feature in the music of Mozart, a composer particularly sensitive to issues of forward flow, as is evident in this exposition. Except for the PAC in m. 37, the exposition's only non-elided phrases are HCs, where the dominant energy continues to push forward.

As both Figures 5.1 and 5.2 show, m. 24 is what Hepokoski and Darcy would call the Essential Expositional Close (EEC), the point at which "the secondary theme ... produces the first satisfactory perfect authentic cadence in the second key."[25] Measure 24 is also the site of an elision and it launches the drive to the end of the exposition. Elisions continue over mm. 24–39, evident in Figure 5.2. They are distinguished by an afterbeat melody that makes possible a clear arrival of a five-bar group on a downbeat and a clear beginning of a new group on beat 2, as is the case in m. 28, for instance. Such afterbeat beginnings are reminiscent of baroque practice. The sixteenth-note rhythm and Alberti bass accompaniment continue to m. 37 where two thick chords make a PAC to announce the end of the exposition.

Measures 36–39

Though the exposition's final four measures, mm. 36–39, form a single hypermetric unit, the cadence in m. 37 precedes the conclusion of the hypermeasure. Measure 35 obviously makes a PAC going into m. 36. However, the continuing sixteenth-note motion drives through to m. 37, a moment of rhythmic closure to match and

---

[24]   Hasty 1997, 204.

[25]   Hepokoski 2002, 134. See also Hepokoski 2001–02, and Hepokoski and Darcy 2006, Chapter 7.

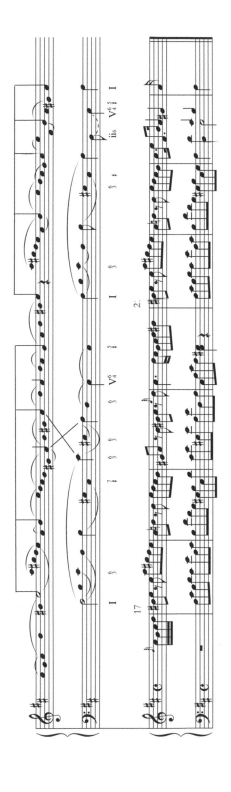

Example 5.2 Mozart, Piano Sonata in D Major, K. 311/i, harmonic structure of second theme, mm. 17–24

confirm m. 36's harmonic closure. And, indeed, m. 37, lying within the four-bar hypermeasure, contains an emphatic PAC that closes the exposition. Following a bar of rest and a change of dynamic from *forte* to *piano*, a two-bar tag, an afterthought, fills out the hypermeasure.

Like themes of the FTA or the STA, tags present a characteristic behavior. In particular, cadential tags tend to be unremarkable. While discussing the structure of a sentence, Caplin introduces the idea of liquidation, by which he means "[the] systematic elimination of characteristic motives."[26] His example is the first eight measures of Beethoven's Op. 2, No. 1/I, and he points out that the last two measures of the passage gradually eliminate the ascending arpeggio and the sixteenth-note triplet, two characteristic motives in mm. 1–2. Caplin then amplifies the idea of liquidation:

> A cadential idea contains not only a conventionalized harmonic progression but also a conventionalized melodic formula, usually of falling contour. The melody is conventional because it lacks motivic features that would specifically associate it with a particular theme.[27]

The figure of mm. 38–39 is such a conventional one. I cite three instances of this ubiquitous anticipation figure in other literature: Beethoven, Op. 31/2/i, m. 3ff.; Haydn, Hob. XVI: 2/i, m. 2; Haydn, XVI: 22/i, m. 12ff. In K. 311/i, mm. 38–39 tend to be trumped by the motivic content of the FTA and the STA.

The same sort of tag closes the exposition of Mozart's String Quartet in G Major, K. 387/i, where it literally is an afterthought, as shown by Mozart's sketches.[28] In K. 387/i, the two-measure tag is a punctuation mark: it returns to usher in the standing on the dominant at the end of the development and it also returns at the end of the recapitulation where it closes the movement.

Example 5.3 shows mm. 38–39. Level a of the example shows the actual music; aligned above are different reductions. Level b rewrites repeated eighth notes as quarter notes to emphasize the result of anticipation; the quarter notes appear "shifted to the left." Level c removes the anticipation, restoring the underlying on-beat quarter-note motion. Finally, level d emphasizes the cadential motion. Measures 38–39 repeat the PAC that has already taken place; in their underlying melodic structure $\hat{2}$ falls to $\hat{1}$, with $\hat{2}$ embellished by a filled-in skip down from D.

In levels c and d, various stepwise motions become apparent. We could attune our ears to hear an overall descent through a diminished fifth, marked with a

---

[26]   Caplin 1998, 11.

[27]   Ibid.

[28]   Irving 1998, 27, comments, "Incidentally, bars 53 and 54 were an afterthought – Mozart's exposition originally ended at bar 53 with the *pianissimo* cadence on D." Finscher 1980, comments similarly, "In the first movement, the exposition originally ended with bar 53—the 'punctuation mark' of bars 54–55 apparently came as an afterthought." Finscher's Facsimile 19, p. 152, reproduces Mozart's sketch of these measures. I am indebted to Paul Crabb for bringing these measures and their sketches to my attention.

Example 5.3 Mozart, Piano Sonata in D Major, K. 311/i, measures 38–39

bracket, as the melody traverses the interval from D down to G♯. We could listen for the descending fourth of level d, also marked with a bracket. Or we could listen for descending thirds, shown slurred in the example.

All of these intervals share a stepwise descent—typical of cadential ideas—that recalls stepwise descents earlier in the STA as well as rhyming stepwise ascents in the FTA. Example 5.4 lists some of these occurrences for comparison, aligning analysis above the music. Example 5.4b examines mm. 34–38. A descending fifth is shown in mm. 35–36 by the upward beaming in the analytical staff; another, larger, descending fifth is bracketed over mm. 36–38. Within the larger descending fifth, a descending third moves in even quarter notes, harmonized in parallel tenths, and recalling the opening of the movement, shown in Example 5.4a. There, an ascending third is shown in the analytical staff and it, too, moves in even quarter notes and is harmonized by parallel tenths. Example 5.4a also shows an ascending fourth in m. 2, highlighted by its separation in register and its absence of accompaniment. Indeed, to my ear, the descending lines that characterize the

STA tend to balance out and, in some sense, resolve the energetic ascents of the FTA.[29]

Development, mm. 40–57

The Standard Model usually presents the development as the part of the form where material from the exposition is fragmented, sequenced, and forged into new contrapuntal combinations. Yet it is no secret that not all developments behave in such a manner.

For example, the development may introduce a so-called "new" theme. Beethoven's *Eroica* Symphony, first movement, introduces such a theme at m. 284, though its connection with the main theme has long been recognized.[30] Mozart's Piano Sonata K. 332/i introduces a new theme at m. 94 to begin the development. David Gagné shows how that new theme emerges from the close of the exposition through linkage technique.[31] Both of these analyses show the derivative nature of the new theme, one consequence of which is a strengthening of the Standard Model.

K. 311/i relies on linkage technique in which, in the words of Oswald Jonas, "a new phrase takes as its initial idea the end of the immediately preceding one and then continues independently."[32] In both the *Eroica* and K. 332, apparently new themes conceal their derivation from earlier material. In K. 311/i, however, there is no question that mm. 40–57 derive from mm. 38–39.[33] What is surprising is that an idiomatic, unremarkable tag trumps the other available motivic material from the exposition to become the motivic source for the entire development. Just as the gradual elimination of characteristic motives is liquidation, "precipitation" can name the prominence given mm. 38–39 by the development. Brendel's recording makes the precipitation vivid. Measure 37 is a compelling conclusion played at the

---

[29]   I am reminded of the suggestive underlying physics of a Schenkerian *Anstieg*: lifting the *Kopfton* through some interval puts energy into the system while the descent of the *Urlinie* dissipates the energy, creating a kind of resolution. In a similar way, the many descending motions in the STA respond to and resolve the ascending motions in the FTA.

[30]   See, for example, Rosen 1971, 393.

[31]   See Jonas 1982, 7–9 for a discussion of linkage technique. For a discussion of how the end of the exposition is linked to the beginning of the development in K. 332/i, see Gagné 1990, 28–30.

[32]   Jonas 1982 , 7.

[33]   Newman 1963, 145, remarks on the relation of the end of the exposition to the beginning of the development: "… there is a lessening of the sense of departure again when not the initial idea [main theme] but a continuation of the closing figure occurs after the inner double-bar, making for a smooth transition rather than a clear break, as in Mozart's [K. 311/i, mm.] 38–55." Mozart's Piano Concerto, K. 537/i, is similarly constructed. The solo piano begins the development at m. 236 without a pause by taking over and continuing the cadential tag of mm. 234–235. I am indebted to Sean Johnston for bringing this example to my attention. See also Hepokoski and Darcy 2006, 564–9.

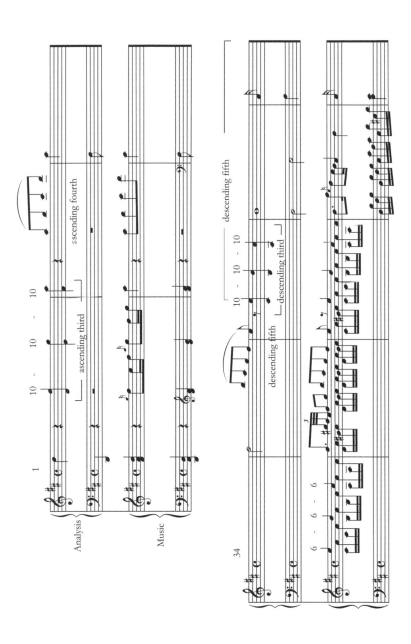

Example 5.4 Mozart, Piano Sonata in D Major, K. 311/i, some motivic rhymes with mm. 38–39

indicated *forte* dynamic. Measure 38 sounds nearly as much like the beginning of the development as it sounds like a tag on the end of exposition, in part because, to begin the development, Brendel scrupulously preserves the same *piano* dynamic that was indicated in m. 38.[34]

The development of K. 311/i is sketched in Example 5.5. Over mm. 40–47, the tag is treated within a circle of fifths sequence. On the musical surface the melody of the tag cycles through different voices. For example, in its guise as a diminished fifth it occurs in the soprano in m. 40 and the alto in m. 41. The bass of m. 43 straightens it into a descending perfect fifth. Measures 44–47 continue the treatment sequentially. On a deeper level, Example 5.5 shows a large-scale descending third, A5–G5–F♯5, spanning mm. 40–47 in the soprano and recalling the descending thirds in Examples 5.3 and 5.4. Reaching over in m. 48 produces the harmonic sixth D6/F♯5 that initiates the next section of the development. Over mm. 48–52, 7–6 syncopes in the right hand recall the stepwise motion in imperfect consonances in Example 5.3b and in Example 5.4.

Measure 52 begins the final portion of the development. As Example 5.5 shows, a bass arpeggiation starting in m. 48 moves from D through B to G, the bass of an augmented sixth chord in B. The music reaches B minor in m. 55. The final two measures of the development, mm. 56–57, move through a perfect fourth. The hands move through the same scale pattern, but in different directions. The right hand ascends by half step, then by two whole steps while the left hand descends by two whole steps, then by half step. Example 5.5 marks a half step as "H" and a whole step as "W" and it beams together the interval of a fourth.

Measure 57 contains vii^{ø7}, an unusual dominant-function chord in a place where one would expect some form of the dominant (V, V^7, or one of their inversions). Also uncharacteristic is the absence of any standing on the dominant. The recapitulation begins after two beats of rest in m. 58.

---

[34]   Brendel 2003.

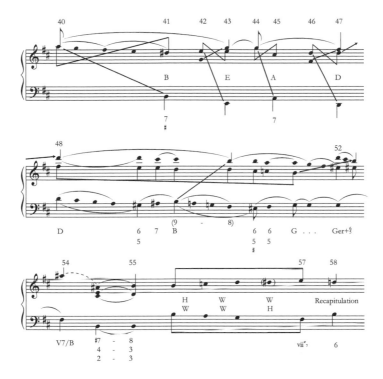

Example 5.5 Mozart, Piano Sonata in D Major, K. 311/i, harmonic sketch of development, mm. 40–58

The Recapitulation

As shown in Figure 5.2, K. 311/i has a subdominant recapitulation: it begins in the subdominant and then moves to tonic to close the movement. Beginning the recapitulation in the subdominant is atypical, of course, but the reader may recall that some of the theory texts reviewed earlier did, in fact, recognize the possibility. The first movement of Schubert's Piano Sonata in B major, Op. 147, features a subdominant recapitulation in which the material of the exposition is transposed literally down a perfect fifth. Thus, just as the exposition moved from tonic up a perfect fifth to the dominant, the recapitulation moves from the subdominant up a perfect fifth to the tonic. Mozart's own Piano Sonata in C Major, K. 545/i also contains a subdominant recapitulation that, while not quite literally transposed, nevertheless remains very close to the structure and proportion of the exposition.[35]

---

[35] Mozart's exposition in K. 545/i contains a nonmodulating transition that necessarily must be rewritten in the recapitulation (Schubert's three-key exposition relies on modulating transitions.). There are also some alterations in the harmony of the recapitulation.

To put it crudely, the transposed subdominant recapitulation can be a laborsaving device.

But K. 311/i also features a reversed recapitulation, as shown on Figure 5.2. To describe it briefly, material from the STA is recapitulated before material from the FTA. One consequence, of course, is that any labor saved as a result of the subdominant recapitulation will be lost to the rewriting required by the reversed recapitulation.

The recapitulation begins in m. 58 with closing 2 in G major. The reader may recall that the development eschewed standing on the dominant. There is no literal dominant but, instead, a $vii^{\varnothing 7}/G$. And there was no standing since $vii^{\varnothing 7}/G$ is on the scene for all of two beats. Thus, one might hear m. 58 butting in too quickly, almost thoughtlessly. One might even count the subdominant, reversed recapitulation itself as evidence of excessive haste.

Understanding aspects of the subdominant recapitulation of K. 545/i may help to clarify our interpretation of the recapitulation in K. 311/i. As summarized by Gordon Sly, analytical work on Mozart's K. 545/i views subdominant material as, one way or another, preparing an upcoming dominant.[36] That dominant would usually have arrived at the end of the development and the following tonic harmony would usually have been coordinated with the thematic return to begin the recapitulation. Sly refers to work by Heinrich Schenker and Edward Laufer, both of whom view the eventual tonic arrival in the recapitulation at m. 59 as deferred and misaligned.

K. 311/i, analogous to K. 545/i, begins its recapitulation with a subdominant that defers and prepares an upcoming dominant. An elided cadence in m. 66 brings in the transition, modulating from G major to D major (specifically, to V/D). We have already remarked upon the hasty approach to m. 58 in which a preparatory standing on the dominant is lacking. Measure 75, however, initiates an entirely satisfactory, four-bar standing on the dominant that prepares the recapitulated second theme beginning at m. 79.

Measure 75 concludes the transition, nonmodulating in the exposition and modulating in the recapitulation. Harmonically, the passage binds the subdominant G to the dominant A. It is devoted to a virtuosic composing-out of a large-scale 5–6 motion that transforms a five-three chord over G, in m. 66, into a six-three chord over G in m. 73.

Example 5.6 sketches the transition. It shows the first system, mm. 66–71, in G. The second system begins by repeating m. 71; it interprets its events in D. Measure 66 is the point of an elided cadence linking the end of closing 2 to the beginning of the transition. A stepwise melody first brings in B4 over G harmony and then D5 over a first inversion D chord, V/G. The D harmony, labeled "D" for dominant on the example, is prolonged over mm. 68–71 first by voice-exchange and by a 5–6 sequence. The G harmony returns in m. 71, shifted an octave higher.

---

[36]   See Sly 2001, Laufer 1981, and Laufer 2001.

In the treble staff a dotted line connects B4 from m. 66 to B5 in m. 71; in the bass staff a dotted line connects G4 to G3.

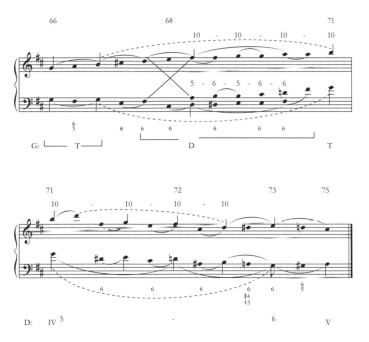

Example 5.6 Mozart, Piano Sonata in D Major, K. 311/i, harmonic sketch of transition, recapitulated, mm. 66–75

Over mm. 71–73 the example shows outer-voice tenths leading from a root-position G harmony to a first-inversion E harmony, the dominant-preparation chord preceding m. 75's satisfactory dominant. The sequence over mm. 71–73 is a varied descending-third type. In m. 72 the D chord, V/G, diverts the sequence from the expected target of C; that is, Mozart composes the underlying root movement G–E–D rather than G–E–C. Launching now from D in m. 72, the sequence proceeds in descending thirds, D–B–G, stemmed in the bass of Example 5.6, with an E-minor six-three substituting for the expected G chord. The E-minor six-three, of course, completes the large-scale 5–6 motion that controls mm. 66–73.

Thus, K. 311/i, like K. 545/i, misaligns thematic and tonal returns (assuming that closing 2 marks the beginning of the recapitulation). The subdominant beginning to the recapitulation, then, is the result of a dilation of harmonic progression without a corresponding alteration in the thematic structure.

Measures 79–86 recapitulate the periodic second theme (in the tonic) with two significant departures. Measures 17–24 formed a parallel interrupted period. However, the second phrase in the recapitulation, mm. 83–86, ends in a HC, making mm. 79–86 an open-ended phrase group.[37] And mm. 79–86 are in D minor, the parallel minor. Measures 87–99 continue in G major, recapitulating closings 1 and 2, as though returning to correct the earlier hasty entrance of closing 2 in the subdominant. Measures 87–99 loyally transpose mm. 24–36 from the exposition.

The cadence in m. 99 is elided, tying together the end of closing 2 with the beginning of the main theme. Measure 99 corresponds to the downbeat of m. 1 and is obviously also related to the downbeat of m. 4. The reader may recall that, where m. 1 sounds almost like a fanfare, kicking off the first phrase, m. 4 very easily can sound like an ending. Though, like m. 4, m. 99 is an ending, to my ear it tends to sound more like a beginning, largely because of $\hat{1}$ in the soprano. At least in retrospect, a listener will recognize the parallelism with m. 1. For the pianist it is difficult to play smoothly and seamlessly from m. 98 into m. 99. The technical challenge of moving from the trill on the last beat of m. 98 to the downbeat of m. 99 can cause a small break that only emphasizes m. 99's initiating function. Whether present by choice or necessity, this small break is audible in Brendel's performance.[38]

Measures 99–104 literally repeat mm. 1–6, with the exception of the eighth notes in the left hand of m. 102. But where the exposition made an elided cadence in m. 7, the recapitulation makes no cadence at all. The first-inversion tonic chord in m. 105 evades a cadence and sets in motion the sixteenth notes that drive to m. 110.

The material that closed the exposition in mm. 36–39 returns to close the entire movement. Measures 109–112, like mm. 36–39, form a four-bar hypermeasure but, unlike the expositional passage, mm. 109–112 feature a deceptive move in m. 110 whose main consequence is to make mm. 111–112 necessary rather than auxiliary, to transform a tag following a cadence into the cadence itself.

The Reversed Recapitulation

I have been speaking of the recapitulation as "reversed"; both Newman and Rosen also refer to it in this way.[39] However, more recent scholars are very careful about such a label. Caplin as well as Hepokoski and Darcy are inclined not to recognize a truly reversed recapitulation. Caplin remarks:

> If the recapitulation deletes the opening of the main theme, these ideas usually
> return later in the movement. This procedure is often referred to as a "reversed"

---

[37] See Green 1979, 54.

[38] Brendel 2003.

[39] See Newman 1963, 146, 158. Rosen 1980, 95 cites K. 311/i as "a recapitulation in reverse order … . [I]n the Piano Sonata in D major, K. 311 … the order of recapitulation is: 'second' theme, first two closing themes, opening theme, short coda, final closing theme. The 'second theme' is clearly a solo, the main theme is in orchestral style, and the coda … is a burst of concerto-like virtuosity." See also p. 274.

recapitulation. Caution must be exercised in speaking in this manner, however, for it suggests that the composer simply shifted around the main and subordinate themes of the recapitulation in an almost mechanical manner. Yet a careful examination of individual cases reveals that main-theme ideas are sometimes incorporated in the actual subordinate-theme area of the recapitulation. At other times, main-theme material does not return in a reversed recapitulation but in a subsequent coda.[40]

When Caplin offers K. 311/i as an example of "main-theme ideas … incorporated in the actual subordinate-theme area of the recapitulation," he does not tell us exactly where this happens. Presumably he is referring to the material over mm. 66–78, a recomposition of the exposition's nonmodulating transition.[41]

It is the distinction Caplin draws between recapitulation and coda that is especially germane. Hepokoski and Darcy help clarify this point by locating the ESC (Essential Structural Close) parallel to the EEC (Essential Expositional Close) in the exposition. The EEC and the ESC are the first satisfactory closes in their respective keys and are inevitably PACs. For Hepokoski and Darcy, material following the EEC is, by definition, material of the coda. As an example, Hepokoski offers the following:

> This is not the place to enter into the discussion of the misunderstanding of the so-called reversed recapitulation or mirror form—a claim (often incorrectly applied, for example, to K. 306/i and K. 311/i, whose codas begin with references to the [main] theme in the tonic) that is historically unjustifiable.[42]

In fact, K. 311/i is parallel to K. 306/i in more than their common key of D major. Though K. 306/i does not feature a subdominant recapitulation, both pieces appear to omit the return of the main theme in the recapitulation, deferring it to the coda. Thus, it will be instructive to compare the recapitulations of the Violin Sonata in D Major, K. 306/i with K. 311/i.

Figure 5.3 outlines the exposition and the recapitulation of K. 306/i. The two columns show that the recapitulation is a faithful transposition of the exposition's STA. In m. 22 the exposition arrives at the EEC, that point at which a compelling PAC is achieved in the second tonal area. Thus, mm. 52–72 affirm a goal already reached; this passage comprises the closing material. Finally, a scalar passage, marked *forte*, brings in a repetition of m. 72's PAC, making mm. 72–74 a codetta. The recapitulation follows an identical trajectory up to m. 159. There, instead of a three-bar codetta, the recapitulation is more expansive, launching into a 14-bar coda

---

[40]   Caplin 1998, 173–4.

[41]   Caplin 1998, 278, n. 36, also gives the example of K. 525/iv in which the recapitulation proper deletes the main theme, deferring it until the coda, explicitly marked as such by Mozart.

[42]   Hepokoski 2002, 138, n. 71. See also Hepokoski and Darcy 2006, 368–9.

based on the main theme. Measures 159–172 do not belong to the recapitulation proper because the harmonic goals have all been achieved by m. 159. The ESC came in m. 139, a goal affirmed and celebrated by mm. 139–159. The melodic/motivic content of mm. 159–172 is subordinate to the harmonic structure of the recapitulation. Hence, Hepokosi and Darcy regard this as a recapitulation of the STA only, plus a coda that is based on the main theme.

As we have already seen, Mozart is highly sensitive to forward flow and to the potentially bad braking effect of a PAC. A common strategy Mozart uses to maintain forward flow is to elide the PAC with the beginning of the next phrase. K. 306/i displays a similar concern: in the passages diagrammed in Figure 5.3, every internal PAC is elided.

Exposition of K. 306/i		Recapitulation of K. 306/i	
STA 26-31	IAC	STA 113-18	IAC
32-9	HC	119-26	HC
40-52	PAC (EEC)	127-39	PAC (ESC)
Closing *52-72	PAC	Closing *139-59 PAC	
Codetta *72-4	PAC	Coda (FTA) *159-72 PAC	

Figure 5.3   Mozart, Violin Sonata in D Major, K. 306/i, form of the recapitulation

Despite their similarities, it is my contention that K. 311/i presents a formal drama fundamentally different from that of K. 306/i. In K. 311/i, the development of the tag measures and the intentional avoidance of a PAC in m. 86 are decisive. In K. 306/i the ESC arrives at the end of the recapitulated STA, in m. 139, where it is elided with the closing. The closing itself is subsequently elided with the coda, based on the FTA. But K. 311/i rejects a PAC at the end of the recapitulated STA that could have served as the ESC. Indeed, the passage stands out all the more because of its minor-mode cast, as though highlighting its lack of closure.

By m. 87 (in K. 311/i), the movement has still not achieved a satisfactory tonic close. In the exposition, mm. 24–39 affirm a goal already reached: these measures follow the EEC. But the corresponding measures of the recapitulation are moving toward the ESC, not away from it. When the ESC finally arrives in m. 99, it is weakened both by the elided cadence and the technical difficulty of connecting m. 98 to m. 99.

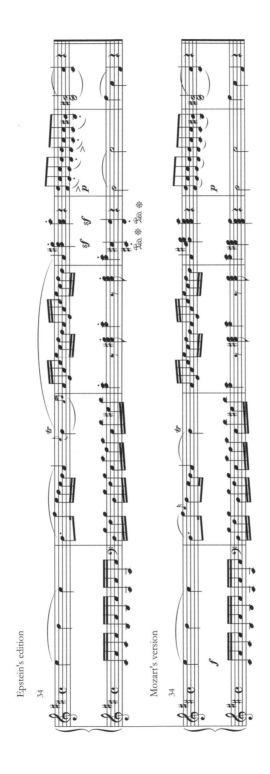

Example 5.7 Mozart, Piano Sonata in D Major, K. 311/i, comparing Epstein's edition with Mozart's version, mm. 34–39

Richard Epstein's 1918 Edition of K. 311/i

To highlight the drama surrounding the tag measures, mm. 38–39, we turn to Richard Epstein's edition of the Mozart piano sonatas.[43] Epstein is apparently firmly committed to the view that the recapitulation should be thoroughly in the tonic. Further, the recapitulation's ordering of material should be identical to the exposition. He is a Standard-Model literalist. One can only speculate about the discomfort Epstein may have felt concerning the subdominant, reversed recapitulation, which remains intact in his edition.

In Epstein's edition, however, m. 37 in the exposition has been "adjusted" to conform to the recapitulation. Example 5.7 compares the two passages. Mozart wrote a PAC in m. 37 and a deceptive cadence in the corresponding spot in the recapitulation, m. 110. Epstein offers the deceptive cadence in both spots. Naturally, most of us cringe at such editorial heavy-handedness. We would be similarly uncomfortable with retouching a painting of Picasso or changing a word in a poem of Yeats.

Epstein's editorial hand helps to highlight what, for me, is the essence of the movement; to wit, the dramatic treatment of mm. 38–39. A physician might refer here to a non-specific symptom: the motivic content of mm. 38–39 can be found in any number of pieces by any number of composers, just as a cough might be symptom of an allergy, a cold, or an exotic viral infection. I can easily imagine that it was precisely this common quality of these measures that inspired Mozart to take up the challenge of transforming the quotidian into the remarkable.[44] Put in terms of sonata-form physics, K. 311/i precipitates the liquidated.

Epstein's adjustment damages Mozart's drama. On the small scale, Epstein's matching deceptive cadences means that the tag in both spots is essential. On the large scale, however, the movement-spanning drama is destroyed. In Epstein's edition, mm. 38–39 and mm. 110–111 are harmonic appendages. In Mozart's version, because mm. 110–111 are necessary, the meaning of mm. 38–39 is transformed. In retrospect, the exposition's tag is all the more remarkable precisely because of its superfluity.

Closing

In harmonic terms, K. 311/i falls short of being unprecedented. For Hepokoski and Darcy, it is one of five sonata types—specifically, a "Type 2" sonata, one which

---

[43] Mozart 1918.

[44] McCreless 1991 addresses "marking." Put very simply, marking, a term borrowed from structural linguistics, refers to the circumstances and causes for some particular item to stand out in some context. McCreless is specifically interested in chromaticism, but motivic structures are also a type of marked structure. Hatten 1994 treats marking extensively.

"[lacks] a full recapitulation."[45] Despite the fact that the recapitulation omits the first theme, it does fulfill its harmonic obligation: as we have seen, the ESC comes in m. 99.

Yet for me there is something unsatisfactory about conceiving the drama of K. 311/i in exclusively or even primarily harmonic terms, despite my earlier claim that harmonic structure—specifically, harmonic drama—is usually best understood as being logically prior to all else. I am not persuaded by m. 99's force of closure. Because of the development's concentration on the tag measures, the rejected PAC at m. 86, and the elided cadence at m. 99, the music continues to push forward, ostensibly aiming at m. 110.

Measure 110, though, does not follow the script: a deceptive move forcefully contradicts a potentially affirming PAC. As a result, mm. 111–112 become necessary and are called upon to close the movement, using a triple retardation to draw out the long-awaited, satisfactory tonic arrival. These features in particular strive to pull mm. 99–112 from the coda back into the orbit of the recapitulation, and to transform the thematic recapitulation of the FTA into a structural event.

Mozart brings his operatic, dramatic sensibility to bear on this instrumental work. The musical events are the cast, and the subject is sonata form itself: themes refer to one another and to sonata practice in general; motives appear, are concealed, become transformed, and converse across the movement.[46] Our understanding of the music is a matter neither of confirming nor rebutting any particular theory of sonata theory. Indeed, these theories provide the point of view that enables us better to appreciate and comprehend Mozart's music.[47] Insight grows out of the concrete music playing against our more general and more abstract knowledge.[48] What is

---

[45]   Hepokoski 2002, 137. In Hepokoski and Darcy 2006, 262, n. 11, K. 311/i is regarded as a "Type 3 sonata [Standard Model] that converts midstream ... into a Type 2."

[46]   Haimo 1995, 7–8, offers as characteristic of Haydn's thought the "normative principle," closely related to the idea of dialogue among musical components within a work and between concrete musical components and more abstract ideas. Haimo comments: "This principle suggests that a normative sequence of events requires no special response, no further answer. By corollary, a significant infringement of norms will require some kind of compensatory response, something that will resolve the instabilities occasioned by the violation of norms. There are two basic kinds of norms: inter-opus and intra-opus. Inter-opus norms are the commonly recognized stylistic norms from the time when the composition was written. Intra-opus norms, by contrast, are determined by the internal details of the composition."

[47]   Gadamer 1975, 238, makes the point explicit in his discussion of prejudice: "a person trying to understand a text is prepared for it to tell him something ... . But this kind of sensitivity involves neither 'neutrality' in the matter of the object nor the extinction of one's self, but the conscious assimilation of one's own fore-meanings and prejudices. The important thing is to be aware of one's own bias, so that the text may present itself in all its newness and thus be able to assert its own truth against one's own fore-meanings."

[48]   See also Bharucha 1994, 216, who develops the ideas of schematic and veridical expectations: "Schematic expectations are the automatic, culturally generic expectations ...

given us, then, is Mozart's own subtly and beautifully composed commentary on sonata form.

Bibliography

Benjamin, William, Michael Horvit, and Robert Nelson. 1998. *Techniques & Materials of Tonal Music.* Belmont, CA: Wadsworth Publishing Company.

Benward, Bruce, and Gary White. 1993. *Music in Theory and Practice*, 5th ed., Vol. 2. Madison, WI: Wm. C. Brown Communications, Inc.

Bharucha, Jamshed J. 1994. "Tonality and Expectation." In Rita Aiello with John A. Sloboda, eds, *Musical Perceptions.* New York: Oxford University Press.

Brendel, Alfred. 2003. *Mozart: Piano Sonatas K310, 311 & 533/494, etc.* Phillips Compact Disc.

Caplin, William. 1998. *Classical Form: A Theory of Formal Functions for the Music of Haydn, Mozart, and Beethoven.* New York: Oxford University Press.

Citron, Marcia J. 2000. *Gender & The Musical Canon.* Urbana and Chicago: University of Illinois Press.

Finscher, Ludwig. 1980. "Aspects of Mozart's Compositional Process in the Quartet Autographs: I. The Early Quartets, II. The Genesis of K. 387." In Christoph Wolff, ed., *The String Quartets of Haydn, Mozart, and Beethoven: Studies of the Autograph Manuscripts*, (Cambridge, MA: Harvard University Press).

Gadamer, Hans-Georg. 1975. *Truth and Method*, translation edited by Barrett Barden and John Cumming. New York: Seabury Press.

Gagné, David. 1990. *Trends in Schenkerian Research* (New York: Schirmer Books, 1990).

Green, Douglass. 1979. *Form in Tonal Music*, 2nd ed. Fort Worth: Holt, Rinehart, and Winston, Inc.

Haimo, Ethan. 1995. *Symphonic Forms: Essays on Compositional Logic.* Oxford: Oxford University Press.

Hasty, Christopher. 1997. *Meter as Rhythm.* New York: Oxford University Press.

Hatten, Robert. 1994. *Musical Meaning in Beethoven.* Bloomington: Indiana University Press.

Hepokoski, James. 2001–02. "Back and Forth from Egmont: Beethoven, Mozart, and the Nonresolving Recapitulation." *19th Century Music* 25/2–3: 127–54.

——. 2002. "Beyond the Sonata Principle." *Journal of the American Musicological Society* 55/1: 91–154.

Veridical expectations are for the actual next event in a familiar piece, even though this next event may be schematically unexpected."

Hepokoski, James, and Warren Darcy. 1997. "The Medial Caesura and its Role in the Eighteenth-Century Sonata Exposition." *Music Theory Spectrum* 19/2: 155–83.

——. 2006. *Elements of Sonata Theory: Norms, Types and Deformations in the Late-Eighteenth-Century Sonata.* New York: Oxford University Press.

Irving, John. 1998. *Mozart: The 'Haydn' Quartets.* Cambridge: Cambridge University Press.

Jonas, Oswald. 1982. *Introduction to the Theory of Heinrich Schenker.* New York: Schirmer Books.

Kostka, Stefan, and Dorothy Payne. 2004. *Tonal Harmony*, 5th ed. Boston: McGraw Hill.

Laufer, Edward. 1981. "Review of Henirich Schenker's Free Composition." *Music Theory Spectrum* 3: 158–84.

——. 2001. "Revised Sketch of Mozart, K. 545/I and Commentary." *Journal of Music Theory* 45/1: 144–6.

Lerdahl, Fred, and Ray Jackendoff. 1983. *A Generative Theory of Tonal Music.* Cambridge, MA: MIT Press.

McCreless, Patrick. 1991. "Syntagmatics and Paradigmatics: Some Implications for the Analysis of Chromaticism in Tonal Music." *Music Theory Spectrum* 13/2: 147–78.

Mozart, Wolfgang Amadeus. 1918. *Wolfgang Amadeus Mozart; Nineteen Sonatas for the Piano*, edited by Richard Epstein. New York: G. Schirmer.

Newman, William S. 1963. *The Sonata in the Classic Era.* Chapel Hill: The University of North Carolina Press.

Ottman, Robert W. 2000. *Advanced Harmony: Theory and Practice*, 5th ed., Vol. 2. Upper Saddle River, NJ: Prentice-Hall.

Pinsky, Robert. 1998. *The Sounds of Poetry: A Brief Guide.* New York: Farrar, Straus and Giroux.

Roig-Francoli, Miguel. 2003. *Harmony in Context.* New York: McGraw-Hill.

Rosen, Charles. 1971. *The Classical Style.* New York: Viking Press.

——. 1980. *Sonata Forms.* New York: W.W. Norton & Company.

Rothstein, William. 1989. *Phrase Rhythm in Tonal Music.* New York: Schirmer Books.

Sly, Gordon. 2001. "Schubert's Innovations in Sonata Form: Compositional Logic and Structural Interpretation." *Journal of Music Theory* 45/1: 119–50.

Stein, Deborah, ed. 2005. *Engaging Music: Essays in Music Analysis.* New York: Oxford University Press.

Yeats, W.B. (William Butler). 1928. *The Tower.* London: Macmillan and Co., Ltd.

Chapter 6

Design and Structure in Schubert's Sonata Forms: An Evolution Toward Integration

Gordon Sly

In a wonderful passage from the Preface to *Roderick Hudson*, Henry James speaks of 'developments' as "the essence of the novelist's process ... the very condition of interest," but also of his abiding "ache of fear ... of being unduly tempted and led on by [these] developments." For, he observes, "really, universally, relations stop nowhere, and the exquisite problem of the artist is eternally but to draw, by a geometry of his own, the circle within which they shall happily *appear* to do so."[1]

James's apprehension reflects very well the dilemma one confronts in writing about an evolving single characteristic in the sonata-form practice of an individual composer. The intricate and—at least in part—arcane web of influences that attaches to this form, to this tacitly appointed subject of composers' broad conversation and commentary within and across eras, means that its relations do indeed seem to stop nowhere. This concern notwithstanding, however, I propose here to encircle only those features of compositional design that interact closely with the harmonic-contrapuntal structure in a small selection of sonata-form movements by Franz Schubert. A circle of modest radius to be sure, but one whose focus I believe illuminates a remarkable evolution in Schubert's work.

In an earlier article I made a series of observations and arguments that will serve as a springboard for the ideas explored here.[2] These proceeded as follows:

1. Schubert follows highly idiosyncratic tonal designs in many of his sonata-form movements. Some of these derive from his fondness for the tonal balance between exposition and recapitulation that he achieves by using the same broad modulation scheme in both sections. This strategy frequently requires that the tonal motion of the later section issue from a key other than the tonic. As well, many works present broad tonal designs whose shapes mimic a motivic idea that appears in the opening measures. This obtains whether or not an attempt to create tonal balance between exposition and recapitulation is evident, and whether or not the recapitulation begins away from the tonic.

---

[1]   James 1917, vi–vii. Emphasis is his.

[2]   Sly 2001.

2. These adventurous tonal plans are evident in the early efforts of a very young teenager, and continue through 1817, becoming especially daring toward the end of this period. Then for an extended time—roughly 1818 through 1823—Schubert all but ceased to write sonatas. The last years of his career, beginning in 1824, witness a renewed involvement with the form. All of this suggests, perhaps, a protracted preoccupation with some compositional problem and its eventual resolution.

3. Although such brave designs are found in sonata-form movements composed on either side of the hiatus, one quality of the music changes from earlier to later works: in the former, idiosyncratic tonal designs frequently stand *in place of* the interrupted voice-leading structure that Schenker held to be definitive of sonata form;[3] in the latter, these designs invariably stand *along with* that interrupted structure.

If I am correct in my view that Schubert felt these symmetries and motivic influences in his tonal plans to be compromising the effectiveness of his sonatas, their formal stability, perhaps, or their dramatic strength—if this was the reason for the hiatus—it would follow that what occupied Schubert during 1818–23 was the working-out of a type of tonal design that would allow for the unfolding of a contrapuntal-harmonic structure that is in some sense captured by Schenker's definition of the form. That definition, as is well known, carries two absolute constraints—two, that is, beyond the self-evident requirements of beginning and ending in the tonic. First, the fundamental line must descend to $\hat{2}$ at the point of interruption, supported, either actually or conceptually, by dominant harmony.[4] And second, the primary tone, either $\hat{3}$ or $\hat{5}$, supported, again either actually or conceptually, by the tonic, must initiate the recapitulation.[5] This is a conception of

---

[3]   Schenker 1979. Schenker's treatment of sonata form begins with the assertion that "only the prolongation of a division (interruption) gives rise to sonata form" (134).

[4]   In some works, the dominant is understood to control the development section even though that harmony is not literally present at the conclusion of that section. Beach 1983, for example, discusses a number of Mozart's sonata-form movements whose developments participate in a long-range descending arpeggiation of the tonic triad, leading from the V that concludes the exposition, through III♯ in the development, and on to I at the outset of the recapitulation. In some cases, a connecting V appears at the end of the development; in others, it does not. Beach argues that the presence or absence of this connecting dominant does not in and of itself determine structural interpretation.

[5]   While this does not bear directly on the present discussion, readers will have noticed that a descent from $\hat{8}$ is excluded. Schenker 1979 is not entirely consistent on this point, but this does seem to represent his view. In his discussion of the division of the fundamental line, he distinguishes the $\hat{8}$-line from those initiated by $\hat{3}$ and $\hat{5}$, noting that the former cannot be interrupted at $\hat{2}$ because the descending seventh would be heard as an ascending second, contravening an essential feature of the fundamental line (33–4, 40). Instead, division of the $\hat{8}$-line occurs at $\hat{5}$, and that division gives rise to the two- and three-part forms illustrated in Figure 27 (Schenker 1979, 40). Figure 27b includes the designations "exposition,"

the form that aligns itself with Beethoven's dramatic practice. A tonal opposition is established and intensified by a drive toward closure that is thwarted at the point of interruption; a recommencement ensues that recasts that tonal relationship and achieves closure. By preventing this interrupted structure from unfolding, many of Schubert's early tonal designs forfeit the dramatic power that attaches to it. Reclaiming that dramatic power, while retaining his idiosyncratic tonal designs, proved an intractable problem. Where the design called for an off-tonic return, a seeming impossibility was required: a recapitulation that begins both away from and in the tonic. Even designs that included a tonic return could be obstinate, since these still frequently involved symmetries that had to be reconciled with a fundamentally asymmetrical voice-leading structure.

In the pages that follow, we will consider five sonata-form movements.[6] Two were composed late in the period prior to the hiatus; two more were composed late in the period following. The final sonata is one of very few that dates from 1818–23, composed just about midway through that span. Taken together, these works light a path that I believe Schubert followed, as they illuminate a relationship between design and structure that evolves from uneasy coexistence to balanced integration.

Symphony No. 4 in C Minor, D. 417, First Movement

The 4th Symphony's opening movement exposition marks the first occurrence in Schubert's sonatas of the two-key scheme i–VI. Even more striking, though, is the design of the recapitulation, which progresses v–III before moving to a closing tonic late in the movement. The recapitulation, then, transposes the tonal motion of the exposition to the upper 5th. Figure 6.1 summarizes the tonal design of the two sections.[7] It is likely that the tonal level of the recapitulation was motivated by Schubert's desire to maintain both the interval between successive keys and the modal quality of the keys involved, and to do so using diatonic degrees: given a

---

"development," "recapitulation," suggesting, of course, that Schenker understood a descent from $\hat{8}$ with its division at $\hat{5}$ as a possible progenitor of sonata form. However, in this section Schenker is careful to maintain a distinction between the general idea of division and the more specific one of interruption, reserving the latter term for the case of division following $\hat{2}$. All subsequent discussion and examples pertaining to sonata form are confined to $\hat{3}$- and $\hat{5}$-lines, and his later discussion of the rondo distinguishes it from sonata form by noting that "the latter involves a forward thrust to [$\hat{2}$ over V]" to which Oster adds "where an interruption in the sense of the structural division occurs" (Schenker 1979, 142). It appears, then, *pace* Figure 27b, that Schenker considered $\hat{3}$- or $\hat{5}$-lines, with their divisions following $\hat{2}$, the only viable bases of sonata form.

[6]   Two of these, the opening movements of the 4th Symphony and the B♭ Trio, are discussed in detail in Sly 2001.

[7]   The exposition proper begins in m. 30, following a 29-measure introduction.

minor-mode exposition that moves from the tonic to the submediant, a dominant-to-mediant return is the only way to achieve this. The A♭ major that controls the second tonal area (STA) of the exposition is prolonged by a sequential passage that moves along a chain of major thirds (that is, A♭ major moves to E♭ major, through C major, and on to A♭ major).[8] At the corresponding point in the recapitulation, Schubert moves abruptly from the key of the STA, E♭ major, up a semitone into E♮ major, in order to regain this same major-3rd chain. Now, of course, only a single stage in the sequence, from E to C major, is needed to provide the movement with its closing tonic (compare mm. 236 ff. to mm. 89 ff.).

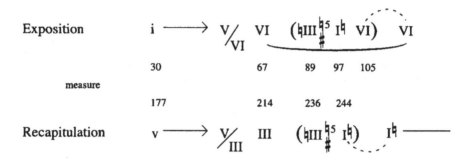

Figure 6.1   Schubert, Symphony No. 4, D. 417, 1st movement, tonal design of exposition and recapitulation

The awkwardness of the tonal adjustment from E♭ to E♮ at m. 236 as well as the compromise to major-mode closure for the movement suggest that the parallel between corresponding passages from exposition to recapitulation was paramount in the work's design. Schubert was perhaps experimenting with the extent to which the sense of formal balance carried by this design might mitigate the absence of a regained tonic at the point of recapitulation. In any case, it is precisely this absent tonic that is our first concern here.

Non-tonic beginnings—whether they occur at the outset of a piece or movement, or within the musical structure—occupy a more central place in Schenker's work than is generally appreciated. This is likely because the form in which the idea ultimately found expression, as the "auxiliary cadence" (*Hilfskadenz*) in *Der freie Satz*, borders on the cryptic.[9] Since Schenker's final written work is the most frequently consulted source for this interpretive idea, the resulting uncertainty about the idea itself, as well as appropriate analytical applications, has doubtless prompted many to steer clear of it altogether. But *Free Composition* is not our sole

---

[8]   Sly 2001 describes a motivic relationship between stages of this sequential motion and the opening melodic idea of the movement's main theme. See pp. 136–37 and example 7.

[9]   See Schenker 1979, 88–90.

source of Schenker's thinking in this area. In an early passage from *Harmony*, for instance, Schenker presents the idea in the form of an analogy. Several versions of a sentence are given, each with different word order. These shift the statement's subject from first position, which it occupies in the "model" version, to later positions in the sentence. Schenker's point is that while the basic meaning remains unchanged (that is, in musical terms, while the tonic still controls the passage), a certain tension is created by the subject (the tonic *Stufe*) being temporarily withheld.[10]

Viewed through the lens of this analogy, the idea itself is plain enough: an auxiliary cadence is an incomplete transference (replication) of a form of the fundamental structure—incomplete because the initial tonic *Stufe* is omitted. The result: a musical passage that begins as though already underway; a passage that, owing to the harmonic ambiguity of its opening stages, is strongly "end-weighted" and charged with dramatic intensity.

It is very much in the application of this interpretive idea that difficulties arise, particularly when such a "non-tonic beginning" occurs *within* a musical structure, as it would here. Example 6.1 shows three different conceptions of the movement's tonal structure. The first two interpret $\hat{3}$ as primary tone; the third reads the movement from $\hat{5}$, which is more strongly supported by the design of the slow introduction than it is by the movement proper. All three invoke the auxiliary cadence idea. The readings given as Examples 6.1a and b both show III as support for the $\hat{3}$ that initiates the second branch of the interrupted *Urlinie*. Both sketches also show that the $\hat{2}$ of the initial descent does not arrive within the exposition or even the development, but only at the point of thematic recapitulation, supported, in the first reading, by the minor dominant that initiates that section and, in the second, by the dominant of the mediant that follows. In both cases, then, the interruption is pushed well into the thematic return. This is due in part to the lack of a dominant to support $\hat{2}$, but also because $\hat{3}$ cannot return at the outset of the recapitulation, since neither G nor B♭ harmonies can support it.

---

[10] See Schenker 1954, 31–7. This passage is cited by Poundie Burstein in his fine explication of the auxiliary cadence. See Burstein 2006, 3. Comparing the presentation of this idea in *Harmony* to that in *Free Composition* reminds us of the stark contrast that can emerge between the intensely musical, "bottom-up" development of Schenker's ideas and their "top-down" presentation in his final written work that at times conceals their origins. His recourse to analogy in the earlier writing evinces both musical sensitivity and pedagogical instincts. To introduce the idea of the auxiliary cadence in my own graduate Schenker class, I use an approach derived from this passage from *Harmony*, asking students to imagine themselves audience members at a stage drama in which the curtain opens to a conversation already underway. They get the idea instantly.

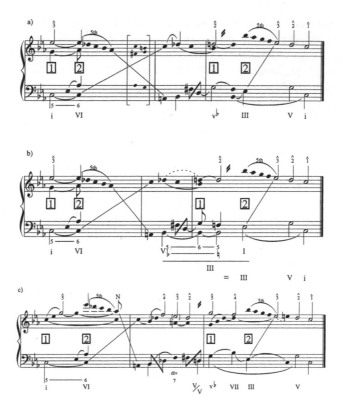

Example 6.1   Schubert, Symphony No. 4, D. 417, 1st movement, middleground
            interpretations: divided structures

The essential difference between these two readings turns on the interpretation of the minor dominant that begins the recapitulation. The first views that dominant as a background harmonic step, while the second understands it to arise as a result of a contrapuntal motion within a governing B♭ harmony. This harmony, prolonged through the development and into the recapitulation, is eventually "corrected" from minor to major to allow its local function as dominant of the mediant that controls the second theme and supports the reestablished primary tone.

The third reading, given as Example 6.1c, differs markedly from the first two. Here, the auxiliary cadence extends back beyond the mediant, all the way to the minor dominant that begins the recapitulation. In this reading, the anomalies involving the unfolding of the fundamental line are not temporal, but harmonic: the arrival of $\hat{2}$, the interruption, and the recommencement on $\hat{5}$ all occur at the usual points in the structure; but $\hat{2}$ and $\hat{5}$ are supported, respectively, by V/V and v♭. Also problematic is the setting of $\hat{3}$ of the initial branch as the seventh of a back-relating dominant of B♭ minor.

As fraught with difficulties as these readings may be, the central problem with the auxiliary-cadence interpretation in each is that its initiating harmony, whether the mediant of the first two or the minor dominant of the third, is not "closed off," in Schenker's words, from what precedes it.[11] That is, a non-tonic beginning must first be heard *as a beginning*, and to be heard as such requires that it connect solely to forthcoming harmonies, and not to what precedes it. Both of the harmonies in question are not merely connected to what comes before—they are prepared emphatically by motions to their respective dominants.[12]

These three, or other conceivable such readings, are musically unconvincing because the conception of the form as a two-part structure articulated by interruption and recommencement is so clearly at odds with a design in which the tonic is recovered only after the essential tonal plan of the movement has played itself out. That is, this tonal structure expresses a single harmonic journey—one that moves away from, and returns to, the tonic. The internal recovery of that harmony upon which the divided structure depends simply does not occur, and cannot be understood to occur in the form of an auxiliary cadence.

Example 6.2 presents three readings that acknowledge this basic quality of the work's design; each presents an uninterrupted fundamental line that spans the whole, supported by a harmonic bass voice, similarly conceived. The example is organized to parallel Example 6.1, its three readings corresponding in important respects to the earlier three. Example 6.2c brings into focus a striking resemblance between the design of the movement proper and that of the 29-measure *Adagio* that introduces the main *Allegro*. Example 6.3 provides an overview. The main internal punctuation in the introduction is the arrival on a Gb-major triad in m. 10, whose articulation and *fortissimo* dynamic parallel those of the tonic in the opening measure. The Gb triad, though emphasized, is the product of a contrapuntal 5–6 motion over a Bb bass. This parallels a similar motion in the opening measures, which produced an Ab triad. Note the misalignment between the metric-melodic design and the harmonic organization. This misalignment corresponds precisely to that which exists in the movement proper between the thematic-formal design and the tonal structure. The broad 5–6 progression in the exposition carries the music from the FTA to the STA. The second of the introduction's 5–6 motions, in which the derivative is emphasized relative to the initiating harmony, corresponds to the development and recapitulation, where the latter is formally emphasized. The organization of the introduction, then, plays a motivic role, whose global realization shapes the movement as a whole.

---

[11]   Schenker 1979, 88.

[12]   For an in-depth discussion of this feature of the auxiliary cadence, see Burstein, 2006, 23–7.

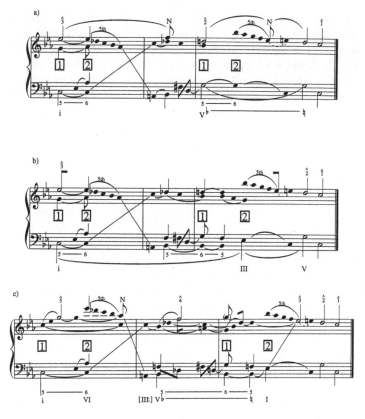

Example 6.2 Schubert, Symphony No. 4, D. 417, 1st movement, middleground
interpretations: undivided structures

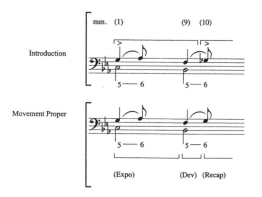

Example 6.3 Schubert, Symphony No. 4, D. 417, 1st movement, "motivic"
designs of introduction and movement proper

In sum, the tonal design of this movement diminishes the dramatic strength usually carried by sonata form. First, the undivided structure depletes the articulative force of the recapitulation, as its failure to regain the tonic denies it the strength of the "double return." Second, the eventual return to the tonic is not only too late, but accomplished unconvincingly. It does not participate centrally in the movement's overarching tonal plan, but rather is grafted on to the end of that plan as an obligatory closing harmony. Schubert addresses both of these problems in the finale of the same symphony.

Symphony No. 4 in C Minor, D. 417, Fourth Movement

In the closing movement, Schubert once again maintains in the recapitulation the broad modulation scheme of the exposition. Here, though, unlike the first movement, the tonal plan is designed so that the tonic can serve as the goal of its motion in the latter section: the three-key exposition scheme i–VI–III is answered at the lower minor 3rd, ♮vi–IV–I. This solves the second problem identified above, but the price of that solution—a recapitulation initiated by the non-diatonic degree of a♮ minor—is steep. Too steep, apparently, for Schubert to tolerate: in an attempt to solve the first problem named above, he alters the passage so that the area controlled by ♮vi can begin in the tonic.

Figure 6.2 illustrates this. The first theme is cast in a rounded binary design. The opening part, comprised of two sentences, modulates to the mediant. The digression sits on the mediant before restoring the tonic in its final measures. The return, labeled "a1," a single sentence, is closed in the tonic. When this passage returns to announce the recapitulation, Schubert adjusts the opening phrase from minor to major, and then transposes the remainder of the rounded form to the lower minor 3rd.

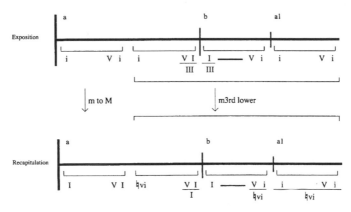

Figure 6.2   Schubert, Symphony No. 4, D. 417, 4th movement, overview of first tonal area design in exposition and recapitulation

The result is really quite ingenious. In the opening section, the second phrase's move to III as a secondary point of tonal emphasis is usual in the minor mode, and foreshadows the larger tonal motion of the exposition as a whole. This mediant, of course, is absorbed by the larger structure, which prolongs the tonic. At the corresponding point in the recapitulation, though, the phrase modulates up a minor 3rd from ♯vi to I, which, in combination with the tonic of the opening phrase, tends to subsume the submediant that began the second phrase within the larger tonic prolongation. And the tonic continues through most of the digression that follows. So, Schubert has taken a four-phrase structure in the tonic, transposed three of its phrases down a minor 3rd, and, paradoxically, produced a structure still apparently controlled by the tonic, moving to the raised submediant minor only at its conclusion. Example 6.4 provides middleground sketches of these passages.

This modification seems to me singularly revealing, and offers powerful evidence that Schubert indeed felt strongly that a tonic return was desirable. Composed during a time of intense experimentation with tonal designs in sonata forms, this passage brings into focus the elusive tonal paradox that I believe Schubert sought: in short, a tonal architecture whose recapitulation begins both in and away from the tonic. Here Schubert unites these two seemingly incompatible recapitulatory strategies with a modest sleight of hand.

But it does not work. The tonal design overpowers the structural return. It is the A minor of the second phrase that sounds like the recapitulation. The C-major phrase is somehow insecure, like a false return. Certainly the modal imbalance plays a part in this. But the real reason runs deeper, I think. A, not C, is the more compelling goal of the movement's tonal motion to this point. Perhaps the major-3rd chain involving A that is so prominent through the development underlies this. Whatever the reason, the motion to the dominant on G in the retransition and thematic return in C feels like a local event, an interpolation within a larger progression. Example 6.5, which may be compared with Example 6.4b, represents how the passage actually works.[13]

---

[13]   This interpretation, in which the expected tonal degree appears at the expected formal point, and is nevertheless denied, is certainly unusual, but hardly unprecedented. Perhaps the most remarkable such reading appears in Schachter 1990. The second movement of Mozart's Piano Concerto, K. 491 is a five-part rondo in E♭ major with episodes in the submediant and the subdominant, respectively. Both episodes lead back to the main theme by way of retransitions organized around what Schachter characterizes as "very strong dominant seventh chords." The theme itself is cast in a three-part design—a1–b–a2, to use Schachter's designations—and is 19 measures in length at its first occurrence. The third and final statement of the theme is altered slightly; the omission of a four-measure repeat shortens it to 15 measures. The second statement, however, is radically truncated. Here the theme is represented by its opening section alone, a1, and is a mere four measures in length. The question Schachter asks is whether the voice-leading structure is best interpreted as comprising two large cadences or just one. That is, does the second statement of the theme represent a return to a tonic harmony of similar structural meaning to those of the first and third statements, or, rather, is it subsumed within the larger harmonic motion from

Example 6.4 Schubert, Symphony No. 4, D. 417, 4th movement, first tonal area
of exposition and recapitulation

episode 1 to episode 2? Schachter favors the latter interpretation. In his view, then, the first
reading represents the tonal design of the movement, whose articulations align with those
of the formal design. The structural reading, however, denies that the abbreviated a1 section
constitutes a true return to tonic harmony. Given the Schenkerian tenet that duration is not
in and of itself a determinant of structural function (Schachter himself (1976) discusses this
idea in the first installment of his important trilogy on rhythm in tonal music); given further
that rondo form provides a natural context for the abbreviation of a thematic statement
without threat to its structural integrity (see Schenker 1976, 142)—given both of these
factors, Schachter's is truly an extraordinary interpretation. In all likelihood it was the
truncation of the theme that prompted him to begin thinking about this alternate reading in
the first place. Nevertheless, it is crucial to note that it is clearly the particular organization
of the movement's tonal design that in the end makes this structural reading persuasive:
"[T]he foreground keys ... fuse into a coherent progression: I (first A section) arpeggiating
through VI (first episode) to IV (second episode), V7 (retransition), and I (third A section)."
It is also noteworthy that Schachter finds his interpretation to be reinforced by a detail
of the movement's motivic design: "The second reading ... receives confirmation from
a most beautiful and refined motivic link: the upbeat that introduces the Ab section is a
reminiscence—disguised but recognizable—of the melodic figure that closes the C minor
episode ... . Thus the second episode begins where the first one had left off, as though the
brief intervening reprise had been a mere digression."

Example 6.4 Concluded

Example 6.5 Schubert, Symphony No. 4, D. 417, 4th movement, interpretation of
          thematic return

If my reading of the Fourth Symphony finale reflects Schubert's dissatisfaction
with the strength of the tonic return, then we ought to find in later works tonal
architectures whose balance of tonal scheme and voice-leading structure is
rethought in order to create an emphasis on the latter.

We now jump ahead a dozen years, well beyond the period of years during which Schubert's production of sonatas had fallen off dramatically, to consider two works composed during what was to be the last year of his life.[14]

Trio in B♭ Major, D. 898, First Movement

In the opening movement of the B♭ Piano Trio, the tonal plan of the exposition proceeds as major-mode works usually do, moving from I to V. The thematic return, however, begins in ♭VI before regaining I. In this work, of course, the off-tonic return is not motivated by a common modulation pattern carried from exposition to recapitulation. Rather, ♭VI is part of a vastly expanded statement of a bass progression that plays a motivic role in the movement. Example 6.6 illustrates this. A foreground reading of the opening section of the first tonal area (FTA) is given as 6.6a. Beneath it, to facilitate comparison with the development, the seven-note harmonic foundation of the main theme is beamed. Example 6.6b summarizes the tonal motion of the development section. Note that the seven-note motive spans the 99 measures from the beginning of the development to the recovery of the tonic harmony at m. 211. The thematic recapitulation, however, appears 24 measures earlier, at m. 187, in ♭VI. Poetically, the thematic return is supported by precisely the same degree in the bass motive as that which supports the melodic apex of the opening theme, which I have interpreted as the movement's primary tone, shown in Example 6.6a.[15]

Schubert has created a context that is analogous in its essential quality to that of the 4th Symphony finale: the movement's design requires an off-tonic recapitulation; its structure demands a tonic return. In the case of the earlier work, I argued that his solution to this dilemma was unsuccessful, that the design overrides the structure. If Schubert felt this way, as I believe he did, we should be able to point to steps he has taken in this later work to ensure that the tonal design does not overshadow the structural organization. Why, in other words, do we hear the tonic at m. 211 as the "real" recapitulation, the *structural* recapitulation? I think that there are two main reasons for this.

First, as he failed to do in the finale of the 4th, Schubert now organizes the development section in such a way that the tonic, not the flat submediant, is the clear goal of that section's tonal motion. Everything points to the dominant harmony of m. 161 as the principal goal of the section. Once gained, this dominant is prolonged for 24 measures, giving way to the D♭ chord that prepares the G♭ return

---

[14] The precise dates of composition of both the B♭ Trio, D. 898 and the String Quintet, D. 956 are unknown; both works are believed to have been written in 1828. See Brown 1980.

[15] The reason for the later alteration in the motivic bass from G to G♭ is that in the theme G♮ roots the minor submediant triad in B♭ major; here $\hat{6}$ carries the return of the main theme, and therefore must support a major triad.

Example 6.6 Schubert, Trio in B♭, D. 898, 1st movement, opening theme and
development

only at the latest possible moment. In this way, Schubert creates the sense of ♭VI
as an interpolation that temporarily disrupts the controlling structural dominant,
in effect signaling the listener at the thematic return that the fundamental point of
articulation is yet to come.

Second, he foreshadows the tonal relationship between thematic and structural
return in the design of the exposition's opening material. Figure 6.3 diagrams the
FTA of the exposition and sets beneath it the corresponding passage of the return.
In the exposition the FTA consists of three brief but distinct sections. The first is
closed in the tonic. The second, beginning at m.12, leads to a D-major harmony in
m. 18. The approach to this harmony, through an augmented-sixth chord, suggests
that it be heard as a dominant, an anticipated harmonic goal following the opening
tonic period. Most of the third section sits on this dominant, assuring us that an
important point of arrival has been reached. We soon learn, however, that while
the rhetoric is appropriate, the logic is not: at m. 24 this D-major chord, V/vi,
gives way to the real dominant that prepares the tonic of m. 26. This deception
fosters a tonal-formal uncertainty associated with the FTA theme that is recalled
at the point of recapitulation. Here, Schubert omits sections two and three from
the FTA, thereby substituting for the major-3rd ascent that those passages would
have effected the deeper-level major 3rd ascent from the ♭VI of the thematic return
at m. 187 to the arrival of I at m. 211. The exposition's opening music and the

ιecapitulation's thematic to tonal return, then, each defined by an eccentric tonal ascent, are mutually clarifying.[16]

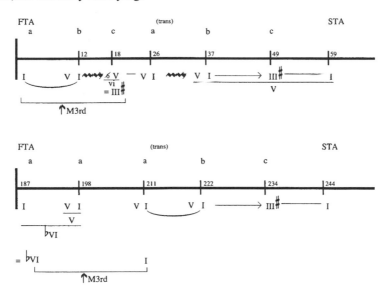

Figure 6.3   Schubert, Trio in B♭, D. 898, 1st movement, overview of exposition and recapitulation opening sections

String Quintet in C Major, D. 956, Third Movement, Presto

We turn now to a work in which Schubert's fondness for symmetrical design features is reconciled with the structural needs of sonata form in a different way. The opening Presto from the third-movement Scherzo of the String Quintet in C Major, D. 956, is based on a tonal design that appears quite restrained. The exposition closes in the dominant; the retransition sits on the dominant; the recapitulation begins in the tonic: none of the more daring features that encumber interpretation as a normative sonata structure occurs. Nonetheless, Schubert's delicate handling of key once again gives rise to sweeping relationships that are very much out of phase with that normative structure.

Although a sonata form of relatively modest proportion, it is one in which Schubert nevertheless indulges his well-known penchant for the three-key exposition. Tonic C major moves through A♭ major, ♭VI, before reaching the

---

[16]   The reader will have recognized the parallel between this major-3rd ascent and the bass voice described earlier. That these motivic ideas are so fundamental in articulating both the opening music and the broadest formal boundaries of the work proposes a breathtaking command of compositional design.

dominant at the conclusion of the exposition. In the recapitulation the music of the exposition's STA reappears in E♭ major, ♭III,[17] thus balancing the third below the tonic with the third above, a strategy Schubert probably borrowed from Beethoven.[18] The development begins in E♭, and progresses through B major on the way to the section-ending dominant. The B major is probably best understood as C♭, or ♭VI/♭III; that is, this progression mimics the first large-scale harmonic motion of the exposition. And, of course, this same progression is replicated as the music is carried on to V. So the initial harmonic motion of the exposition, the major-third descent I–♭VI, gives rise to the broad modulation pattern that shapes the whole of the development section.

A deep-middleground interpretation of the voice-leading is given in Example 6.7. The series of major-third descents emerges as the principal agent of the dominant prolongation from the end of the exposition through the development, effecting an equal division of the G3 to G2 octave.[19]

---

[17]   Readers who know the piece will recall that A♭ and E♭ also control the two occurrences of the second theme in the opening movement of the quintet. There, the order of their occurrence is reversed, E♭ appearing in the exposition and A♭ in the recapitulation.

[18]   Beethoven wrote no sonata movements that follow precisely the tonal plan that Schubert employs here, but there are a number of movements in which the exposition's III is answered by VI in the recapitulation, and vice versa. Beethoven's first experiment with this type of tonal design is the first movement of the Piano Sonata, op. 31 no. 1 in G major. Here the STA of the exposition is in III♯. In the recapitulation the second theme appears in VI♯, but is immediately restated in I. Beethoven returned to this tonal scheme for the opening movement of the "Waldstein" Sonata, op. 53. Again, I moves to III♯ in the exposition. The second theme of the movement is cast as a repeated period, and Beethoven takes advantage of this design to recapitulate this second theme both in VI♯ (in the initial period) and in I (in the repetition). The theme also appears in the tonic in the movement's substantial coda. The design of these two movements, in which III is answered by VI, involves transposition to the lower 5th, which of course maintains the usual relation in major-mode sonatas between the non-tonic material of the exposition and its restatement in the recapitulation. The more unusual major-mode design, which Schubert follows here, in which VI is answered by III—that is, at the upper 5th—was anticipated by Beethoven in only a single instance: the opening movement of the string quartet in B♭, op. 130. In this quartet, as in the Schubert Scherzo, the second theme group is in ♭VI, and returns in ♭III. But Beethoven allows ♭III to dissolve to I within the theme group, in accordance with his general practice. In our Scherzo movement the second theme never does appear in the tonic, exemplifying a practice that Schubert was the first to employ.

[19]   Tonal designs such as this, involving harmonic progression by equal increments— by major thirds in particular—held considerable interest for Schubert. Both opening and closing movements of the 4th Symphony, discussed earlier, feature this type of motion. Another well-known example is the opening movement of the G major String Quartet, D. 887, which is discussed in Beach 1993, and again, from a slightly different perspective, in Beach 1994. Broader and more comprehensive studies that address the phenomenon in 19th-century music generally include Krebs 1980, Chapter II, pp. 109 ff., and Proctor 1978, especially Part Two, Chapters II and IV.

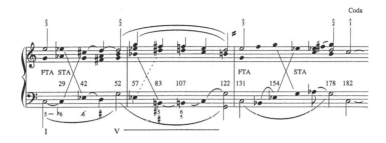

Example 6.7 Schubert, String Quintet in C, D. 956, 3rd movement, Presto, middleground reading

This reading also reflects an intriguing change found in the opening music of the recapitulation, in the approach to the STA's E♭, that, as noted, is counterpart to the exposition's A♭. In the exposition, this ♭VI directly follows the prolonged tonic harmony. There is no transition to it, nor is it preceded by its own dominant. In the recapitulation Schubert could very well have followed this same strategy, and moved directly into an E♭ triad. But he does not: instead, the opening section's tonic is diverted toward ♭III, and, by the time the second theme arrives, E♭ has been well established as local tonic.

A plausible explanation for this alteration might look to the design of the movement's opening, in which the first theme is stated not once but twice: perhaps this restatement over an extended tonic harmony, while appropriate at the outset, would have been tedious at this later point in the piece. But this account begs a larger question. The *unprepared* entrance of ♭VI in the exposition is striking—*the* salient feature of the entire section. Had Schubert wanted to preserve this effect in the recapitulation and at the same time to relieve a drawn-out tonic, he could have done so in any number of ways. He might, for example, have carried the repetition of the opening theme toward the dominant, so as to replicate intervallically the exposition's sudden major-3rd descent to A♭. The recomposed motion into E♭ relinquishes this effect, undermining that marked aspect of the theme's correspondence to its earlier presentation.

This change illuminates a correspondence to another prominent occurrence of ♭III—that at the outset of the development section—and leads one to consider whether these two occurrences of this harmony may be related in some essential way. Assessing the piece from this vantage point quickly brings their parallel contexts into focus.

The reading given in Example 6.8a reflects the analogous roles of the two instances of ♭III within the two large tonal motions, and to that end reinterprets both the flat mediant that initiates the development and the dominant that precedes it, reading the E♭ as the deep-level harmonic successor to the opening tonic. The ascending arpeggiation of the (minor) tonic triad is completed, as ♭III moves on to the dominant at the end of the development. The interpretation of the recapitulation's ♭III recognizes the greater sense of key that attaches to it than to the tonal level of its thematic counterpart in the exposition, which enables it to counterpoise the development's ♭III within the coordinate arpeggiations.

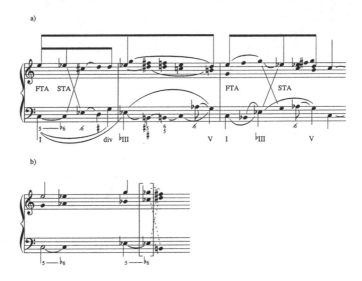

Example 6.8 Schubert, String Quintet in C, D. 956, 3rd movement, Presto, motivic design

   This reading brings into focus the remarkable parallels between the contrapuntal framework that organizes the exposition-development and that of the recapitulation—right down to the augmented-6th chords that precede each dominant. As well, embedded within the upper voice $\hat{3}$–♭$\hat{3}$–$\hat{2}$ descent that spans the exposition-development is a more local statement of that chromatic line confined to the exposition alone. The similar harmonic motion that initiates both exposition and development sections, noted above, is illustrated in Example 6.8b, where the chromatic 5–6 progressions give rise to parallel major-3rd descents. The interpretation of the development's flat mediant as a harmonic point of departure, an initiator of tonal motion, rather than a harmonic point of division internal to the dominant prolongation that a structural reading would embrace, brings emphasis to this kinship.
   These parallels in the global contrapuntal shape of the movement are reflected by another aspect of the musical design—the movement's metric organization.[20] One of the most striking aspects of Schubert's substantial restructuring of the approach to the recapitulation's ♭III, noted above, is that these modifications are

---

[20]   Another study that considers the interdependence of pitch and metric/rhythmic design in Schubert's music is McCreless 1977, which explores aspects of design in the *Moments musicaux*, op. 94 no. 2.

contained within precisely the same musical time as is allotted the opening tonal area in the exposition. By adhering to the larger *metric* context established in the earlier section, the *harmonic* reworking in the recapitulation is made all the more evident. This particular metric correspondence turns out to be only a small part of a rigorously organized overarching design, to which we now turn.

The foreground reading of the movement given in Example 6.9 incorporates an interpretation of the music's metric architecture. Barlines are used to indicate four-measure groupings. That is, each measure in the sketch represents four actual measures of music.[21] Note that throughout the movement, up to the onset of the coda at m. 187, the pattern of four-bar groupings—the four-bar hypermeter[22]—is inviolate, with a single exception. This occurs with the two-measure grouping of mm. 81–82, which belongs to neither the preceding nor the following four-bar unit. Instead, these bars begin a hypermeasure, but are interrupted halfway through by a new hypermetric downbeat, and thus constitute a kind of metric "hiccup" that sets off the descending leap into the B-major passage that initiates the following hypermeasure.

The four-bar groupings are themselves grouped into larger patterns, which are indicated by numbers in larger font. To make these patterns easier to see, the numbers alone have been extracted and set into the schematic given as Figure 6.4. (Note that the sections have been rearranged so that the exposition and recapitulation can be directly juxtaposed.) Schubert's restructuring of the opening music of the recapitulation—the arrival of ♭III *within* the initial four-plus-three grouping rather that at the outset of the second such grouping—is apparent at a glance. Note also the layout of the development. The "hiccup" separates precisely sections of six hypermetric bars each, deployed as a palindrome, into groupings of two plus four and four plus two; a quick examination of the music reveals that the groupings of four are also thematically allied, as are the groupings of two.[23] The retransition occupies, once again, exactly six four-bar units. Each of the three six-unit areas that comprise the development section, then, is demarcated by its own controlling harmony.

---

[21]   This notation derives from those developed in Rothstein 1981 and Schachter 1980.

[22]   The term hypermeter refers to the extension of the metric characteristics of a single measure to a group of measures. In the four-bar hypermeter of this movement, then, units of four measures can be heard as if they comprised a single measure. That is, the measures of a four-bar grouping assume the attributes of the individual beats that comprise a measure in 4/4 time, with alternating strong and weak beats. The measures indicated in Example 6.9, then, each containing four actual bars of music, are called "hypermeasures." This term was coined in Cone 1968, 79. Rothstein 1981 and 1989 present extensive work with hypermeter in particular, and with rhythmic/metric organization in tonal music in general.

[23]   Newbould 1992 details a fascinating example of a musical palindrome in Schubert's melodrama *Die Zauberharfe*.

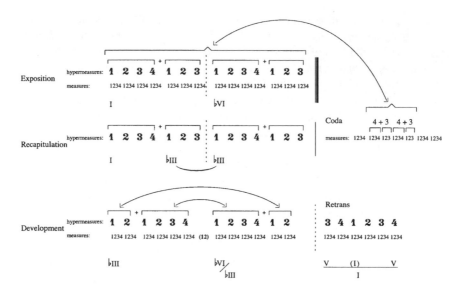

Figure 6.4   Schubert, String Quintet in C, D. 956, 3rd movement, Presto, metric design

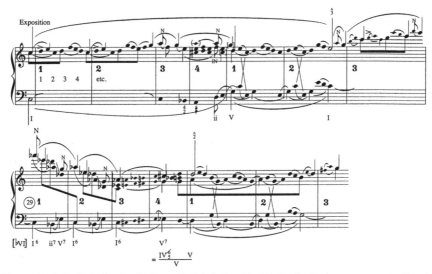

Example 6.9 Schubert, String Quintet in C, D. 956, 3rd movement, Presto foreground and metric interpretation

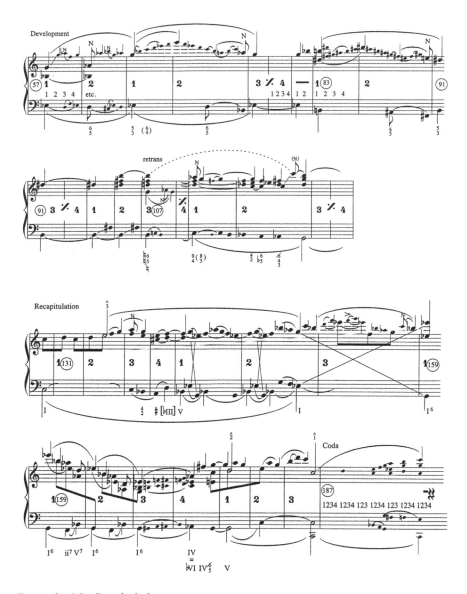

Example 6.9 Concluded

In contrast with the strict metric regularity of the rest of the movement, the clarity of metric organization in the coda seems to break down. What actually takes place is a re-orientation in the *level* of metric grouping, which causes the established metric pattern to fail. Following the first hypermeasure in the coda, these four-bar groupings are abandoned in order to allow the metric design to mimic, at the level of the individual measure, the hypermetric pattern of the exposition and recapitulation. Once the listener recognizes that the large "four-plus-three : four plus-three" designs of those earlier sections are being constructed here with individual measures, the logic of the coda's metric organization becomes clear. Immediately following the completion of the second four-plus-three pattern, the music returns to the four-bar hypermeter for two concluding hypermeasures. This explains why Schubert includes a full bar rest as the movement's penultimate measure, a detail that should be noted in performance, since it makes clear that the final chord we hear occurs as the second measure—the weak "beat"—of the final hypermeasure.

The essential strategy evident in the metric scheme, then, is an alternation of duple and triple hypermetric groupings. In the exposition, recapitulation, and coda this strategy is expressed in the four-plus-three groupings. The development, as described, is organized into three broad hypermetric units. The two four-plus-three groupings of the exposition, then, followed by the development's division, extend this duple-triple alternation to a deeper level of the design, forming a large such pattern that embeds the exposition's occurrences of the basic metric alternation within it. As a result, a precise analog is drawn between the large-scale contrapuntal and metric architectures. Figure 6.5 illustrates this.

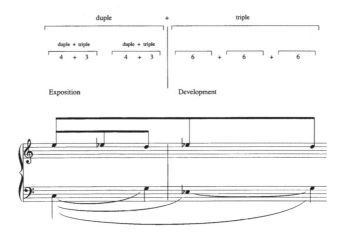

Figure 6.5   Schubert, String Quintet in C, D. 956, 3rd movement, Presto, comparison of contrapuntal and metric designs

In this work we observe a tonal design and a tonal structure that, once again, follow distinct courses. These are directly at odds at prominent points of formal articulation—in their interpretations of the dominant that concludes the exposition and of the mediant that initiates the development. But once again, as it did in the Trio, the tonal design accommodates the structural division and recommencement basic to sonata form.

Quartett-Satz in C Minor, D. 703

The final work to be considered is the string quartet movement in c minor, D. 703 (*Quartett-Satz*), which dates from December, 1820. This work represents the sole instrumental sonata form Schubert composed during 1820–21. So unusual is the design of the recapitulation that the work's very status as a sonata form has been questioned.[24] This uncertainty is due to the fact that the return begins both off-tonic *and* away from the opening theme, which begs the question as to how it is recognizable as the recapitulation at all.

The broad organization of the movement is illustrated in Figure 6.6. It begins with an animated figure that describes a descending tetrachord from tonic to dominant. This figure is treated canonically by the four voices, and thereby expanded into a complete antecedent phrase (labeled "1" in the figure). Its consequent modulates to the submediant, which prepares a lovely, typically Schubertian, melody (labeled "2"). The juxtaposition of these two passages creates the effect of an explosive introduction leading to the exposition proper. When the return is carried by the *cantabile* second theme, the listener simply assumes that the "introduction" will not be recapitulated in its original position—not at all uncommon, of course. As Figure 6.6 also shows, Schubert has postponed, not omitted, the restatement of the opening material, which returns to close the movement, functioning as a brief coda.

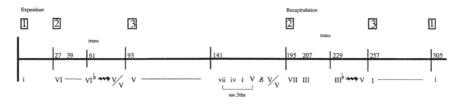

Figure 6.6   Schubert, *Quartett-Satz* in c minor, D. 703, overview of design

But the thematic reordering is not the only unusual feature: the recapitulation at m. 195 is in B♭ major. This appears to be related to the falling tetrachord that opens the movement, from which springs much of the motivic life of the piece. In addition to numerous more local statements, both transposed and at pitch, enlarged versions of the tetrachord, absent its second member, shape the essential bass motions of the exposition, and, once again, from the dominant that concludes the exposition across to the end of the development section. The B♭ of the return forms

---

24   Webster follows a comment regarding what he refers to as the movement's *exposition* with the qualification "even though the movement as a whole is not in sonata form" (1978: 26). Unfortunately, he does not elucidate this self-contradictory characterization. In any case, his comment does point up an essential feature of the piece: through the exposition and development of this sonata form, things proceed fairly routinely.

part of the broadest such statement, which extends from the opening tonic to the dominant of m. 255.

David Beach has given an account of the unusual organization of this piece.[25] His argument relates the B♭ of the restatement to the opening tetrachord, and demonstrates how a key area arises as part of the unfolding of a linear progression. He does not provide a comprehensive interpretation of the work's voice-leading structure, and it is beyond the scope of his concern to address how this linear progression relates to the tonal structure of this sonata form. This, of course, is the question that concerns us here, and it is to it that we now turn.

Example 6.10 gives a middleground reading. The music moves to $\hat{2}$ at the usual point and it is supported across the development by a motion to the D-major harmony that concludes that section. I have interpreted this as a back-relating dominant that prolongs the exposition-ending home dominant. The B♭ of the return, of course, cannot support the recovery of $\hat{3}$. But this problem points to an intriguing modification that Schubert has made to the theme that initiates the return. In the exposition, the second theme appeared as a closed period in A♭. The antecedent reached a half cadence on the dominant; the consequent both reestablished and closed in the (local) tonic. With the return of this music at mm. 195 ff., the antecedent moves, as expected, to the dominant of B♭, but the consequent is altered so that it both begins and ends a fourth higher, in E♭. This allows the B♭ of m. 195 to be heard not as a local tonic, but as the dominant of E♭, in effect, a lead-in to that harmony. Beach does not hear the passage this way. He feels that the E♭ is subsumed within the B♭ harmony, functioning as its subdominant, and in support of this interpretation points to the internal emphasis on the subdominant within the theme itself.

On the face of it, this seems a reasonable view. Yet to assert that E♭ arises within the context of the controlling B♭ scale step is simply to explain away a substantial alteration to the theme, to assert, tacitly, that the change in the theme's design is essentially gratuitous. Why would Schubert not simply have allowed the theme to remain in B♭, just as the earlier version remained in A♭? Surely the recomposing of the tonal level serves some purpose.

I suggest that this modification reflects an intermediate stage in Schubert's search for a satisfactory balance between the conflicting impulses that underlie his tonal architectures. It is, in fact, the crux of that search in this work. The B♭ is there as part of the motivic design. The E♭ is there to provide structural stability, to initiate the second stage of a two-part dramatic-tonal conception. No, it is not the tonic. But there are compelling reasons to believe that Schubert may have felt it to be a convincing surrogate for the tonic at this point in the piece. First, B♭ cannot prepare C as a structural harmonic goal with the same power as it can E♭. If B♭ is indeed required at this point in the return as part of the broad motivic design, then E♭ presents itself as the only possible stable tonal goal within that context. Second, E♭ solves the modal problem that attaches to the restatement of the second theme in

---

[25]   Beach 1994.

minor mode sonatas generally. Many major-mode themes translate to minor very poorly, and the A♭-major theme from this exposition would do so with particular discomfort.[26] Finally, recapitulating the exposition's submediant material in the mediant balances the 3rd below the tonic with the 3rd above, a procedure that Schubert used elsewhere, including the Quintet Scherzo discussed above.

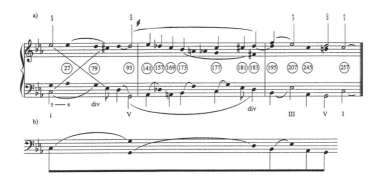

Example 6.10   Schubert, *Quartett-Satz* in c minor, D. 703, middleground reading and motivic tetrachord in bass voice

We do not know whether or not Schubert considered the movement a success; that he had apparently intended a full quartet, but abandoned it—41 measures of a second movement, an Andante in A♭, are extant—is perhaps telling. But it is revealing to try to locate, in terms of the perspective described here, this work in relation to the other four. Along a continuum whose extremes might be characterized, at one end, as an awkward pairing of design and structure and, at the other, as a synthesis, the opening movement of the 4th Symphony would be placed

---

[26]   Difficulties associated with recapitulating major-mode (III) material in minor-mode sonata forms can be seen in the various approaches used. Bringing back the STA material in the tonic major (I) is common, of course, but other solutions abound. In K. 310, Mozart simply recapitulates the C major STA material in tonic a minor (compare mm. 23 ff. with mm. 104 ff.; note the use of the Neapolitan in the recapitulation in place of the exposition's supertonic, avoiding the diminished triad). In K. 457, however, the E♭ (III) melody that begins in m. 23 is omitted from the recapitulation, having been replaced by a subsequent STA theme that sounds in tonic c minor. The reason seems clear: the melody of mm. 23 ff. does not work in minor, while that of mm. 36 ff. (recapitulated at m. 131) does. Another solution is to recapitulate the STA melody first in the tonic major, and reserve the tonic-minor version for later in the section. Mendelssohn opts for this approach in the opening movement of the Violin Concerto. Still another strategy is to recapitulate the major-mode STA material in a non-tonic major key, and then "correct" things to the tonic minor. See, for example, Beethoven's 5th Piano Sonata, op. 10/1 (1st movement), where the E♭ (III) STA is recapitulated first in the major subdominant at mm. 215 ff., then quickly corrected (with the right hand playing in octves) to the tonic minor at mm. 233 ff.

closest to the former extreme. Here Schubert sets in motion a symmetrical tonal architecture within which a divided structure cannot unfold. A little further along we would set the finale of the same piece. This movement's recapitulation, by means of a clever alteration to the music of the opening theme, begins in the tonic. But it is only an apparent tonic. All signs point to the subsequent submediant as the stronger return. Nearing the other extreme would sit the B♭ Trio. The organization of this movement takes a lesson from the 4th Symphony finale. As in that earlier movement, the design calls for a recapitulation in the key of the altered submediant, while the structure requires a tonic return: but the latter must be *heard* to articulate a two-part dramatic structure. To achieve this, Schubert reverses the placement and roles of the two harmonies. Perhaps even further along should be placed the String Quintet Presto, in which a symmetrical design merges effortlessly with the interrupted structure.

Reflecting its chronological place, the *Quartett-Satz* would be set roughly at the mid-point of this evolutionary continuum. Interpretation of this work as an interrupted structure is possible, provided we accept the mediant as a convincing substitute for the tonic at the outset of the second part. Importantly, Schubert takes steps, both thematic and tonal, to mark the arrival of this harmony within the broad organization of the movement. This we may understand as an attempt to remedy the 4th Symphony finale's structural shortcoming—the insertion of a tonic of too-local significance at the point of recapitulation. The effect that he fosters at the outset of the work, that of an introduction leading to the movement proper, can be understood to be calculated for the role it will play later in the piece, where B♭, the key of the design's recapitulation, must place emphasis on E♭, the key of the structural return.

***

The works explored here suggest that tonal architecture in sonata form remained a preoccupation with Schubert throughout his career. Comparisons among the earlier two movements, composed in 1816, the middle one, from the end of 1820, and the later two, from 1828, reveal a marked evolution in the relationship between Schubert's concern for strength and location of the recovered tonic harmony and his interest in large-scale motivic and tonal design—what might be thought of as two tonal sub-plots.[27] This evolution represents, I believe, a quest that occupied Schubert until the very end of his all-too-brief but remarkable career—a quest that sought to reconcile these sub-plots, to bring into synthesis the established structural norms that had come to define the form, and a sensitivity to large-scale modal, intervallic, and motivic symmetry that just as surely had come to define the composer.

---

[27]   The idea of thinking about an overarching tonal organization in terms of a dramatic plot comes from McCreless 1983, 69.

Bibliography

Beach, David. 1983. "A Recurring Pattern in Mozart's Music." *Journal of Music Theory* 27/1: 1–29.

———. 1993. "Schubert's Experiments with Sonata Form: Formal-Tonal Design versus Underlying Structure." *Music Theory Spectrum* 15/1: 1–18.

———. 1994. "Harmony and Linear Progression in Schubert's Music." *Journal of Music Theory* 38/1: 1–20.

Brown, Maurice J.E. 1980. s.v. "Schubert, Franz (Peter)." *New Grove Dictionary of Music and Musicians*, ed. Stanley Sadie (Basingstoke: Macmillan).

Burstein, L. Poundie. 2006. "Schenker's Concept of the Auxiliary Cadence." *Essays from the Third International Schenker Symposium*, ed. Alan Cadwallader (Hildesheim, Zürich, New York: Georg OlmsVerlag), 1–36. The symposium (12–14 March, 1999, at Mannes College of Music) featured four papers on the auxiliary cadence, three of which appear in this volume. The others are Roger Kamien's "Quasi-Auxiliary Cadences Beginning on a Root-Position Tonic Chord: Some Preliminary Observations" (pp. 37–50), and Lauri Suurpää's "Non-Tonic Openings in Three Beethoven Introductions" (pp. 51–66).

Cone, Edward. 1968. *Musical Form and Musical Performance* (New York: Norton).

James, Henry. 1917. *Roderick Hudson*. Rev. ed. (Boston and New York: Houghton Mifflin).

Krebs, Harald. 1980. "Third Relation and Dominant in Late 18th- and Early 19th-Century Music." PhD Dissertation, Yale University.

McCreless, Patrick. 1977. "Schubert's Moment Musical No. 2: The Interaction of Rhythmic and Tonal Structures." *In Theory Only* 3/4: 3–11.

———. 1983. "Ernst Kurth and the Analysis of the Chromatic Music of the Late Nineteenth Century." *Music Theory Spectrum* 5: 56–75.

Newbould, Brian. 1992. "A Schubert Palindrome." *19th-Century Music* 15/3: 207–214.

Proctor, Gregory. 1978. "Technical Bases of 19th-Century Chromatic Tonality: A Study in Chromaticism." PhD Dissertation, Princeton University.

Rothstein, William. 1981. "Rhythm and the Theory of Structural Levels." PhD dissertation, Yale University.

———. 1989. *Phrase Rhythm in Tonal Music* (New York: Schirmer).

Schachter, Carl. 1976. "Rhythm and Linear Analysis: A Preliminary Study." *The Music Forum*, Vol. IV (New York: Columbia University Press), 281–334.

———. 1980. "Rhythm and Linear Analysis: Durational Reduction." *The Music Forum*, Vol. V (New York: Columbia University Press), 197–232.

———. 1990. "Either/Or." *Schenker Studies*. ed. Hedi Siegel (Cambridge: Cambridge University Press), 165–79.

Schenker, Heinrich. 1954. *Harmony*. ed. Oswald Jonas, trans. Elisabeth Mann Borgese (Chicago: University of Chicago Press).

———. 1979. *Free Composition*. trans. and ed. Ernst Oster (New York: Longman).

Chapter 7

On Chopin's *Fourth Ballade*

Edward Laufer

This study proposes to consider some aspects of the *Fourth Ballade* (Op. 52, 1842), in particular its form and motivic associations, with some references to the *First* and *Third Ballades*.[1] The formal designs of the *Ballades* are perhaps controversial inasmuch as different commentators read them differently, and music that is controversial and problematical is often particularly intriguing just on that account. For example, Schenker's reading of the g-minor *Ballade*, in *Der freie Satz* (Fig. 153; given here as Example 7.1), shows a ternary form. But in hybrid fashion, the *Ballade* also resembles a sonata movement.

Each *Ballade* follows its own original formal design: none is an actual classical sonata form, as Chopin's title "Ballade" indicates, but in specific ways the *Ballades are* related to the traditional view of sonata form, with Chopin's characteristic modifications.[2] In coming to terms with these, some commentators—Alfred Cortot, for instance, citing Schumann quoting Chopin himself—have suggested that the *Ballades* were inspired by certain specific narrative poems by Mickiewicz.[3] Whatever the poetic inspiration of the *Ballades*, it is probably better to regard their formal and tonal designs and motivic aspects *not* as being programmatic representations of any particular literary work, but as expressing a narrative, poetic character in the most general sense—like the "Im Legendenton" in Schumann's *Fantasy*, or Schumann's *Novelettes*. And in this very general sense, narrative character, like changing events in a story, might suggest many rapid *changes* of musical character, and these we do find in the *Ballades*, and in fact these changes and contrasts are a feature.

---

[1]   The present study is an abbreviated adaptation of a paper presented at the *Fourth International Schenker Symposium* at the Mannes School of Music, New York, March 17, 2006.

[2]   By "traditional view" of sonata form I am referring both to a description (not definition) such as in Tovey 1959, 214 ff., and also, less traditionally, to Schenker's concept of *interruption* as a quintessential, distinguishing feature of sonata form.

[3]   For the *Fourth Ballade* Alfred Cortot writes: "The Three Budrys – or the Three Brothers – are sent away by their father to far distant lands, in search of priceless treasures. Autumn passes, then winter. The father thinks that his sons have perished at war… Amidst whirling snow-storms each one, however, manages to return; but one and all bring back but a single trophy from their odyssey – a bride." (Cortot n.d.)

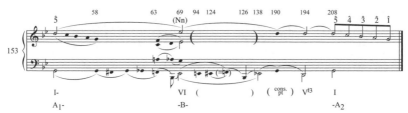

Example 7.1 Chopin, g-minor *Ballade*, Op. 23: reading by Schenker from *Der freie Satz*

Schenker's quick sketch of the g-minor *Ballade* (Example 7.1) was meant to illustrate his discussion of form rather than to provide a "finished" reading of the *Ballade*; he would very likely have revised this hasty reading had he lived. His primary tone of d^2 ($\hat{5}$) is surely inexact: there is no marked d^2, neither at the outset nor, certainly, at m. 194. The descent at the coda, mm. 208 ff., is not supported harmonically; the very striking A-major section (mm. 107 ff.) is altogether absent. For reasons of space the present study cannot discuss the fascinating and complex foreground and middleground features of this work, but can only offer an overview (background) sketch, in order to consider the question of the relation to sonata form. Example 7.2 proposes either a ternary design, or a modified four-part, or modified sonata form. In the latter two, the B section is on VI (E♭), and the returning A_2 not on the expected I but on V—unusual, if plausible. But a ternary reading, rather willfully, would have to regard the section—and it is a section—between the B_1 and B_2 as merely an enormous parenthetical interpolation; so one might rather regard the section as an extension or expansion of the B_1 (thus a modified four-part form: $A_1 B_1 - A_2 B_2$ with the order of the latter A and B reversed) or, even better, as a developing episode (thus a modified sonata form: first and second subjects, extension, recapitulation, with order reversed in the recapitulation).

In what sense *modified?* A classical development section would expand or move to the V, but this is not the case here: so let us rather speak of a *developing episode*. Lacking the V, there is no interruption in the Schenkerian sense. Both second-subject appearances (B_1, B_2)—that is, in both exposition *and* recapitulation—are on VI, which tonal procedure would be unknown in the classical canon. The order of subjects is reversed in the recapitulation, something occasionally met with in classical works, for motivic or dramatic reasons. Sonata form or not? The designation is more than pedantic quibbling over nomenclature: for the formal and tonal designs set off Chopin's original and poetic adaptations of classical procedures, adaptations which presumably incorporate the "narrative" aspect of the title, with its possible programmatic implications and concomitant changes of mood. One thinks, for instance, in the g-minor, of the E♭–A dichotomy of the middle section (developing episode), a dichotomy in a poetic, not voice-leading sense, since the A is a passing note as shown in the sketch, and not connected to the E♭.

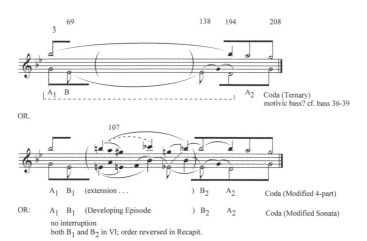

Example 7.2   Proposed readings of Chopin's g-minor *Ballade*, Op. 23 in relation
to sonata form

I may now summarize some preliminary observations comparing the *Ballades*
with certain aspects of sonata form (see Figure 7.1).

- *First* – Character. A broad generalization, which I think contains some
  measure of truth, would be to say that whereas a classical sonata typically
  has three or four movements, comprising three or four *main* contrasting
  moods spread over the three or four movements, the *Ballades* incorporate
  the three or four *main* contrasting moods within a *single* movement, these
  contrasts perhaps corresponding to an unfolding narrative idea. (My own
  interpretations are suggested in Figure 7.1.)
- *Second* – Form. The formal designs suggest sonata form, inasmuch as
  there are the first and second subject groups, a development (which I have
  called a developing episode because unlike the classical sonata there is
  here no main harmonic direction to nor extension of the dominant), and a
  recapitulation.
- *Third* – Interruption. Without this harmonic direction to the dominant, as
  noted, there can be no interruption, which is crucial to Schenker's concept
  of sonata form, and which is why he reads the g-minor *Ballade* as a ternary
  form, even though other traditional sonata features are somehow in place.
  Other general observations will be noted later.

Some general observations

1. Classical sonata typically 3-4 movements, comprising 3-4 contrasting moods in 3-4 movements; Chopin's Ballades incorporating 3-4 moods within single movement (interpretation is subjective . . .) as do many classical movements. (Do these changes have to do with "narrative" character??)

2. Form

3. no interruption – crucial to Schenker's view of sonata form; hence, impression of 3- or 4-part form. But certain sonata-form features – 1st and 2nd subjects (groups); exposition, development, recapitulation

4. reversal of order of subjects in Recapitulation (g and Ab Ballades) emphasizing motivic association; relationship of 2nd subject to 1st, revealed in Recapitulation, giving special meaning to Recapitulation.

5. parenthetical sections: i.e., parenthetical with regard to background and middleground reading
-no Closing Themes, demarcating Exposition; sense of going on directly

6. "fioratura" sometimes, articulating sections, e.g., g min. Ballade mm. 33, 56ff., 136, 246ff.; Ab Ballade 130ff.; f min. Ballade 74ff., 134.

7. final climactic perorations (cf. also Chopin's Scherzi . . .)

8. motivic continuity, associations; combining of motives (in Developing Episodes); motivic transformations

Figure 7.1   Interpretations of unfolding narrative design in Chopin's *Ballades*

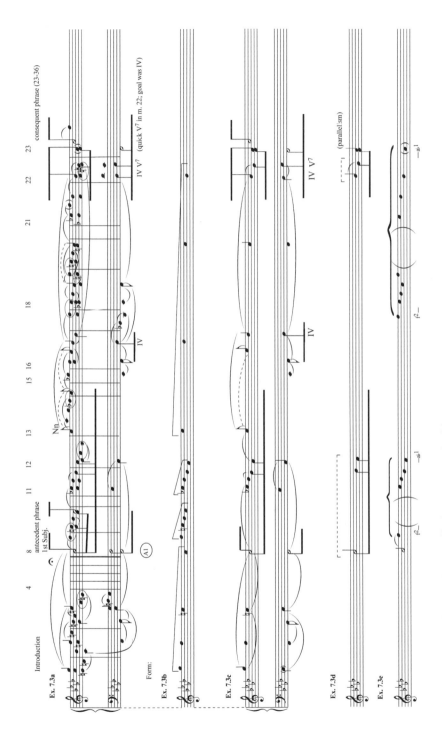

Example 7.3 Chopin, F-minor *Ballade*, measures 1–23

The *Fourth Ballade's* searching quality as expressed in its striving for the subdominant as goal, both on the small scale and on the very largest background level, has often been noted.[4] Example 7.3a shows the IV in m. 16 prolonged to m. 22, with a quick V only to reintroduce the I. Example 7.3b shows a motivic component, bracketed: first prepared in the introduction (Example 7.3c), then as the 4th-motive of the first theme, then in variants, and in the enlargement, from m. 13. As in Example 7.3d, an initial middleground 3rd, c^2–$a\flat^1$, continues as $b\flat^1$–g^1 at that quick V, as if to evade a cadence and start again. A kind of composite of this 3rd, plus the 4th-motive (Example 7.3b) gives rise to the 6th-figure of Example 7.3e, which will become significant later on.

As shown in Examples 7.4a and 7.4c, the contrasting phrase again composes out the IV (mm. 36–57). Example 7.4b shows the 4th-motive from the first subject, here beautifully marking $g\flat^2$, which belongs to the IV.

Examples 7.5a and 7.5c show how the IV underlies the returning phrase of the first subject, and extends into the second subject, joining the two harmonically. That is, quite unlike the procedure in the classical sonata, the second subject here does not *articulate* a new key area, but joins the already established IV, however as IV$\natural$. I draw attention to a few motivic points. At m. 66 (Example 7.5b) the inner voice 6th d^2–f^1 (brace) becomes the top voice of the second subject ($d\natural^2$–f^1 m. 85). The 6th is also worked into the *leggieramente* from mm. 76–80, from top to bass registers (not shown in my sketches). The same 6th becomes, remarkably, the opening figure of the ensuing developing episode (m. 100), the 6th now as the *5th* $a\natural^1$–d^1! Here are subtle motivic links from the first subject to the second to the developing episode—each section nonetheless maintaining its own distinctive character. The middleground top-voice 3rd $d\flat^2$–$b\flat^1$ becomes $d\natural^1$–$c\sharp^1$–$c\natural^1$–$b\flat$ (Example 7.5d), which turns into $d\natural^2$–$b\flat^1$ of the second subject. Example 7.5e shows how, at this point, the connection to the first subject (broken brace) is fleeting, but the association will emerge later.

The transitional passage from about m. 68 to m. 83 reveals a remarkable point-to-point continuity. What might be called "foreground continuity"—the most direct motivic continuity—is illustrated in Examples 7.5f and 7.5g, developing a motive from the first subject (broken braces). The underlying voice leading ("middleground continuity"), artfully concealed, is shown in Example 7.6e, elaborated as in Examples 7.6f and 7.6g; the top line (Example 7.6h) is the 4th-motive from the first subject in enlargement. Example 7.6c, elaborating Example 7.6g, is the middleground basis for the beautiful motivic features of Examples 7.6a and 7.6b: the c^2–$g\flat^2$ (mm. 68–71) expands the first subject's c^2–f^2 figure (Example 7.6f, m. 68); the $e\flat^2$–$g\flat^2$ from this continues in rising parallelisms (mm. 71–73); the next due step would be $b\flat^1$–d^2, which then actually appears, after the *fioritura* (mm. 74–80), as the $b\flat^1$–d^1 of the second subject. What an amazing connection, and what a beautiful paradox: *joining* the first and second subjects harmonically and motivically while *separating* them by the textural break and the *fioritura*!

---

[4]   See Aldwell and Schachter 1989, 430.

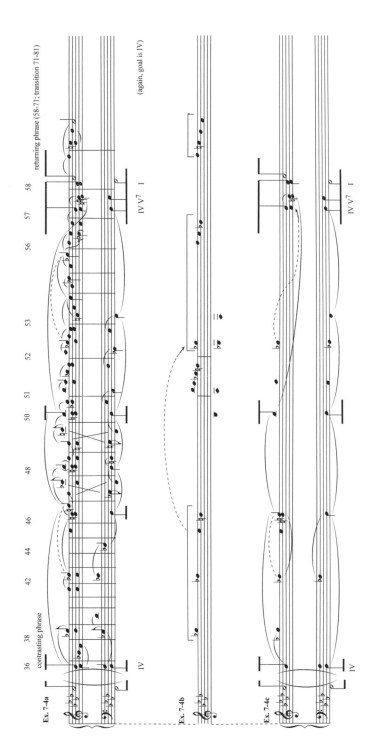

Example 7.4 Chopin, F-minor *Ballade*, measures 36–58

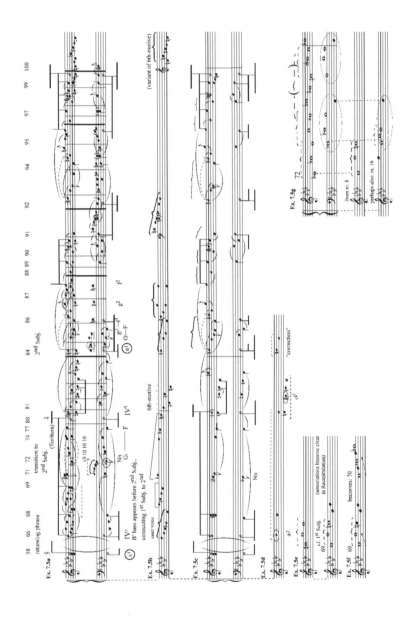

Example 7.5 Chopin, F-minor *Ballade*, measures 58–100

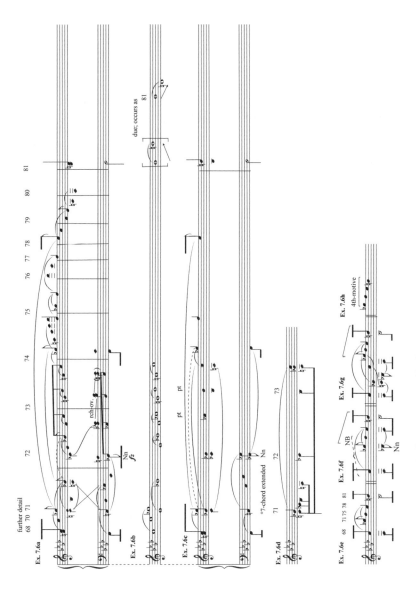

Example 7.6 Chopin, F-minor *Ballade*, measures 68–81

Example 7.6d shows a further motivic detail—enlargement of the third c^1–a of m. 71. If the second subject is much shorter than the first (19 compared to 80 mm.), it is the *nature* of the contrast rather than the *duration* that is significant.[5]

Example 7.7a sketches the developing episode. The force of the IV is such as to extend, in the background, throughout the developing episode and the return and through the second subject again, thus from the second subject, m. 66, all the way to the final V at m. 195! This is a realization of the IV that had already quietly been intimated as the goal as far back as m. 16. There is a *false* reprise at mm. 129 ff., introducing the onset of the return as mm. 1–7 had introduced the first subject in the exposition. A *fioritura* passage articulates the middleground return to the IV following the chromaticism of the developing episode. On the one hand the "A-major" *fioritura* of mm. 134 formally *sets off* the return; on the other, the 5-6 motions (Example 7.7a) *bridge over* the preceding to the beginning of the (false) return, mm. 135–145. The actual return of the first subject (A_2 at m. 152) is for formal balance.

But what seems like a *tonic* return of the first subject here at m. 152 is in fact not so. The F bass is rather the upper fifth of the B♭ of the IV-chord. This return must be read, therefore, as parenthetical. This brings about a quite new emphasis in the return—namely, not a reassertion of the I but a further expansion of the IV. Why would one read it like this? For one thing, the manner of leading back to the IV in m. 145 suggests it and, for another, the rather insignificant V in m. 151 cannot really mark m. 152 (the "quasi I") as a goal. And as the F in m. 153 *means* the upper fifth of the real bass B♭, so the D♭ at the return of the second subject (m. 169) *means* the upper third of the B♭ of the IV-chord, leading to the augmented 6th-chord (m. 194) which decisively signals and marks the final V. Example 7.7b shows how the IV-chords at mm. 66 and 145 are connected motivically and how the parenthetical return (m. 152) easily alludes to the same motive. This is the 6th-figure of the second subject. Here is a marvelous revelation: the second subject, in the return, picks up and transforms the motives of the first subject! The piano's left-hand figuration celebrates this discovery—the very real motivic association with the first subject, a realization which only blossoms forth here in the return. As in Example 7.7c, a vast voice exchange passes over the "f-minor" (parenthetical) return of the first subject. The exchange would technically extend from the IV at m. 66 to m. 194! (Perhaps the extended, bold dwelling on IV has a possible programmatic meaning as well.)

Example 7.8a sketches the second subject return in more detail. In addition to the 6th-figure (Example 7.8b) just referred to, which reveals the association of the second subject with the first subject, Example 7.8c suggests another association with the first subject: the three-note figure from the first subject (broken braces) is worked into the second subject, a triumphant realization of that figure, which had partaken of the searching quality at the beginning and now celebrates that

---

[5]   For an instance of this, see the "unduly" short middle section of Schumann's "Vogel als Prophet" from *Waldszenen*, Op. 82/7.

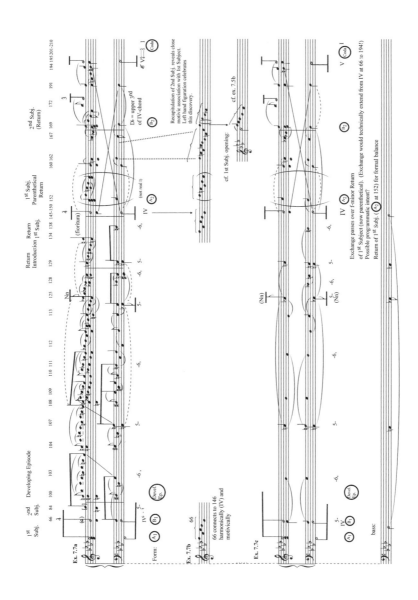

Example 7.7   Chopin, F-minor *Ballade*, measures 66–210

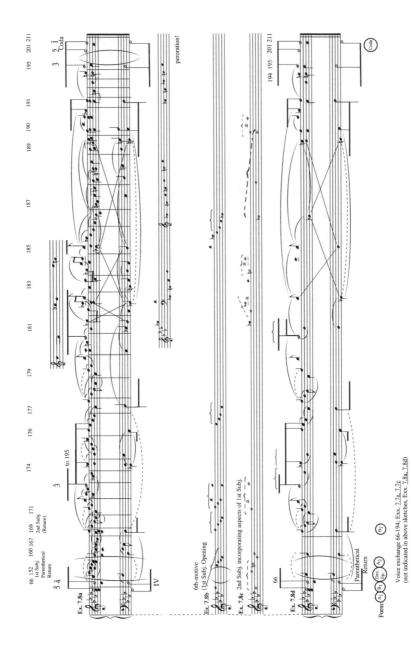

Example 7.8   Chopin, F-minor *Ballade*, measures 66–211

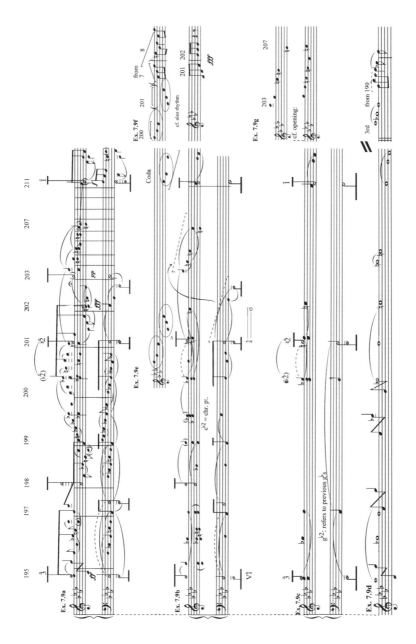

Example 7.9 Chopin, F-minor *Ballade*, measures 195–211

what was sought has been found. The g♭²s are also beautifully reminiscent of their earlier counterparts (e.g., mm. 15 ff. and 38 ff.). Example 7.8d summarizes.

Example 7.9 sketches the music from the arrival at the dominant (m. 195) to the onset of the coda (m. 211). Creating the climactic intensity at the arrival of the long-awaited V are not only the agitated note-values and dynamics, but especially the concentration of motivic references, such as the 3rd a♭²–f² which refers to the second subject (Example 7.9d); the encircled three-note figure, from the first subject (Examples 7.9e and 7.9f); the rhythmic reference (Example 7.9f); and the association of b♭²–a♭²–g♭²–f² (mm. 190–191) with the 4th-motive f²–e♭²–d♭²– c² (mm. 8–9), making the close of the second subject here especially poignant; and (Example 7.9g) the wonderful, long sustained chords which pause on and draw out the V and refer to the very opening, like a deep breath, before rushing into the pell-mell excitement of the coda. (How many pianists rush through these chords, not counting out the dotted half-notes but giving each chord the length of about an eighth-note, thereby robbing them of their extraordinary sense of arrival…). As in Examples 7.9b and 7.9c, the g♭² subtly associates with previous g♭s and in so doing sets off the g♮² (m. 201), the ♮2̂ of the fundamental line.

Example 7.10 sketches the coda. The purpose of a classical coda was to take care of features still left unresolved, and the *Ballade* does this in extraordinary manner. As in Example 7.10a, Chopin evades a strong close on 1̂, in order to restate certain motivic features: the 3rd a♭¹–f¹ from the second subject (cf. mm. 190–191 and Example 7.9d) is restated again and again, and takes on not only a reminding but a cadential function. Combined with this and conveying the same intent is the 4th-motive from the first subject (brackets), worked in repeatedly, permeating all registers from lowest to highest (Example 7.10a). Here too, at m. 217, the first subject's three-note figure (Example 7.8c) is worked in again. The IV is no longer the goal, having already made its point—having encompassed the extended parenthetical return; the IV now progresses directly to reaffirm the cadential V (mm. 218–222).

On the downbeat of m. 220 a strong cadence on I is evaded, in order to restate the cadence: a top f¹ is elided, and the bass is A♮, not F. Measures 221–222 (Example 7.10d) present a contraction of mm. 186–190 as a kind of summing-up of that aspect of the second subject. Example 7.10c suggests a very striking— possibly programmatic—compositional idea: the 4th-motive from the first subject with its characteristic augmented 2nd e♮¹–d♭¹ (circled) is "corrected" to e♭¹–d♭¹ now at the coda, as if to say that this dramatic aspect of the augmented 2nd has been resolved. There is a beautiful dichotomy here: the opening 4th-motive with the augmented 2nd suggests a plangent, lyrical character, but the dramatically charged, unstable augmented 2nd e♮²–d♭² would suggest an *agitato* character. Yet this unstable opening 4th is calmly plangent in character, and marked *piano*. The paradox, however, is that the coda's "corrected" 4th with its *stable* major 2nd e♭²– d♭² would thereby suggest calm and resolution; but here the stable 4th-motive is *forte* and *agitato*—the opposite of what one might expect. (Perhaps this represents a celebratory outburst, as if the problematic nature of the augmented 2nd were

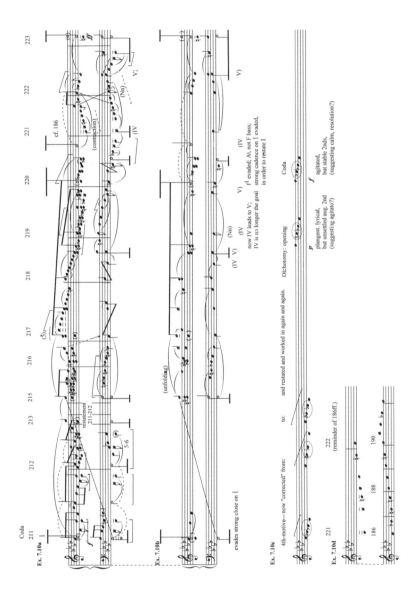

Example 7.10   Chopin, F-minor *Ballade*, measures 211–223

resolved just here at the coda.) Indeed, the magnificent peroration towards the end is a feature of the *Ballades*, as has been noted—but not really typical of the classical sonata.[6]

Examples 7.11a and 7.11b conclude the coda, prolonging the top voice $\hat{1}$ over the tonic bass, and continuing the 4th-motive, once again evading a strong cadence at m. 223 through an elision of the due f^2. Heretofore restatements had been avoided, so when they occur now, as in mm. 225–226 and 229–230, they dramatically signal the final cadence. Another subtle and beautiful way of marking the cadence is indicated in Example 7.11c: here is what Schoenberg would have called "liquidation" of the 4th-motive—the rushing sixteenth-notes are not merely bravura, but engage in "getting rid of" the motive. That is, we can regard the four notes of the motive in mm. 223–224, as being shortened to three (the neighbor-note figure in m. 227), then cut down to just the neighbor-note figure in mm. 228–229, these figures embellishing the triad c^2–ab^1–f^1 which is itself contracted as in m. 233. Finally, the descending 4th-motive is transformed as in Example 7.11d to become an *ascending* figure, as if thereby to conclude the story of the many adventures of that motive.

Earlier I noted that these *Ballades* display certain features of classical sonata form but with Chopin's very individual modifications, so that we would not speak of sonata forms in the traditional understanding of the term. I should like briefly to review certain similarities along with some of Chopin's salient "modifications." First, as to the character of the *Ballades*: I proposed earlier that whereas a sonata typically expresses three or four contrasting *main* moods, one in each of three or four movements, the *Ballades* compress three or four main moods into a single movement, perhaps programmatically alluding to changes of events in an unfolding narrative. Second, certain basic formal features of sonata form are retained: an exposition with first and second subjects, a development (developing episode), a recapitulation (return). But, third, there is no closing theme demarcating an expositional close, and no interruption—both "omissions" giving a sense of the music's going on directly, without marking any formal articulations. The development, as already noted, does not extend nor reach for a main V, which is why there can be no interruption and why the designation "developing episode" is preferable. The lack of interruption gives rise to the impression of a three- or four-part form. Fourth, the g-minor and Ab *Ballades* reverse the order of first and second subjects in the return—an infrequent event in the classical sonata—here perhaps responding to a possible programmatic aspect and stretching the traditional bounds of sonata form. Apropos this re-ordering in Chopin and in other classical works, there is an underlying compositional intent: the second subject contains (often in hidden guise), or is a transformation of, motivic features of the first, so when in the recapitulation the second subject appears in place of the expected first, now in the tonic, these motivic associations are often suddenly and strikingly brought to the

---

6   Compare also the Scherzos in Db Major and C# Minor and the Impromptu in F# Major.

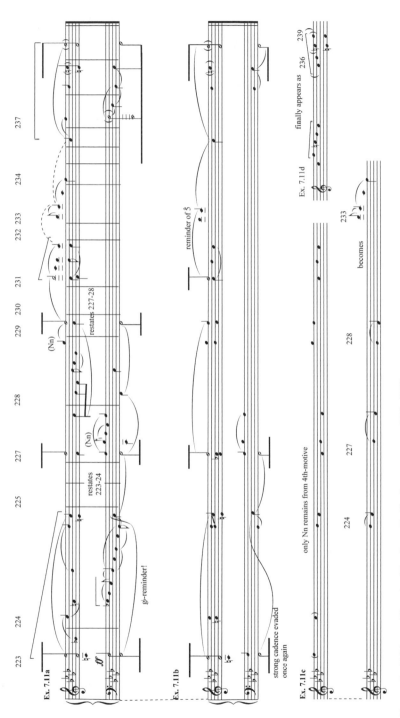

Example 7.11   Chopin, F-minor *Ballade*, measures 223–239

fore.[7] Fifth, as in Figure 7.1b, the formal designs show parenthetical sections—that is, parenthetical with regard to background and middleground readings. In a voice-leading sense the developing episodes (marked C in Figure 7.1b) in the g-minor and A♭ *Ballades* are parenthetical, and in the f-minor the return of the first subject, as discussed earlier, must be read as parenthetical with respect to the larger voice-leading design.[8] Clearly, these parenthetical passages—of relatively infrequent occurrence in the classical sonata literature—also denote another aspect of Chopin's "going beyond" classical sonata procedures. Sixth, another Chopinesque feature of the *Ballades* is his writing of elegant *fioritura* passages—short, more or less cadenza-like flourishes which serve to articulate sections—such as, in the f-minor *Ballade*, the approach to the second subject (mm. 74 ff.), and the return of the first (m. 134); in the g-minor, at mm. 33, 56, 136; in the A♭ at mm. 130 ff. [9] Seventh, typical also of the *Ballades* (see footnote 6) but not really of the classical sonata, is the final climactic peroration, the exuberant and triumphant blossoming, the burst of energy and high point to which the preceding passages had been building, marked (as discussed in the f-minor *Ballade*) by intensity of motivic concentration, or expansion of the opening subject (A♭ *Ballade*), or further transformation and compressing of motivic features (f-minor).

Despite those aspects which depart from a traditionally described classical sonata design, the *Ballades* are characterized by their classical background basis, classical point-to-point motivic continuity, combining of motives (especially in the developing episodes), and interplay of motivic associations and transformations—all features which belong to the great classical sonata tradition.

---

[7]   See, for instance Mozart's Piano Sonata K. 311, and Cherubini's *Medea Overture*. In the latter, in addition to the motivic associations, there is also a dramatic purpose. For if the first subject portrays Medea's fury and the second her loving pleading, the course of the drama dictates that the characterization in the Overture too must conclude with the first subject's expression of the wild rage of a woman spurned. Chopin's B♭-minor Sonata starts the recapitulation with the second subject and omits altogether the return of the first, because it had been constantly worked throughout the development. And here too, the motivic association of second subject to first is subtly reaffirmed and revealed just in the recapitulation.

[8]   Just how remarkable *is* this vast, drawn out IV going to its augmented 6th may be all the more appreciated by comparison with a small-scale instance, of which there are many, such as Chopin's motivically slightly similar f-minor *Nocturne*, Op. 55/1 (mm. 62–69). For a parenthetical or bridged-over return, see for instance footnote 5 again: Schumann's "Vogel als Prophet," m. 24, bass e♭; return m. 25; bass e♭ to e♮ and f (mm. 26–27) to III$^{5-6}$ (mm. 28–35), IV (m. 36–38), V (m. 39), I (m. 40–42). The return (A_2) thus has an harmonic meaning quite different from the A_1, a symmetrical formal balance is avoided, and there is a sense of direction of the A_2 reaching ahead to m. 40. For a "parenthetical" return of a tonic, which functions as a kind of reminder of the original tonic in the course of a main bass progression I–VI–IV (i.e., I–VI–[I]–IV–V), compare Mozart, Piano Sonatas K. 281, Rondo; and K. 570, Larghetto; Trio K. 498, Rondo; Trio K. 548; and Concerto K. 491, Larghetto.

[9]   Cf. Beethoven, Piano Sonata Op.2/3: the cadenza at m. 232.

Bibliography

Aldwell, Edward and Carl Schachter. 1989. *Harmony and Voice Leading*, second edition. Harcourt Brace Jovanovich. San Diego, New York.

Cortot, Alfred. n.d. *Students' Edition of the Ballades*, Salabert, Paris and New York.

Tovey, Donald. 1959. "Sonata Forms." In *The Forms of Music*. Meridian Books, New York.

Chapter 8

Committing to Opening Theme Possibilities: How Beethoven's Sketchbook Struggles are Reflected in Two Symphonic Movements[1]

Alan Gosman

Determining an opening theme for a movement is a critical step in the compositional process.[2] Beethoven's sketches for an opening theme often stretch over many pages of his sketchbooks, and the possibilities he explores range from slight variants of the final version to fundamentally different creations. This attention to the opening theme is fitting, given the extent to which this theme influences choices during the composition process.

In this paper I will examine Beethoven's search for the opening themes in two symphonic movements: the first movement of his Eighth Symphony, and the fourth movement of his Second Symphony. In each case, the movement grows not just out of the final version of the opening theme, but also out of the questions and alternative possibilities that Beethoven explores while working out the final version of this theme. As a listener familiar with the final version of each of these themes, it is easy to treat alternative sketch possibilities as curiosities that the composer wisely transformed or discarded. These two movements demonstrate, however, that what strikes a modern ear as an awkward version of a theme still has the potential to influence dramatically the structure of the music. Indeed, a knowledge of these sketches can direct attention toward various dramatic elements of the final version of a work.

The impact of alternative sketch possibilities for the opening theme is most strongly heard when the opening theme returns during a movement or in the music leading up to this return. The repetition, or expected repetition, of a theme provides fertile ground for thoughts and possibilities from the sketchbook to reseed themselves. In sonata form, this repetition occurs at the recapitulation; in sonata-

---

[1]   I would like to acknowledge the excellent comments from Lewis Lockwood and David Lewin that contributed to this paper.

[2]   I will define the opening theme as theme number one of the first theme group. Caplin 1998 labels this section *main theme one* of the main-theme group. There can be one or more main themes in this group, but this chapter will only focus on the first of these themes.

rondo form, there are multiple refrains that follow couplets. These structural points will be the focus of this study.

Beethoven – Symphony No. 8 in F Major, Op. 93

For a listener, the search for the exposition's opening theme holds few challenges. It either begins the piece or follows a slow introduction. The opening theme of Beethoven's Eighth Symphony, presented in Example 8.1, bursts forth with no hesitation.

Example 8.1   Beethoven, Symphony No. 8, first movement, opening theme

The sketchbooks reveal this overwhelmingly confident theme was born out of a less certain past. Beethoven contemplated a wide variety of options for this opening, and his sketches provide valuable snapshots of the work's compositional possibilities. A knowledge of alternative versions can help us to avoid the illusion that a theme could not have taken any other shape. The sketches show a theme born of choices, hesitations, and doubts. What is fascinating is that one of the alternative possibilities for the theme that is not chosen for the exposition nonetheless does find its way out of the sketchbook's pages to influence the final version of the work.

The majority of Beethoven's sketches for the first movement of his Eighth Symphony are in the Petter Sketchbook between leaves 35r and 51v. The first sketch related to this theme is shown in Example 8.2a. Gustav Nottebohm, after comparing the first sketch to the final version (Example 8.1), writes, "How widely the sketches were from the final version can be seen by this."[3] George Grove's commentary, based on Nottebohm, emphasizes the long path from this sketch to the final version. Grove writes, "Twenty-six large pages are occupied with attempts in this direction before the actual present opening passage is arrived at."[4] Oswald Jonas, in his discussion of the composing-out of chords, also compares the first and final versions of the theme. He states, "A sketch by Beethoven of the first theme of the Eighth Symphony together with the theme itself shows how a finely

---

[3]   Nottebohm 1887, 111.
[4]   Grove 1962, 283.

honed, almost chiseled melodic line emerges from a simple arpeggiation, initially only rhythmically shaped."[5]

One could imagine a rather direct path to the final version of the theme from Beethoven's first sketch. Example 8.2b–e provide the next four sketches of material for the opening theme. Each of these sketches contributes to the realization of the final version of the exposition's opening theme. Sketch 2 composes out the arpeggiation.[6] Sketch 3 presents the theme as eight bars long. Sketch 4 reestablishes the upper register for the exposition's opening, and sketch 5 interpolates a four-bar phrase that goes to an imperfect authentic cadence, resulting in the exposition's twelve-bar version of the theme.

Example 8.2 Beethoven, Symphony No. 8, the first five sketches of the opening
theme.

Many of the differences among the sketches in Example 8.2 relate to three features: the length of the theme, the melodic register, and the tonic harmony support in bar one. Most of the sketches in Example 8.2 are discontinued before the opening theme is complete—after just two or four bars. Example 8.2c and e are the exceptions, lasting eight and twelve bars respectively.[7] The register for the

---

5   Jonas 1982, 39.

6   The complete version of this theme in the final score has a half note F. Curiously, this motive ending with the quarter note F only occurs in one place in the score—as the last two bars of the piece.

7   The downbeat note in m. 8 of Example 8.2c is difficult to read. It is either an F, in which case the phrase is an eight-bar phrase, or it is a G, in which case the second beat A would suggest a retardation into an imperfect authentic cadence, to be followed by an omitted repetition of four bars, going to a perfect authentic cadence. Three items suggest

melody is lowered one octave in each of the first three sketches before Beethoven reestablishes the upper octave for the melody in Example 8.2d. It is interesting that once Beethoven returns to this upper octave, his next full version of the theme introduces registral variation of its own in mm. 7–8. The registral play is tied to the lengthening of the theme.

The tonic harmony support at the beginning of the theme is quite varied in these early sketches and deserves careful consideration. The two-bar introduction that opens Beethoven's first sketch establishes clear tonic harmony support before the theme begins. This, along with the appearance of the melody in an upper voice, secures a strong tonic harmony for the beginning. Beethoven's third sketch of the theme is the only one among these early sketches to contemplate the theme starting with C in the bass clef.[8] The bass-clef version suggests that the melody is the lowest voice. The prominent $\hat{5}$ that would occur as the first note of the bass could, however, threaten the stability of the opening tonic harmony. The melody takes one bar to arpeggiate the tonic triad and arrive at $\hat{1}$, but, even then, the strength of $\hat{5}$ asserts itself as the melody continues the arpeggiation down to another C. The C's prominence is a feature that must be negotiated if the theme is to occur in the bass. The registral shift of the theme to an upper voice in Example 8.2d eliminates the potential for harmonic instability. A bass F can sound along with the opening melodic C. The sketch in Example 8.2d abruptly ends after just two bars, perhaps because these two bars are sufficient to eliminate the harmonic implications that accompany the bass version.

The sketch in Example 8.2e is found only two pages later, but it is quite close to the final version used in the exposition. The first four bars present the theme in the upper melodic register, and mm. 7–8 are in a lower register.[9] In addition, Example 8.2e is the first version that definitively establishes the theme as twelve bars long.

Example 8.2's sketches provide a wealth of thematic possibilities. The theme could extend eight or twelve bars, appear in a bass or upper voice, follow

---

that an F is the correct reading. First, Beethoven's next sketch of the theme, which is twelve bars in length, does not include a dissonant G at bar 8 (see Example 8.2e). Second, there is never a time in which the notes G and A in m. 8 are preceded by the descending eighth notes A and G as would be the case if m. 8 of Example 8.2c were a G resolving to A. Finally, there is no evidence that Beethoven intended to repeat mm. 5–8 for mm. 9–12. The sketch shown in Example 8.2c quickly breaks down after the downbeat of m. 8. Bar 8 contains four quarter notes rather than three, and bar 9, which starts with a quarter note D, does not suggest the eventual twelve-bar rendering of the theme.

[8]   Thayer 1865, No. 170, transcribes Example 8.2c in the treble clef instead of the bass clef. Therefore, his version is in D major, rather than F major. There are two reasons that the D major reading seems unlikely. First, the music is written on the lower of two staves that are paired by a brace. Secondly, in m. 5, the accidental looks more like a natural sign than the sharp sign that would be required in D to $\hat{4}$.

[9]   The next sketch (Petter, 37v, I–iii) has mm. 5–8 all in this lower register as is found in the final version.

an introduction or be heard immediately. Sketch seven of the theme, shown in Example 8.3, is nearly identical to the exposition's version of the theme.

Now that the exposition's opening theme is established, the listener might expect this chosen version to be featured again as the beginning of the recapitulation.

Example 8.3 Beethoven, Symphony No. 8, sketch seven—Petter, 39v, v and vii.

Beethoven could repeat the exposition's version, perhaps with a few embellishments, as soon as the music reaches the development section's concluding dominant. The first sketches for the end of the development and beginning of the recapitulation, shown in Example 8.4, suggest that this was Beethoven's initial plan. Example 8.4a confirms the predictable harmonic boundaries of the two sections. Example 8.4b reveals the entire theme, which is the same upper-voice, twelve-bar version that began the exposition. Example 8.4b's first four measures also introduce the possibility of leading into the opening theme with an ascending scale.

Example 8.4 Beethoven, Symphony No. 8, sketch of the end of the development and beginning of the recapitulation.

Almost all of the material from Example 8.4 is preserved in the final version of the movement, which is shown in Example 8.6. In bars 184–187 of the development, the cellos and basses present the exact dominant pedal figure that opens Example 8.4a. Example 8.4b's scalar ascent to the opening theme's first note is worked into mm. 188–189 as a continuation of the dominant pedal. And in m. 198, the flutes, supported by the tonic F in the timpani, initiate the twelve-bar version of the opening theme in the same upper register as the sketches.

Although Example 8.4's sketch material survives to the final version, there is one significant difference between the sketches and the final version. Beethoven inserts eight bars between what had been the end of the development and the beginning of the recapitulation to create the most striking effect of the movement. In this new space appears a previously rejected sketch of the opening theme at a *fff* dynamic—only one of four times that Beethoven uses this dynamic in his symphonies, and the only time outside of a coda.[10] The change forces the listener to reckon with the presence of another version of the opening theme.

The new possibility for the beginning of the recapitulation first appeared on Folio 48v, i–iv, as shown in Example 8.5. Example 8.6 provides the final version of the score for this passage.

Example 8.5 Beethoven, Symphony No. 8, Petter, 48v, i–iv. Sketch of the end of the development and beginning of the recapitulation.

---

[10]   The other *fff* dynamics are found in the coda of the Seventh Symphony's finale (two occurrences), and the coda of the Eighth Symphony's first movement (one occurrence).

Example 8.6   Beethoven, Symphony No. 8, final version of score, mm. 180–212.

Example 8.6   Concluded

The exposition's version, which seemed so obvious a choice to begin the recapitulation, is repositioned. In its place, Beethoven introduces a version of the theme that is identical to the melody's first extended sketch (previously transcribed as Example 8.2c), and one that is older than the exposition's version. This version is eight bars long and has the melody in the bass. The only differences between mm. 190–197 and the early sketch are a few minor rhythmic adjustments to the end of the phrase.

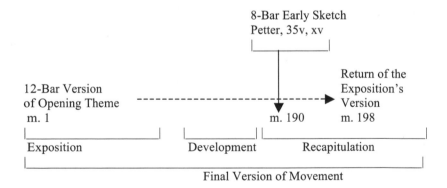

Figure 8.1   Beethoven, Symphony No. 8, insertion of early sketchbook version of the opening theme into the final version of the movement

Figure 8.1 displays the intrusion of the early sketch into the recapitulation. The relationship between the themes at m. 190 and m. 198 is deceptive. The two themes fundamentally share the same melody, but m. 190 presents an early conception of the theme, while m. 198 presents a polished version already tested in the exposition. The later version at m. 198 is secure with its tonic opening, whereas the version at m. 190 seems unable to escape from dominant harmony. This is partly a result of the opening $\hat{5}$ being heard in the bass rather than an upper voice. But the dominant dependence is even more an effect of Beethoven's orchestration. Most notably, the timpani and trumpets, having just anchored the dominant pedal of the development's final six bars, continue on the pitch C until the very end of the bass melody. From m. 190 to m. 196 they do not cooperate with the expected return to tonic harmony. Beethoven's choice for the timpani is particularly interesting because the exposition begins with the timpani on F for two bars.

Other features that distinguish the two versions are the dynamic, the melodic register, and the instrumentation. Two sibling themes have grown up to be remarkably different from each other. Many recordings deemphasize this difference by performing a decrescendo from m. 196 to m. 197. This links the two versions together smoothly. Beethoven does not indicate this marking, however, suggesting that the presentation of the two themes ought to emphasize rather than obscure their differences.

The dissimilarities between the exposition's version and the two statements of the theme in the recapitulation are quite marked. Typically, one can explain changes to a recapitulation's presentation of material as either an abbreviation or an embellishment of the exposition's version. Both of these explanations initially provide plausible accounts for mm. 190–197, but the reentry of the theme in m. 198 causes each explanation to fail.

The shortening of the exposition's twelve-bar version to the recapitulation's eight-bar version might be justified by the fact that the material has already been presented sufficiently in the exposition and development. But this reason breaks down because the twelve-bar version *is* presented immediately after the eight-bar version in m. 198. In retrospect, one wonders whether an eight-bar phrase also belongs at the beginning of the exposition. A simplified form would be more comfortable in m. 1 than in m. 190. Perhaps the listener, thinking back to the beginning, should hear the existing theme at m. 1 as a continuation of the compositional process rather than simply a beginning.

Except for the length, the eight-bar version can be heard alternatively as an embellishment of the exposition's longer version. The positioning of the melody in the bass triggers a more complex harmonic presentation of the theme. As noted earlier, the bass melody weakens the expression of tonic harmony and the orchestration further stresses the dominant harmony. In these ways, mm. 190–197 are more complex than mm. 1–12. But embellishment does not satisfactorily explain these bars either, because the theme in m. 198 takes the unusual step of backtracking to the more straightforward version from the exposition.

The insertion of the theme at m. 190 challenges expectations about what should be used in sonata form. Measures 190–197 stand out in a variety of ways. But perhaps their greatest impact comes from the fact that Beethoven could so easily have omitted them from the piece. He could simply have left this version in the sketchbook, always to be overshadowed by scholars' discussions of the distinctive first attempt. But instead he introduces the sketchbook struggles into the finished work.

Beethoven – Symphony No. 2 in D Major, Op. 36

The fourth movement of Beethoven's Symphony No. 2 is in sonata-rondo form. Beethoven's sketches of this movement's opening theme are at least as varied as those of the Eighth Symphony's first movement. And these early experiments can again be heard to influence the final version's move into the recapitulation as well as refrains 2 and 4. Beethoven's first sketches for this movement are in Landsberg 10. However, the majority of his work on this piece is found in the Keßler Sketchbook. Example 8.7 shows the initial sketch of the opening theme above the final version of the theme.

a) Sketch 1—Landsberg 10, 128, v

b) Final version of the opening theme's melody

Example 8.7 Beethoven, Symphony No. 2, first sketch and final version of the opening theme.

Beethoven conceived of the theme in a 2/4 meter as opposed to the cut-time marking of subsequent versions. Many other features of the first sketch are similar to the final version, but it is impossible not to be struck by the abrupt end to Example 8.7's antecedent and consequent phrases when comparing it to the final version. The original sketch is a period divided into two eight-bar phrases (or two four-bar phrases when the meter is converted to cut-time). In the final version, the meter is cut-time, and each phrase is lengthened to six bars.

Beethoven's second sketch of the theme, shown in Example 8.8, adjusts the bar-line placement to reflect the change in meter. If the only change to the theme were the time signature, the D that ends the opening theme would have been played mid-measure. The D arrives, however, on the downbeat after the "etc." marking. Most commentators have interpreted the "etc." to mean that Beethoven knew the remainder of the theme and had no need to write it out.

Example 8.8   Beethoven, Symphony No. 2, sketch 2, Keßler, 17r, i

Kurt Westphal, for example, goes so far as to suggest that not only does the shorthand notation demonstrate Beethoven's certainty about what would fill the empty space, but that Beethoven was thinking of the theme's final version (Example 8.7b).[11] Cecil Hill largely concurs with this opinion. He states that the opening "may well at this stage have taken exactly the shape of bars 1–18 [of the final version]; the doubt contained in the 'etc.' … seems too small to be worth questioning, though [the third sketch] may be worth noting here."[12] Though Hill does leave open the possibility that Beethoven had not composed the final version by the time this second sketch was written, he nonetheless demonstrates a decided preference for this conclusion.

By concluding that the final version was established early in Beethoven's compositional attempts, Westphal and Hill downplay the dramatic turns that this theme takes later in the sketchbook. Beethoven continues to experiment in the next four sketches. It seems appropriate, then, to be skeptical that Beethoven had determined the theme by the second sketch.

Beethoven's third sketch of the opening theme, provided in Example 8.9, shows how dramatic the continued thematic experimentation is. Here, Beethoven deletes the first two bars of both the antecedent and consequent phrases. He balances this action with the addition of two bars to the ends of both phrases. In Example 8.9, Beethoven maintains the eight-bar periodic form but immediately establishes a stable, tonic harmony. Through this sketch Beethoven radically rethinks the opening of the theme. The previously unquestioned dominant-harmony material from Example 8.8 loses its grip on the theme. The harmonic surprise of beginning with the dominant harmony is gone, along with any need to justify or integrate a non-tonic opening in the movement. In addition, Beethoven reveals a preference for two four-bar phrases at this early compositional stage. Both Example 8.9

---

[11]   Westphal 1965, 65.
[12]   Hill 1980, 93–4.

and Example 8.7a (when converted to cut-time) show the theme as a four-bar antecedent plus a four-bar consequent.

Example 8.9 Beethoven, Symphony No. 2, sketch 3. Keßler, 18r, xii–xiii

At this point in the sketches, it might seem that the opening attention-grabbing bars have been rejected. But echoes of the now-missing opening are found in the continuation of Example 8.9's sketch. Example 8.10 provides this continuation, and the constant references to the opening motive are marked with brackets.

Example 8.10   Beethoven, Symphony No. 2, continuation of sketch 3 (Example 8.9). Keßler, 18r, xiii–xiv

The next complete sketch of the opening theme makes clear that the original bars 1 and 2, which I will call the "dominant-harmony motive," have not been removed from the movement at all. Rather, Beethoven recasts the motive to end the section that precedes the opening theme's return. Example 8.11 shows the fourth sketch.

Example 8.11   Beethoven, Symphony No. 2, sketch 4. Keßler, 19r, xii and xiv. Labels are added

The refrain, which is familiar from Example 8.9, is labeled with a bracket. The dominant-harmony motive (mm. 5–6 of the example) is adjacent to the opening theme's tonic arrival, but its role is now associated more with ending the preceding couplet. The motive is now part of a set of three statements over six bars that progresses from tonic to subdominant to dominant harmony. Furthermore, the dominant-harmony motive no longer occurs midway through the refrain as an initiation to the consequent phrase. The new positioning of the dominant-harmony motive makes the refrain a four-bar plus four-bar construction.

Beethoven's early sketches open up two possibilities for the dominant-harmony motive. One is that the motive is a starting point for the opening theme—an introduction attached to both the antecedent and consequent phrase. The other is that it concludes a section that precedes the refrain. This distinction is particularly important when the opening theme is considered in the context of the entire movement.

Typically, a dominant arrival precedes the return of an opening theme. In sonata-rondo form, all three couplets normally conclude with the dominant. Couplet one in a major-key movement modulates to the dominant and can end with a retransition that reestablishes the dominant as V/I rather than I/V. Couplet two is the development section, which arrives at dominant harmony. Couplet three stays in the tonic but will also lead to a dominant chord in order to prepare the return of the refrain as part of the coda. Each of these dominant-harmony arrivals would anticipate, and potentially weaken, the opening theme's harmonic surprise if it were to start with dominant harmony. The listener could miss the harmonic punctuation meant to accompany a new formal section.

Example 8.12   Beethoven, Symphony No. 2, hypothetical positioning of dominant-harmony motive as both the end of a couplet and beginning of an opening theme

The worst-case scenario is that the dominant-harmony motive, which the various sketches recognize as either beginning the refrain or ending the preceding section, occurs in both places. The unfortunate result of this repetition is given as a hypothetical passage in Example 8.12. This version illustrates the problem of the same material fulfilling two different formal roles. The opening theme is

Example 8.13   Beethoven, Symphony No. 2, end of couplet 1 into refrain 2

Example 8.13   Concluded

extremely compelling when it begins with the dominant-harmony motive, but it loses its appeal in the example when the preceding section anticipates the surprise beginning.

Although it would seem wise to reserve the dominant-harmony motive for one position or the other, Beethoven repeatedly explores how elements of the motive can continue to occupy both ending and starting positions. A compelling aspect of this movement is the extent to which the section preceding the opening theme refuses to give up its tie to the dominant-harmony motive, almost as if it is daring the piece to sound the unusable version presented in Example 8.12.

The music from couplet one to refrain two is the first time Beethoven flaunts aspects of the dominant-harmony motive in adjacent sections. The music seems designed to accentuate—rather than to solve—the problem of whether the piece is devoted to one sketch approach or another. Example 8.13 provides the music from just before the dominant arrival at the end of couplet one to refrain two. The dominant harmony begins in m. 94, and the refrain begins with the dominant-harmony figure in m. 108. Bars 94–107 do not repeat the complete dominant-harmony motive prior to the refrain, but the motive is signaled by the constant repetition of the F♯–G. The formal juncture is punctuated, not by a harmonic change or by a motivic change, but by the successful sounding of the complete motive.

A sketch for the development (couplet two) to the recapitulation (refrain three) is shown in Example 8.14. This sketch uses nearly the same music heard in couplet one. The dominant is prolonged for nine bars and the F♯–G motive occurs frequently.

Example 8.14   Beethoven, Symphony No. 2, Keßler, 19v, xiv–xv, and 20r, i–iii. End of the development section into the recapitulation

Beethoven's final version of this passage is strikingly different and is shown in Example 8.15. The F♯–G motive is heard two bars before the recapitulation. These notes, marked *pp*, could easily be interpreted as a timid acknowledgement of the motive when compared to the multiple soundings in couplet one. In addition, Beethoven only acknowledges at the last possible moment that the harmonic goal of the development section is the dominant. This is in sharp contrast to the earlier sketch shown in Example 8.14. When the recapitulation begins at the pickup to m. 185, it establishes the dominant much more strongly than the development does.

The development section, on the surface, appears designed to abandon any strong expression of the dominant or the distinctive F♯–G of the dominant-harmony motive. For the most part, the end of the development section is marooned in the distant key of F♯ minor and seems to shirk the responsibility of establishing the home-key's dominant. But this is an illusion. The music escapes from F♯ minor with perhaps the most dramatic sounding of dominant harmony and the F♯ to G motive in the entire movement.

Beethoven strongly establishes the key of F♯ minor from m. 154 to m. 165. At m. 165, however, a root-position F♯ chord is avoided. The bass ascends from A to C♯ in mm. 165–167. The C♯ supports a cadential $^6_4$. Rather than resolve immediately, the $^6_4$ chord is prolonged by a two-bar interpolation from m. 167 to m. 168. In m. 170 the prolonged cadential $^6_4$ resolves as expected. Beethoven repeats the same approach to and arrival at the cadential $^6_4$ in mm. 171–173. This time, however, the $^6_4$ chord is prolonged for nine bars through m. 181. It would seem that there is no better way to avoid the dominant of D major and the associated F♯ to G motive than to prolong the dominant of another key—particularly a distant key such as F♯ minor whose scale has a G♯ rather than G♮. However, a voice-leading trick proves that this assumption would be mistaken.

Example 8.15   Beethoven, Symphony No. 2, final version of the development
                into the recapitulation

Example 8.15   Concluded

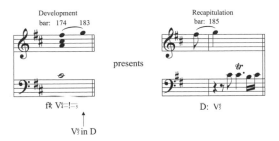

Example 8.16   Beethoven, Symphony No. 2, voice leading at the end of the development section

Example 8.16 shows how the cadential $^6_4$ in the key of F♯ can transform into the V[7] chord in D major by the stepwise ascent of a single note. The F♯, which the listener expects to resolve down by a half step, instead "resolves" up by a half step. The development section does not ignore the dominant-harmony motive. Rather it ends with a powerful, large-scale representation of the motive—a representation that rivals the recapitulation's two-bar presentation of the motive from mm. 185–186.

Moreover, the incomplete neighbor note F♯ from the dominant-harmony motive inspires an entire key in the development section. The development establishes a history for the F♯ that the fleeting presentation of the motive in the opening theme could never provide. The development, by establishing a context for the F♯, reasserts its claim to elements of the dominant-harmony motive.

The opening theme and its preceding section both have one final opportunity to present the dominant-harmony motive. This is when couplet three proceeds to refrain four (the coda).[13] The music is shown in Example 8.17.

Remarkably, the dominant-harmony motive in mm. 294–95 can now be heard to be shared by both sections. Example 8.18 shows that the end of couplet three is derived from two sources, each preparing the listener for a different placement of the dominant-harmony motive.

Bars 282–290 of Example 8.18 transpose the ending from couplet one. Couplet one stressed the half-step motive at the end, but the opening theme distinguished itself by presenting the entire motive. At m. 290, the dominant-harmony motive is expected to begin the opening theme, but it occurs in the wrong key—G major. The key correction that follows uses the material from Sketch 4 (Example 8.11). Bars 290–294 lead to the dominant-harmony motive—this time in the expected key of D major. The dominant harmony motive in mm. 294–295 is heard both as leading couplet three to its correct conclusion and initiating the final presentation of the opening theme.

---

[13]   Marston 1995 provides an excellent account of the sketches for the coda and how the final version of this section provides stability and resolution.

Example 8.17   Beethoven, Symphony No. 2, end of couplet three and beginning
of refrain four

The movement's late inclusion of material from Sketch 4 is a fascinating conclusion to this motive's journey. It is another example of an alternative sketch that is not discarded. This movement of the Second Symphony can be heard as grappling with the alternative sketch's implications throughout, even though the sketch's material is not introduced until almost the end of the finished work.

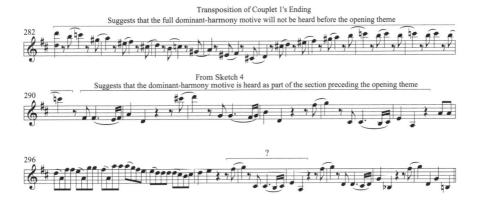

Example 8.18   Beethoven, Symphony No. 2, sources for the end of couplet three.

In both the Eighth and Second Symphonies, the compositional struggle involved with choosing an exposition's opening theme provides insight into a movement's final version. However, the story in these symphonic movements is more complex simply than that of a single version of an opening theme having emerged from a sketchbook of possibilities. A close examination of the score points to the continued influence and presence in the final work of many of the various ideas that find expression in the sketchbook's pages. These ideas shape the piece in surprising and provocative ways, leading into territory that would otherwise not be explored. The story of these sketches, then, is that they continue to assert themselves against the exposition's established version and force us to celebrate Beethoven's compositional choices.

Bibliography

Beethoven, Ludwig van. *Kesslersches Skizzenbuch*. Sieghard Brandenburg, ed. Vol. I: Übertragung. Vol. II: Faksimile (Original in the Beethovenhaus in Bonn). Bonn: Beethovenhaus, 1976–78. Discussed in Johnson, Tyson and Winter 1985, 124–9.

——. *Skizzebuch Petter*. Original in the Beethovenhaus, Bonn, Sammlung H.C. Bodmer. Discussed in Johnson, Tyson and Winter 1985, 207–219.

——. *Landsberg 10*. Original in the Staatsbibliothek zu Berlin.

Caplin, William. 1998. *Classical Form: A Theory of Formal Functions for the Instrumental Music of Haydn, Mozart, and Beethoven*. New York: Oxford University Press.

Grove, George. 1962. *Beethoven and his Nine Symphonies*. New York: Dover Publications.

Hill, Cecil. 1980. "Early Versions of Beethoven's Second Symphony." *MusicologyAustralia* 6: 90–110.

Johnson, Douglas, Alan Tyson, and Robert Winter. 1985. *The Beethoven Sketchbooks: History, Reconstruction, Inventory*. Berkeley and Los Angeles: University of California Press.

Jonas, Oswald. 1982. *Introduction to the Theory of Heinrich Schenker*, translated and edited by John Rothgeb. New York: Longman.

Kinderman, William. 1982. 'The Evolution and Structure of Beethoven's "Diabelli" Variations.' *Journal of the American Musicological Society* 35: 306–328.

——. 1991. "Compositional Phrases and Analysis." In William Kinderman, ed., *Beethoven's Compositional Process* (Lincoln: University of Nebraska Press), 20–23.

Marston, Nicolas. 1995. "Stylistic advance, strategic retreat: Beethoven's Sketches for the Finale of the Second Symphony." In Christopher Reynolds, Lewis Lockwood, and James Webster, eds, *Beethoven Forum* (Lincoln: University of Nebraska Press), Vol. 3, 127–50.

Nottebohm, Gustav. 1887. *Zweite Beethoveniana: Nachgelassene Aufsätze*, ed. E. Mandyczewski. Leipzig.

Thayer, Alexander. 1865. *Chronologisches Verzeichniss der werke Ludwig van Beethoven's*. Berlin: F. Schneider.

Westphal, Kurt. 1965. *Vom Einfall zur Symphonie*. Berlin: Walter de Gruyter & Co.

Chapter 9
A-Major Events[1]

Brian Alegant

Initial Considerations

My preoccupation with the development sections in A-major works began in the late 1990s, while teaching an undergraduate Form and Analysis course. We studied a number of works in this key, including the first movements of a Haydn Trio, Hob. XV: 18, Mozart's Concerto, K. 488 and Clarinet Quintet, K. 581, Beethoven's Piano Sonata, op. 2, no. 2 and Violin Sonata, op. 12, no. 2, and the outer movements of Schubert's Piano Sonata, op. 120. The students and I were intrigued to find a host of common features and procedures in these compositions, particularly in their development sections.

I focus solely on the key of A major for two reasons. First, the repertoire of works written in this key is substantial yet manageable: significantly more works are written in A than in, say, B, F♯, or D♭, but far fewer than in C, G, D, F, or B♭. A survey of the literature suggests that this key represents an outer limit of commonly used tonal regions in the eighteenth century. Even a casual glance through the collected works of Classical era composers reveals a preponderance of key signatures having zero through two sharps or flats.[2] Second, concentrating on the development sections in A-major compositions reveals a curious phenomenon: the dominant, E major, seems to present a conceptual barrier that discourages—even prohibits—further motion to the keys of B, F♯, or C♯.[3] Where three general

---

[1] An earlier version of this essay was delivered at the annual Society for Music Conference held in Philadelphia, PA, 2001. I would like to thank Deborah Rifkin, whose comments were helpful in revising this essay. To date I have not encountered literature on the idea of an E-major "barrier," or for the examination of sharpwise and flatwise motion in development sections as a whole. The single-key approach resembles in some fashion Anson-Cartwright 2000, which discusses aspects of key-specific characteristics in E♭-major works of the Classical period.

[2] We find many Baroque compositions or movements in keys having four or more sharps or flats (The *Well-Tempered Clavier*, of course, has two of *everything*), but few in the Classical era. Mozart, for instance, wrote no piano sonatas or symphonies in the keys of E or A♭ major; Beethoven wrote seven piano sonatas in keys with four sharps or four flats, and one in F♯ major (an exception, to be sure), but none in B major. Perhaps this preference was a continuation of the procedure of mean tone temperament.

[3] Issues of tuning and temperament loom large here, of course. While there is a vast literature on the topics of *Affekt* and tuning, I have yet to find any specific discussion of

trajectories in the tonal designs of development sections should be in evidence, then—namely, moving up the circle of fifths, down the circle of fifths, or staying close to home, to which I will refer, respectively, as sharpwise, flatwise, and stationary strategies—in A-major works only the latter two are fully realized. The four-sharp barrier exerts a powerful influence on the first-named strategy, which plays out in several distinct ways.

This essay proposes a conceptual framework for hearing and analyzing the development sections of A-major compositions written in the eighteenth and nineteenth centuries.[4] It views the developmental landscapes through a lens that brings into focus two specific aspects of tonal design: the key areas that are realized and the types and degrees of sharpwise and flatwise motions between them. This highlights both the overarching trajectories of development sections as well as surface events that are often rhetorically charged or "marked."[5] Analyses of sonata-form movements by Mozart, Haydn, Beethoven, Brahms, and Schubert suggest ways in which composers employ bait-and-switch tactics (promise a key or strategy but substitute another); delay arrivals on keys (most often F♯); refuse to commit to a key altogether; and juxtapose stationary, sharpwise, and flatwise strategies. The analyses also uncover some overlooked (or at least undisclosed) commonalities among different pieces.[6]

---

the ways in which the choice of an original key may influence the sorts of modulations and tonal motions that might occur. For interesting, accessible works on tuning in Bach's time, see Bradley Lehman 2005, and also http://larips.com. While any exploration of historical tunings would far exceed the scope of this essay, I shall make two main points. First, although equal temperament was not universally adopted by 1770, unequal and well-tempered tunings were in place before and during Bach's time; such systems allowed composers easily to travel to and cadence in any key. Second, we can find a number of compositions written during the latter stages of the eighteenth century that were written in (or modulate to) more sharpwise keys than E. Haydn's piano sonatas offer a number of examples: Sonatas Hob. XVI: 13, 22, and 31 are in E major (and naturally modulate to the dominant within the exposition); Hob. IX: 26 is in F♯ major (as is the "Farewell" Symphony). From this, we may conclude that classical composers *could* modulate to B, F♯, and even C♯ during the course of a sonata-form movement. My point is not that they were *unable* to do so, but rather that they were *unwilling*.

[4]   Repertoire for this study is given in an appendix. The sample includes A-major Classical and Romantic works in sonata, concerto, and rondo-sonata forms.

[5]   "Marked" is a term coined by Robert Hatten (1994).

[6]   The list of references at the end of this essay includes studies that deal specifically with development sections (most of these approaches are Schenkerian in orientation), and those that discuss key characteristics (such as Steblen 2002). To my knowledge, no one has specifically considered sharpwise/flatwise motions in an effort to understand the topographies and commonalities among development sections.

Let us begin with some basic definitions. Figure 9.1 shows a line of fifths ranging from G♭/e♭, on the far left, to F♯/d♯ on the far right. It also gives the number of sharps and flats for each pair of relative major and minor keys.[7]

G♭	D♭	A♭	E♭	B♭	F	C	G	D	A	E	B	F♯ ...
e♭	b♭	c♭	c	g	d	a	e	b	f♯	c♯	g♯	d♯ ...
6♭	5♭	4♭	3♭	2♭	1♭	0	1♯	2♯	3♯	4♯	5♯	6♯

Figure 9.1   A line of fifths, oriented around C

Figure 9.2 reconfigures the line of key pairs into a wheel of fifths, fixing A/f♯ at the top. In this representation, clockwise motion moves us to sharper keys, and counter-clockwise motion moves us to flatter keys.

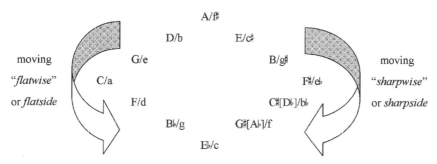

Figure 9.2   A wheel of fifths, oriented around A

---

⁷   Throughout this study I pair each major key with its relative minor key, and I use upper-case to designate major keys and lower-case for minor keys. Thus A goes with f♯, F with d, and so on. This method of relating keys has both advantages and shortcomings: keys are grouped according to the number of sharps or flats, and distance is measured by the number of common (or uncommon) accidentals. As a result, relative key relationships are privileged over parallel ones, and a "space" is invoked that is rather distinct from the distances between keys in Riemannian, neo-Riemannian, or Schoenbergian orientations. Further, modal mixture creates a difficulty, since, for instance, C major and D minor in this scheme are "closer" than are C major and c minor. It would be entirely possible to pair keys in other ways. For instance, parallel major and minor pairings or pairings of keys related by chromatic-thirds might more effectively model the development sections in later nineteenth-century compositions. Nevertheless, I would argue that the method I have chosen offers distinct advantages when tracing the trajectories of development sections.

Figure 9.3 displays the tonal landscape in another way, showing A major as "home," with flatwise keys to the left and sharpwise keys to the right. Several keys are missing here; I will explain these in a moment.

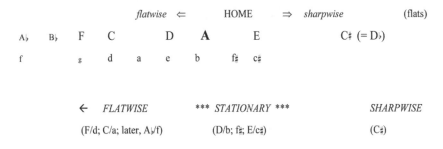

Figure 9.3   Navigating in A major

Stationary developments stray no farther than one sharp or flat from the tonic, A. They typically hover around the keys of A/f♯, or use E/c♯ or D/b. Flatwise developments travel counter-clockwise through the circle of fifths; they shed sharps, so to speak. In sonata-form movements in the 1770s and 1780s, C/a and F/d represent the extremes for flatwise developments. Early nineteenth-century composers (Beethoven being the first) extend that limit to A♭/f; later composers visit even more distant harmonic regions and eventually "break through" the enharmonic barrier. Sharpwise developments, of course, would travel clockwise through the circle of fifths. As noted above, the barrier that seems to occur at four sharps causes modification to this strategy. When developments do continue in the sharpwise direction, composers tend to skip over B and F♯ major and jump directly to C♯. More typically, sharpwise motions are combined with and subsumed by stationary and flatwise strategies, which are examined below. Before we leave Figure 9.3, though, note the remaining keys that are absent. These are keys that composers avoid in the development sections of A-major pieces. They include B/g♯, G (although e is not uncommon), and E♭/c.[8]

---

[8]   It is interesting to speculate on the reasons why composers avoid these "dark zones." It makes sense to avoid G major (the subtonic), g♯ minor, and E♭, the tritone pole; it is not easy to integrate these keys into the tonal design of a sonata or concerto movement. Other avoided keys, though, are more puzzling. For instance, while the fourth movement of Mozart's String Quartet in G major, K. 387, touches on the keys of e♭ and b♭ minor in the development, the corresponding regions for a movement in A major—f minor and c minor—occur in no piece of which I am aware. As another example, Beethoven's Sonata for Cello and Piano, op. 5, which is in F major, jumps immediately to A major at the beginning of the development. A similar motion in an A-major composition would leap to C♯ major, but I am unable to find examples of such leaps in the literature.

Stationary Developments

Stationary developments share several common traits. First, composers announce their stationary intentions immediately—invariably during the initial two to four measures of the development. Typically, the music gravitates toward f♯ (vi), which can be taken as the "default" setting; the second most popular destination is D (IV), followed—at some distance—by c♯ (iii).[9] The main portion of the development usually involves a restatement of the opening theme on f♯ or D, but rarely both. If either c♯ or f♯ appear, they are likely to be foreshadowed in the exposition; that is to say, the seeds for these keys are invariably planted in the P zone.[10] As a rule, stationary developments have recessive dynamics, they are harmonically straightforward, they are shorter than flatwise developments, and they have perfunctory, uncomplicated retransitions.

Stationary developments also feature a limited number of entrance strategies, or voice-leading patterns that afford easy access to the keys of f♯ or c♯. Example 9.1 shows the standard stationary entrance strategies. The primary agent in most stationary developments is the chromatic fragment E–E♯–F♯, shown in Example 9.1a. This string is often counterpoised by an exit strategy that involves an augmented sixth chord moving to the dominant. In this way, E–E♯–F♯ and its counterpart, (F♯)–E♯–E, serve to frame the development section as a whole. Example 9.1b and c offer two common harmonizations for E–E♯–F♯.[11] Example 9.1d illustrates a chromatic line that is often used to introduce the key of c♯. This line is a literal transposition of the string that moves to f♯; it can also be understood as the composing-out of a 5–6 voice-leading motion above E.[12]

---

[9]   Ratner notes Haydn's predilection to move to (and occasionally end on) vi in the development section of his early sonata forms.

[10]   I shall use the terminology used by Hepokoski and Darcy 1997 to identify the sections of sonata form. Briefly, the components are the P zone (also called by other theorists the primary theme area or first theme group); transition; S zone (also knows as the secondary theme area or subordinate group); and the closing zone.

[11]   Works that incorporate the voice-leading fragments in (b) and (c) include Beethoven, op. 18, no. 5, iv; Beethoven, op. 69, i; Mozart, K. 169, i; and Schubert, op. 120, i and iv.

[12]   Mozart's Violin Concerto No. 5, K. 219, i, and Fauré's Sonata for Violin and Piano, i feature this entrance strategy. Incidentally, no standard entrance strategy exists for development sections that begin on IV; more often than not, there is no transitional link: the development begins with a restatement of the primary theme material in the subdominant. A clear example is Mozart's Symphony, K. 201, i.

Example 9.1 Common entrance strategies to the keys of f♯ and c♯.

Example 9.2 offers a reduction of the development section of the first movement of Schubert's Piano Sonata, op. 120, which is a fairly straightforward illustration of this procedure.[13] I divide the development into five discrete stages. In this and subsequent examples, the stages of a development are delineated according to sharpwise, flatwise, and stationary motions or impulses—and not according to changes in thematic content, texture, or other features. (Of course, changes in the tonal landscapes invariably coincide with shifts in texture, dynamics, and thematic content.) Stage 1 opens by restating the P theme in the key of f♯ minor (vi); the dotted bracket identifies one of the standard entrance ideas for stationary developments: E–E♯–F♯. This tonal direction is abandoned, however, when the main melody is repeated on the dominant (V). Stage 2 introduces a new idea that promises another stationary key, c♯ minor. The augmented sixth and *fz* arrival on the octave G♯s pave the way for a perfect authentic cadence in c♯ minor that is asserted with a *forte* dynamic. Stage 3 accepts c♯ minor as a temporary key—and immediately begins to undermine it. The energy increases, bolstered by *sforzandi*, at two-measure intervals, helping drive the descending chromatic line F♯3–F♮3–E3 toward the dominant. Stage 4 initiates the retransition, which restates the two ascending chromatic gestures of the development: the first, B–B♯–C♯, recalls the key of c♯ minor, while the second, E–E♯–F♯, references the opening of the development (and the thwarted key of f♯ minor). There follows a parenthetical return to the tonic (m. 24), followed by three more projections of E–E♯–F♯ in the left hand, the latter of which frames the entire development.[14] In sum, the inner workings of the

---

[13]   Space limitations make it impractical to provide full scores for all of the development sections. Edward Laufer analyzes the development section in his "Voice-leading Procedures in Development Sections" (1991); his reading, which appears as Example 10 on p. 90, is similar in terms of voice leading.

[14]   At a deeper level, the reader can appreciate the expansion of B–C♯–B across the section, with the C♯ in measures 10–12, 20–21, and 27 serving as upper neighbors to B, and the C♯ in measure 29 as an anticipation of the *Kopfton* that heralds the recapitulation. Additionally, although not shown in this example, the primary theme zone of the exposition (and the recapitulation) features the submediant (f♯), and thus prepares the opening gambit of the development section. Also of interest are two hypermetric irregularities in the established two-measure patterns. The first occurs in the measure immediately before the arrival on c♯ minor (in the ninth measure); the second occurs immediately before the arrival on the structural dominant.

development section are defined by the composing-out of two chromatic ideas, B–B♯–C♯ and E–E♯–F♯, and with the struggle, or interplay, between the keys of f♯ and c♯.

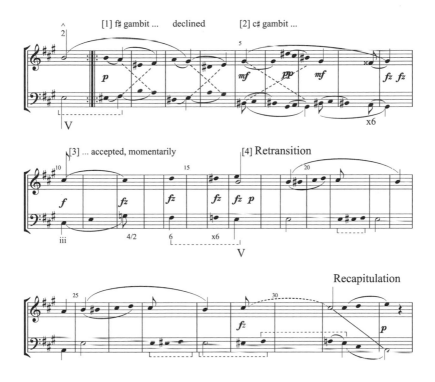

Example 9.2 Summary of Schubert, Piano Sonata, op. 120, i, development

The development section of Haydn's trio in A major, Hob. XV: 18, portrays a much more complicated stationary landscape. Example 9.3 is a reduction that identifies the development's main stages. Dotted bar lines designate subsections, and the number of measures is indicated for each segment or chord. I shall make two analytical passes through the section. Stage 1 begins with a fifth descent from the dominant toward the subdominant, setting the stage for the development proper.[15] Stage 2 begins as expected, by restating the primary theme material in the subdominant key. However, it quickly dissolves in an ascending sequence that accrues sharps: in turn D♯, A♯, E♯, and B♯. A *sforzando* marks the end of the sequence, and places into relief an E♯–F♯ dyad in the upper voice. The bass note, D, now supports an augmented sixth that progresses to a C♯-major chord; F♯–E♯ is

---

[15]   The E and A octaves shown in the reduction are decorated by double-neighbor-note figures in the music. These figures appear throughout the movement.

transferred to an inner voice. An eight-measure oscillation of this E♯–F♯ strongly asserts the C♯-major chord as V of f♯; to borrow a phrase from Edward Laufer, f♯ is "due."

Example 9.3 Summary of Haydn, Trio in A major, Hob. XV: 18, i

Stage 3, however, begins not with the expected f♯ minor, but with a chord that appears to be V⁷ of E♭.[16] Here, in an unusual progression of sustained chords, Haydn seems to lose his way. While a normal continuation for the second chord might be a cadential $^6_4$ or passing $^6_4$ (such a continuation would move to V$^4_2$ of E♭ and create a voice exchange between B♭ and A♭ in the bass and alto), we instead get V⁷ of E followed by V⁷—i in c♯. An augmented sixth leads to a second perfect authentic cadence in c♯, shown at the end of the second system. One explanation for this excursive harmonic progression is that it is a "pun" on E♯–F♯. We have every right to expect that E♯–F♯ will go directly to f♯ minor. Instead, the following chain of events unfolds: first, E♯ is respelled as F; next, F♮ goes not to E(♮) but to F♯; and finally, F♯ behaves not as a tonic but as the seventh of V⁷ of c♯ minor. The

---

16   Interestingly, Haydn writes on the downbeat of this measure B♭ octaves in the piano but A♯ in the cello. As an aside, this is a wonderful teaching piece, with a host of interesting structural features, including a two-measure passage that recurs throughout the first movement, and a monothematic orientation that restates the entire secondary theme in the recapitulation.

resulting hard-won perfect authentic cadence in c♯ is emphasized by a *sforzando* and *forte* dynamics. In a sense, this progression instances a "bait-and-switch" tactic: f♯ minor is promised through an augmented sixth–V progression and an eight-measure expansion of a C♯-major chord, but c♯ minor is delivered instead. Rather than reconcile the conflict between the keys of f♯ and c♯ minor, stage 4 exploits the ambiguity between them. While c♯ minor enjoys another perfect authentic cadence, f♯ minor chords surface twice—as shown by the E♯–F♯ motions bracketed in the left hand. The piano dynamics seem to underscore the harmonic indecision; moreover, the vii°7–i in f♯ minor with which the stage closes is hardly definitive. Nevertheless, having reached f♯, Haydn's work in the development section is finished. A brief retransition—absent any bass support whatsoever—leads to the recapitulation.

Placing the above observations in a broader context, this development exploits the E–E♯–F♯ idea common to stationary developments, but in an unusual way. Over the course of the development each of the three possible stationary keys is referenced or asserted. D major (IV), offered at the beginning of stage 2, is summarily rejected. Subsequently, eight measures of F♯–E♯ oscillations over a C♯ pedal lead us to expect f♯ minor, but this key is rejected in favor of c♯ minor. The piano dynamics in stage 4 seem to suggest a change of heart, with the result that f♯ minor is tentatively proposed and (begrudgingly) accepted. After such a harmonically ambiguous development, the recapitulation seems terribly anti-climactic.

An overview of A-major compositions reveals many variations on stationary developments, ranging from simple examples such as the Schubert to more complex offerings like the Haydn. Yet virtually all stationary blueprints share a set of structural characteristics, chief among them an immediate move toward f♯, D, or c♯; a chromatic entrance strategy; a cadence on a stationary key that is foreshadowed in the exposition; and a brief retransition.

Flatwise Developments

Flatwise landscapes tend to involve only a handful of possible keys. The most common of these are shown below in boldface.

D♭	A♭	E♭	B♭	**F**	**C**	D	G	A	E
b♭	f	c	g	**d**	**a**	b	e	f♯	c♯

Like their stationary counterparts, flatwise developments share a number of traits. Composers invariably announce their intentions almost immediately in the development, and they foreshadow flatwise keys by invoking modal mixture in the exposition, typically in the S zone. (In fact, a significant presence of modal mixture in the S zone virtually guarantees a flatwise development.) Flatwise developments also tend to feature multiple retransitions that are based on dominant pedal points. As a rule, the first pedal point incorporates minor-mode inflections (specifically F♮ and C♮) whereas subsequent passages "correct" these to F♯ and C♯, restoring the major mode mediant and submediant and paving the way for the tonic re-entry at the recapitulation.[17]

Flatwise landscapes also share common entrance strategies. Example 9.4a shows perhaps the easiest and most common way to enter a flatwise region: modal mixture. Converting E major to e minor effectively "sheds" three sharps; it is easy to move from e minor to C major (♭III), which routinely functions as a temporary tonic or as the dominant of F major (but not f minor). Textbook examples of this progression include the first movement of Mozart's Clarinet Quintet, K. 581, i, and the first movement of the Piano Concerto no. 23, K. 488, i, which is nearly identical in terms of structure and flatwise characteristics. Example 9.4b shows that a common-tone modulation also effects an immediate shift from E major to C major. Classic cases of this entrance strategy include Beethoven's Piano Sonata, op. 2, no. 2, i the first movement of Symphony no. 7, op. 92, and the fourth movement of Schubert's A-major Sonata (1828). A third way to move flatwise is through a descending fifth progression, either diatonic or chromatic (see Example 9.4c). The two most popular points of arrival in this strategy are, again, C and F major.

Example 9.4   Common flatwise entrance strategies

Finally, two types of flatwise developments occur in the literature. I call these pure and mixed. Pure developments contain no trace of stationary keys or procedures; their middleground structures resemble those of minor-mode sonata forms. In contrast, mixed developments "modulate" from flatwise into stationary or (rarely) sharpwise landscapes. Needless to say, such shifts in orientation are signal events in their developments. I shall now consider three flatwise developments, two pure and one mixed.

---

[17]   I adapt a term used by Caplin in *Classical Form* (1998) to describe the juxtaposition of minor- and major-mode inflections above pedal point. Caplin uses the acronym "SOD" to represent "standing on the dominant." Henceforth I use *sod* to indicate a dominant pedal point with minor-mode colorations (C♮ and F♮) and *SOD* to indicate a dominant pedal with major-mode elements (C♯ and F♯). Incidentally, one often finds a D♯ toward the end of the *SOD*. The most typical pattern for flatside retransitions is *sod, sod, SOD*.

Example 9.5 provides an annotated score for the development of the opening movement of Beethoven's Violin Sonata, op. 12, no. 2; Example 9.6 provides a reduction and summary. The reduction divides into three discrete stages. Stage 1 includes a literal restatement of the P theme, transposed to the flatwise key of C major. The move from E (at the end of the exposition) to C is achieved by a common-tone modulation, as shown in Example 9.4b, above; note the linkage of the chromatic lower-neighbor figure, D♯–E. After a restatement of the main theme,

Example 9.5 Beethoven, Sonata for Violin and Piano, op. 12, no. 2, i, development

Example 9.5 Concluded

a descending-third sequence travels one fifth further into flat territory, from C/a to F/d. Stage 2 displays the cascading thirds, each of which is marked by a *sforzando*. The sequence stops on a *fortissimo* iv chord (recall that this chord is, at this point in the eighteenth century, the limit for flatwise developments). A chromatic voice exchange extends predominant function and leads to the retransition, shown in stage 3. The retransition contains three statements that appear over a dominant pedal point. The first two gestures exhibit the feature of standing on the (minor) dominant, or *sod*, with flatwise inflections of C♮ and F♮; the third corrects *sod* to *SOD*, incorporating, at the last minute, C♯ and F♯.

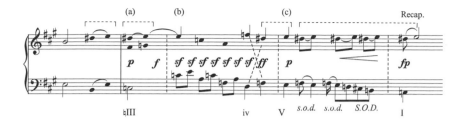

Example 9.6 Beethoven, Sonata for Violin and Piano, op. 12, no. 2, i, development
summary

Three other aspects of the development section deserve mention. One is the
D♯–E idea, which figures prominently in stages 1 and 3 and also appears as the last
notes of the exposition and the first notes of the recapitulation. (This is a piece-
specific feature, not a by-product of flatwise developments in general.) A second
point is the key profile of the development section, specifically the total absence
of any sharpwise or stationary characteristics. With the exception of the last two
measures of the final *SOD* passage (in the retransition), the harmonic profile of this
development replicates a minor-mode paradigm: ♮III–iv–V ‖. Finally, the flatwise

Example 9.7 Beethoven, Piano Sonata, op. 2, no. 2, i, opening of the
development

motion in this development is foreshadowed in the secondary theme zone of the
exposition. (It is also recalled by the same zone in the recapitulation, of course.)
Thus, the flatwise turns in a development section like this are not isolated events;
rather, they form a network of associations that spans the entire movement.[18]

Example 9.7 shows a portion of another pure flatwise development. This excerpt
is taken from the opening of the development of Beethoven's Piano Sonata, op. 2,
no. 2, i, which begins in an almost identical fashion as the Mozart Quintet. First, in
the lead-in to the development, model mixture inflects E major to e minor, setting
the stage for a stationary protocol. The first true stage begins by stating the P theme
in C major (♮III). However, the *fortissimo* octave Gs resolve deceptively to A♭
major, which is realized by the P theme in the bass voice. This harmonic event is
significant because A♭ major is uncharted territory—no previous composer (to my
knowledge) asserts this key in the development section of an A-major sonata. Our
appreciation of this outburst is particularly enhanced by the *fortissimo* dynamics,
which seem to underscore the boldness of the harmonic move.[19]

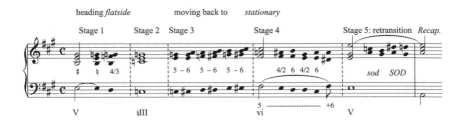

Example 9.8 Mozart, Clarinet Quintet, K. 581, i, reduction of the development

---

18   An examination of the score reveals that the secondary theme zone not only takes a
great deal of time to work itself to V, but also begins on the "wrong" key. The S zone takes
a detour into the unlikely keys of G major and F major before finally achieving a perfect
authentic cadence in the dominant—and this only after a 25-measure delay. *Sforzandi*
accentuate these flatside keys in the exposition (just as they do in the development). The
development of Mozart's Piano Concerto, K. 488, i, is strikingly similar: stage 1 (mm.
143–156) begins in E major, using material from the closing area; stage 2 (mm. 156–170)
immediately shifts to e minor, which is followed by a sequence through e, C/a, and F/d;
stage 3 (mm. 171–177) contains a descending fifth sequence that ends with an augmented
sixth; and stage 4 (mm. 178–197) functions as a retransition, with the customary pattern
sod, sod, SOD.
19   As the development continues we realize that this A♭ is only a temporary diversion.
A sequential passage leads from A♭ to a fermata on a C-major chord (m. 161), which leads
to F major (m. 162)—a "normal" flatside key. Subsequent fragmentations flirt with d minor,
g minor, and a minor, in a procedure that might be described as a "holding pattern"; the
ensuing retransition (mm. 203–225) features *sod* and *SOD* characteristics.

The development of the first movement of Mozart's Clarinet Quintet, K. 581 illustrates a mixed landscape: it modulates from flatwise to stationary territories midway. Example 9.8 divides the landscape into five discrete stages. The initial movement to flatwise keys, in stage 1, is achieved with the progression outlined in Example 9.4a: in rapid succession G♯, F♯, and C♯ are "naturalized" and the stage is set for a flatwise development. Stage 2 establishes the key of C major with the material of the P theme, which closes with a perfect authentic cadence. Stage 3 contains an ascending chromatic 5–6 sequence; remarkably, this sequence climbs out of flatwise territory and travels a tritone to reach the stationary key of f♯ minor. Stage 4 projects a variant of a descending-fifth sequence; this sequence is nested within a 5–6 motion above the bass note F♯. The ultimate chord of this stage, vii°6, heralds the retransition, summarized in stage 5. Typically, the retransition features multiple pedal points: first, the minor-mode inflections of *sod* recall the flatwise characteristics of the first half of the development; the major-mode inflections of *SOD* prepare the recapitulation.

(a) opening of the movement

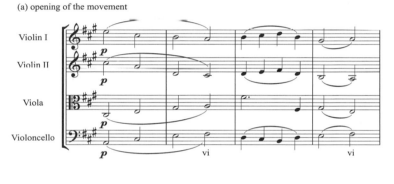

(b) near the end of the S zone in the recapitulation

Example 9.9 Mozart, Clarinet Quintet, K. 581, i, opening and mm. 167–168

Arguably, the most intriguing facet of this development is the motion from C major to f♯ minor in stage 4: it is almost as if f♯ minor exerts a gravitational pull and disrupts what would otherwise be a normal flatwise outcome. In this light, it is significant that f♯ is marked in the opening measures of the exposition (and recapitulation). Example 9.9a shows that the first half of the opening phrase contains not one but two deceptive root progressions to vi. The excerpt in Example 9.9b occurs well into the recapitulation, immediately before the perfect authentic cadence that concludes the S zone. Note that the accented chord and its resolution replay at pitch the chords at the center of the development. This brief moment of intensity recalls at once all of the previous excursions to f♯ minor—especially the conclusion of the 5–6 sequence that occupies (indeed, defines) the center of the development. What is more, this manifestation of f♯ is the only significant change in the second half of the recapitulation; the remaining materials of the secondary and closing zones are literally transposed. A second point of interest is the fact that both facets of the mixed development are foreshadowed in the exposition. The flatwise characteristics are prepared by modal mixture in the S zone (the theme is presented first in E major and then, syncopated, in e minor), whereas the stationary characteristics are pre-established by the repeated motions to f♯ mentioned above.

Extensions and Variegated Landscapes

Generally, as movements throughout the nineteenth century become longer and more tonally complex, their developmental landscapes become increasingly elaborate and tend to combine developmental strategies. My final example illustrates one such landscape drawn from late in the century. Example 9.10 provides a partially annotated score of the development section of the first movement of Brahms's Sonata for Violin and Piano, op. 100.[20] The following analysis focuses primarily on aspects of key organization; as a result, I shall gloss over many intriguing aspects of thematic transformation and voice leading.

I subdivide the development into six discrete stages. Stage 1 (mm. 89–96) contains an eight-measure phrase that states the opening theme in the key of the dominant. The development thus begins by suggesting a stationary orientation. Measures 95–96 feature a hemiola, hairpin dynamics, and a foreign tone, F♮, which destabilizes the key of E major, converting it from a temporary tonic to the dominant of A. Precisely at this point the right hand projects B–B♯–C♯, an entrance strategy typical of stationary landscapes. Stage 2 (mm. 97–105) replays the material of stage 1 in A major (using invertible counterpoint). Beginning in

---

[20]   Eric Wen discussed this movement from a Schenkerian perspective at the Third International Schenker Symposium, Mannes College of Music, 1999 in a paper entitled "'*Wie Frühlingsblumen blüht es*': The First Movement of Brahms's Violin Sonata, Op. 100." The analysis here and the accompanying reduction are intended as a complement to his reading.

Example 9.10   Brahms, Sonata for Violin and Piano, op. 100, i, development

Example 9.10   Continued

Example 9.10   Concluded

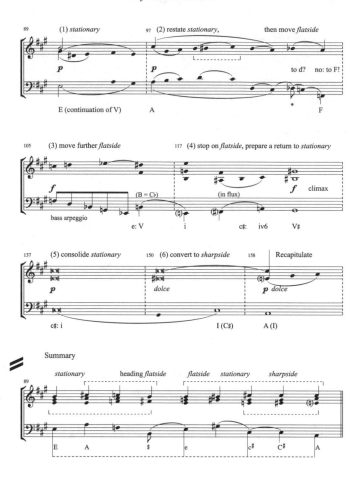

Example 9.11   Satellite view of Brahms, Sonata for Violin and Piano, op. 100,
                i, development

measure 102, the same features—a hemiola, hairpin dynamics, and a foreign note,
now B♭—undermine A major and suggest a flatwise motion. The stage ends with
an imperfect authentic cadence in F major. Stage 3 includes an extended bass
arpeggiation that dives further flatwise, traversing a tritone from F to B♮ (alias
C♭). Imitation, motivic fragmentation, and an acceleration of harmonic rhythm
increase tension and drive toward the next stage. Stage 4 contains the climax of
the development. It introduces a radical shift in character (it is *forte*, *marcato*, and
syncopated) and thematic content (its material is drawn from the conclusion of the
S zone in the exposition). The thematic organization is sentential in design: the
basic idea comprises mm. 117–19; its repetition occurs in mm. 120–23; and the
continuation phase commences with the downbeat of m. 124 and extends the octave
G♯ pedal point that continues throughout the stage. A diminuendo and thinning of
texture lead to stage 5 (mm. 137–49), which marks the long-awaited arrival of the

stationary key of c♯ minor. The final stage introduces a wonderful modal shift (m. 150): c♯ minor is transformed into C♯ major, and we enter the rarefied sharpside domain. The recapitulation—or lack thereof—is also intriguing, as the return to A major is achieved not by a structural dominant but by a common-tone modulation (C♯ is maintained).

Example 9.11 provides a skeletal reduction of the development that summarizes the observations above; the bottom of the example offers an even more condensed view. The first observation we might make about the reduction is that the "soprano" and the "alto" voices project variants of the prototypical stationary entrance strategies, E–F♮–F♯ and B–B♯–C♯. The upper voice projects a near palindrome, with C♯–C♮–B leading us flatwise to e minor, and B–B♯–C♯ taking us back to the stationary area of c♯ minor. Meanwhile, the inner voice incorporates E–F♮–F♯(–G) in a motion toward e minor; it then "toggles" between E♮ and E♯ to move from c♯ through C♯ to A. Another feature of the reduction is the ascending chromatic line in the alto that extends from E4 all the way to A4.[21]

I would argue that thinking in terms of combined development protocols allows us to come to terms with the expansive development sections of such works as Dvořák's Piano Quintet, the second movement of Beethoven's Second Symphony, op. 36, and the first movements of Mendelssohn's Quintet or Italian Symphony— all of which explore broad networks of keys.[22]

Final Considerations

The primary goal of this essay has been to advance a conceptual framework for analyzing the development sections of A-major compositions. The framework is intended to be suggestive rather than comprehensive, and is meant to complement analytical approaches to development sections that focus on voice leading or other aspects of organization. I have sampled several representative development sections in A-major sonata forms, paying particular attention to issues of large-scale

---

[21] A final observation concerns the large-scale connection among the beamed bass notes, E–C♯–A. David Beach points out the use of this structure in the development sections of several Mozart works; this same construct appears in some of Schubert's developments, too. See Beach 1983.

[22] Beethoven's Second Symphony features a quirky development that begins with an immediate flatwise jump, and subsequently employs three enharmonic shifts that drastically alter the tonal landscape. The first shift, from B♭ to A♯, edges us sharpwise; the second shift, G♯ to A♭, moves us back flatwise; and the third shift, which jointly moves A♭ to G♯ and F to E♯, drives sharpwise again to stationary keys of f♯ minor and D major, with which the development concludes. Mendelssohn's Quintet is interesting because the exposition ends in f♯ minor. The development features a remarkable transformation from f♯ to C major and even flatter territories. The retransition is notable for its highly chromatic, almost palindromic sequences and several surprise sharpwise and flatwise feints. The first movement of the Italian Symphony is similar.

form and the delineation of discrete stages that are articulated by shifts in flatwise and sharpwise motions. To review briefly, Schubert's Piano Sonata is a relatively straightforward illustration of a stationary landscape in which f♯ and c♯ jockey for prominence. Haydn's trio is a much more elaborate affair, with a high degree of harmonic ambiguity and intriguing bait-and-switch tactics between the three stationary keys of f♯, c♯, and D. Beethoven's Violin Sonata presents a pure flatwise development characteristic of the late eighteenth century. The development from Mozart's Clarinet Quintet offers a mixed landscape, with flatwise keys followed by stationary keys. Finally, Brahms's violin sonata is emblematic of the mixed landscapes of the latter half of the nineteenth century, which frequently combine stationary, flatwise, and eventually sharpwise profiles.

In addition to providing insight into the broad architecture of A-major developments, unusual harmonic paths can be illuminated by this analytical approach. Consider, for instance, the excerpt shown in Example 9.12, which is taken from Haydn's String Quartet, op. 20, no. 6, i. Level a shows the opening measures of the development, in which two measures of b minor are followed by an extended (German) augmented-sixth chord. As we have observed, though, Haydn simply cannot modulate to B major: this key is "forbidden" in an A-major development. The hypothetical continuation given at level b is, for all intents and purposes, a harmonic impossibility at the turn of the century. Instead, the key of B major is avoided: G♮ rises to G♯, and a series of feints and avoided cadences set into motion what turns out to be a highly irregular development. (Indeed, this development is even more peculiar than the one in the Trio.)

This investigation of development sections of sonata forms in A major from a perspective of prevailing tonal directions reveals a number of useful and interesting observations, among them that: (1) the key of the dominant, E major, represents a boundary that makes further sharpwise motion difficult (though not impossible); (2) some keys seem to be considered forbidden territory; (3) stationary and flatwise developments have their own characteristic entrance strategies; (4) stationary and flatwise protocols are announced almost immediately in the development and are invariably foreshadowed in the exposition; (5) flatwise retransitions are marked by *sod* and *SOD* passages; (6) sharpwise territories are rarely encountered; and (7) stationary, flatwise, and sharpwise impulses may be combined.[23] As a final

---

[23]   One question that has no doubt occurred to readers must be left for another study: are the development sections of A-major works unique or even unusual? Are their strategies and procedures significantly different from those in other keys? A thorough investigation of developments in all keys might reveal that sharpwise motion is a relatively rare phenomenon; it could well be that *flatwise* and *stationary* motions are more common. Certainly, many authors have observed that descending—going flatwise—is easier (more natural) than ascending. At any rate, it would be interesting to explore several possibilities: that each key might have its own "forbidden regions"; that the entrance (and exit) strategies here apply in other keys; and that it is both possible and valuable to categorize and classify development sections along these lines.

thought, I would suggest that this approach can be beneficial in both analysis and musicianship courses, since students are highly receptive to modal mixture and to the color changes that are effected by sharpwise and flatwise motion. It also provides a manageable point of entry into the varied architectures of sonata-form development sections.

(a) Actual

(b) Hypothetical continuation

Example 9.12   Haydn, String Quartet, op. 20, no. 6, i, development (beginning)

Appendix

A-major Compositions Considered

Beethoven
> Piano Sonatas opp. 2/2 and 101
> Sonatas for Violin and Piano, op. 12, no. 2; op. 30, no. 1; op. 47 ("Kreuzer,"
> though the first movement of this latter work opens in a minor)
> Sonata for Cello and Piano, op. 69
> String Quartet, op. 18/5
> Symphony 7, op. 92, Symphony 2, ii (the outer movements are in D, the
> second is in A)

Brahms
> Quartet for Piano and Strings, op. 26
> Serenade no. 2 (for orchestra), op. 16
> Trio in A major (piano, violin, cello), op. post.
> Sonata for Violin and Piano, op. 100

Dvořák
> Quintet for Piano and Strings, op. 81
> String Sextet, op. 48

Fauré
> Romance for Cello and Piano, op. 69
> Sonata no. 1 for Violin and Piano, op. 13

Franck
> Sonata for Violin and Piano (first movement more fantasy than sonata-
> form)

Haydn
> Piano Sonatas, Hob. XVI: 5, 12, 26, 30
> Sonata for Violin and Viola, Hob. VI: 2
> String Quartets opp. 2/1, 3/6, 9/6, 20/6, 55/1
> Symphony no. 87 ("Paris")
> Trios, Hob. XV: 9, 18, 35

Haydn, Michael
> Quartet for Flute, Two Violins, and Cello
> Sinfonia, Perger 6 and Perger 15

String Quartet no. 3, Perger 122

Mendelssohn
    String Quintet no. 1, op. 18
    Symphony 4 ("Italian"), op. 90

Mozart
    Clarinet Quintet, K. 581
    Concerto for Clarinet, K. 622
    Concerto for piano no. 12, K. 414; no. 23, K. 488
    Concerto for Violin no. 5, K. 219
    Quartet for Flute, Violin, Viola, and Cello, K. 298
    Sinfonia Concertante, K. 104
    Rondo for Piano and Orchestra, K. 386
    Sonatas for Violin and Piano, K. 305 (293d) and K. 526
    String Quartet, K. 169, K. 464
    Symphonies, K. 114, K. 134, K. 201

Schubert
    Piano Sonatas, D. 664 (1825), D. 959 (1828)
    Quintet in A major, op. 114 ("Trout")
    Rondo in A major for Violin and String Orchestra, D. 438
    Sonata in A major for Violin and Piano (op. post 162), D. 574

Bibliography

Anson-Cartwright, Mark. 2000. "Chromatic Features of E♭-Major Works of the Classical Period." *Music Theory Spectrum* 22.2: 177–204.

Beach, David. 1983. "A Recurring Pattern in Mozart's Music." *Journal of Music Theory* 27.1: 1–29.

Caplin, William. 1998. *Classical Form: A Theory of Formal Functions for the Instrumental Music of Haydn, Mozart, and Beethoven.* New York: Oxford University Press.

——. 1987. "The Expanded Cadential Progression: A Category for the Analysis of Classical Form." *Journal of Musicological Research* 7.2/3: 215–58.

Harrison, Daniel. 1994. *Harmonic Function in Chromatic Music.* Chicago: University of Chicago Press.

——. 2002. "Nonconformist Notions of Nineteenth-Century Enharmonicism." *Music Analysis* 21.2: 115–60.

Hatten, Robert. 1994. *Musical Meaning in Beethoven.* Bloomington & Indianapolis: Indiana University Press.

Hepokoski, James and Warren Darcy. 1997. "The Medial Caesura and its Role in the Eighteenth-Century Sonata Exposition." *Music Theory Spectrum* 19.2: 115–54.

Jan, Steven B. 1992. "X Marks the Spot: Schenkerian Perspectives on the Minor-Key Classical Development Section." *Music Analysis* 11.1: 37–54.

Jorgensen, Owen H. 1991. *Tuning, Containing the Perfection of Eighteenth-Century Temperament, The Lost Art of Nineteenth-Century Temperament, and the Science of Equal Temperament*. East Lansing, MI: MSU Press.

Laufer, Edward. 1991. "Voice-Leading Procedures in Development Sections." *Studies in Music from the University of Western Ontario* 13: 69–120.

Lehman, Bradley. 2005. "Bach's Extraordinary Temperament: Our Rosetta Stone—1." *Early Music* 33: 3–24.

Lewin, David. 1983. "Transformational Techniques in Atonal and Other Music Theories." *Perspectives of New Music* 21/1: 312–71.

Petty, Wayne C. 1999. "Koch, Schenker, and the Development Sections of Sonata Forms by C.P.E. Bach," *Music Theory Spectrum* 21.2: 151–73.

Ratner, Leonard G. 1980. *Classic Music; Expression, Form, and Style*, New York: Schirmer Books.

Rosen, Charles. 1988. *Sonata Forms*, rev. ed. New York: W.W. Norton & Company.

Schachter, Carl. 1987. "Analysis by Key: Another Look at Modulation." *Music Analysis* 6.3: 289–318.

Schenker, Heinrich. 1979 [1935]. *Free Composition*. Translated and edited by Ernst Oster. New York and London: Longman.

Schoenberg, Arnold. 1954. *Structural Functions of Harmony*. Translated by Leonard Stein. London: Faber and Faber.

Steblen, Rita. 2002. *A History of Key Characteristics in the Eighteenth and Early Nineteenth Centuries*, second edition. Rochester, NY: University of Rochester Press.

Tusa, Michael. 1993. "Beethoven's 'C-Minor Mood': Some Thoughts on Structural Implications of Key Choice." *Beethoven Forum* 2, ed. Lewis Lockwood and James Webster. Lincoln: University of Nebraska Press: 1–27.

Wen, Eric. 1999. "'*Wie Frühlingsblumen blüht es*': The First Movement of Brahms's Violin Sonata, Op. 100." Paper given at the Third International Schenker Symposium, Mannes College of Music.

Willner, Channan. 1988. "Chromaticism and the Mediant in Four Late Haydn Works." *Theory and Practice* 13: 79–114.

Index